Kevin P. Phillips is the author of *The
Emerging Republican Majority*, the
book credited with defining Nixon's
"Southern strategy." He served as the
principal political analyst in the 1968
Nixon campaign, and resigned from
the Nixon administration in 1970 to
write an independent newspaper
column.

MEDIACRACY

MEDIACRACY

American Parties and
Politics in the Communications Age

KEVIN P. PHILLIPS

DOUBLEDAY & COMPANY, INC.
GARDEN CITY, NEW YORK
1975

Library of Congress Cataloging in Publication Data

Phillips, Kevin P
   Mediacracy: American parties and politics in the communications age.

   Includes bibliographical references and index.
   1. Political parties—United States—History. 2. United States—Politics and government. 3. Voting—United States—History. I. Title.
JK271.P46   329'.02
ISBN 0-385-04945-5
Library of Congress Catalog Card Number 74–20070

PREFACE

The purpose of this book is to explain some of the enormous changes that have overtaken American society and politics in the past decade and a half—and to set forth their implications. Too little attention and analysis have been devoted to the political impact of a Post-Industrial, or Communications, Revolution, which appears to be as far-reaching a phenomenon as the Industrial Revolution. In the age of the mass media, the old Republican and Democratic parties have lost their logic. Effective communications are replacing party organizations as the key to political success; and, beyond that, they are becoming an increasingly dominant force in national life. As the first communications society, the United States is on its way to becoming the first "mediacracy."

This relationship between changing social patterns and changing political alignments has been blurred by the ups and downs of U.S. political leadership, notably the confusion, incapacity, and scandal of the Nixon administration. At times, the Nixon people appeared to hold history in their hands, but invariably those opportunities were sacrificed or dissipated. My own experience with the Nixon administration—first serving as voting-patterns analyst in the 1968 campaign, and then trying to make sense of their circumstances from a columnist's standpoint—produced a mixture of incredulity and disappointment. What they might have done under other circumstances will never be known.

In spring 1967, which now seems like another era, I began work on a book describing the coalition I saw taking shape for U.S. presidential elections: *The Emerging Republican Majority*. The book's thesis was that the national GOP was shifting to a southern and western base, and that such a coalition would triumph over northeastern liberalism in upcoming presidential elections. By spring 1968, the first draft of the book was complete, and after Richard Nixon won the May Oregon GOP primary, I took the manuscript and got a job with his campaign.

During the autumn campaign, I worked in New York headquarters as the Nixon organization's chief voting-patterns analyst. Elements of my book were distilled into strategy memos, and one or two bits were distributed to the press. But by 1969, it was high White House policy to deny any connection with the book—in fact to deny even having read it. My role in the 1968 campaign was more peripherical than some accounts have implied, and I don't think that the high command realized the impact the book would have until it was too late.

When it was finally published, in June 1969, the book attracted a lot of attention. Much of the press portrayed *The Emerging Republican Majority* as the Nixon administration's strategic political blueprint. Because of my position as Special Assistant to the Attorney General, the Administration felt obliged to take evasive action. Top officials tried to say, "I haven't read the book." Besides being untrue, this absurd stance for the White House to take toward a volume of statistical and historical analyses—including 47 maps and 143 charts! —epitomized the extraordinary fear of a public-relations-focused Administration to in any way identify itself with a specific philosophic or historic overview. The ultimate posturing occurred in September, when the President himself, responding to a question at one of his infrequent press conferences, denied having read the book. The Attorney General did likewise, and Republican Chairman Rogers Morton told a December 1969 party meeting that I was a "clerk" whose "Southern Strategy" couldn't possibly affect the course of U.S. politics (earlier that year, I had provided galley proofs to the Republican National Committee, receiving a letter from the Deputy Chairman telling me how much he enjoyed the southern chapters). Columnists Evans and Novak reported that John Ehrlichman told a Senate Republican meeting that he had never met Kevin Phillips and never heard "the Southern Strategy" mentioned in the White House. And so forth.

In retrospect, it was quite an episode in Know-Nothingism. The Nixon administration did not burn books; it simply didn't read them. I resigned from the Administration, and since then have been writing a newspaper column on political subjects.

The Administration's lack of interest in history, programs, or philosophy was apparent in many more ways than mere book-denial. Mr. Nixon's chief aides were merchandising men and technicians afraid of being tied to a specific ideology or issue-approach. They had little idea where their 1968 votes had come from and little idea of what to do to hold and develop those electoral loyalties. As a result, they approached the 1970 off-year elections with a mishmash of haphazard domestic programming—from busing, suburban low-income housing and quotas, and continuation of controversial anti-poverty schemes, to pioneering advocacy of a guaranteed annual income—which violated the basic Middle American ideological thrust of the 1968 election. Daniel Patrick Moynihan told the President that "continuity" in these matters would be good for the country; it was a measure of Mr. Nixon's total lack of sociopolitical savvy that he did not appreciate the anti-Great Society analyses that would shortly bloom even in the inhospitable gardens of academe (see chapter 2).

Consequently, as autumn 1970 rolled around, the Administration was obliged to embrace another line of "conservative" attack on "radical liberalism." Since philosophy and sociological percipience were out, the Administration turned to the law-and-order theme set forth by Richard Scammon and Ben Wattenberg in their 1970 book *The Real Majority*. The drawback was that the Scammon-Wattenberg theme—that politicians should drape themselves with pro-police, anti-hippie, and anti-student imagery—was basically designed for *Democratic* politicians caught in a defensive posture because of public reaction against social unrest, urban crime, and racial engineering. Inasmuch as most Democratic politicians were not free to criticize the experimentation and permissive sociology of the Great Society, the law-and-order theme was useful and effective. At the same time, it was a trap for the Republican administration: By campaigning with abrasive superficiality against campus demonstrators, anti-war protesters, and permissive "radical-liberals," while simultaneously eschewing basic social critiques (and indeed perpetuating many of the most egregious programs), the White House only demonstrated the shallowness of its domestic policy posture.

Naturally enough, the electorate was not terribly impressed. The off-year elections were not satisfactory from the GOP point of view; the numbers weren't bad, but a major opportunity went by the boards.

After the elections, some commentators mistakenly sought to portray it as a repudiation of the so-called "Phillips strategy." As the campaign had developed during October, I had criticized the White House superficial law-and-order negativism and failure to develop a broad-based socioeconomic appeal to a Middle America anxious for an alternative to liberal failure. Even the New York *Times* had occasion to note in a pre-election editorial that I had criticized the "sheer negativism" of the White House campaign.* Unfortunately, I don't think many liberals had as yet developed any real appreciation of 1965–69 social-policy failure, and the validity of such analysis in contrast to shrill law-and-order rhetoric.

If anything, the Nixon administration got worse during the first half of 1971: more erratic, unphilosophic, and opportunistic in domestic policy formulation, more and more panic-stricken at the prospect of losing power (and helicopters, Marine guards, and Filipino messboys) in the 1972 election. As subsequently proved, White House planning leaned toward advertising, managerialism, espionage, surveillance, and kindred tools of the communications age, rather than philosophy, program formulation, or grass-roots party commitment.

Hardly anybody in the White House expected or anticipated the rending of the Democratic coalition that was to take shape by early 1972 with the increasing success and bilateral polarization of George Wallace and George McGovern.** But two weeks of the 1972 campaign were like the last weeks of the 1968 and 1970 campaigns: Kafkaesque periods marked not by articulation of any blueprint for the future but by 1) refusal to debate, a dissipating lead, and mushrooming panic (1968); 2) strident student-baiting and harsh "I-am-the-President" rhetoric (1970); 3) preoccupation with Watergate

---

* New York *Times,* November 2, 1970.
** I may have played an unwitting role in Wallace's effort. In the late fall of 1971, I produced an analysis that said George Wallace would easily win if he entered the new Florida, Tennessee, and North Carolina Democratic presidential primaries. One of Wallace's Alabama allies sent him my (newsletter) estimate, and I am told it helped convince him to run—and tear the Democratic Party apart.

charges and loss of any interest in upbeat new-coalition campaigning (1972). By 1972, this lack of depth was clear enough in the electorate's minds so that even though the President won a huge victory against a weak and radical-seeming opponent, there was no desire on the part of the voters to translate that victory into a larger political upheaval. As M.I.T.'s Walter Dean Burnham observed right before the election, a greater man might have fashioned a positive, creative coalition out of the existing political disarray, but the Nixon team was incapable of packaging anything more than a negative triumph.

What *might* have happened may now be water over the dam. Another post-1968 administration might have been able to pull off the *traditional* broad-based sort of U.S. party realignment. But the failure of the Nixon administration consummated in the Watergate morass, followed by the ideological confusion of the Ford administration, makes that prospect less likely. In light of this failure, the Republican/Democratic party system—having been unable to handle traditional realignment—may also be exhausted and obsolete. Conceivably, the Post-Industrial, or Communications. Revolution is shaping new party roles—as well as a new party system—just as the Industrial Revolution did in its time. Perhaps the Nixon administration, instead of being an aberration, was really part of that process.

This book is not about Watergate or the corollary episodes that have prompted such great moral outrage. I don't think that the Nixon administration was all that different, in terms of morality or political practices, from the preceding, Democratic administration of Lyndon Johnson. I did not leave in 1970 with any sense of moral outrage. But while the problem is not really discussed in this book, there is a worrisome truth in the analysis—made by Daniel Bell and others —that morality and post-industrial-*cum*-communications technology do not easily coexist. Strategic politics is an *amoral* (if not immoral) business, as readers of most of the political analysis and strategy books of the past decade know. Even in the wake of Watergate, "integrity" surfaced not as a natural commodity but as the 1974 theme of the political managers and packagers. A lot has been written about the corrupting effect of money on politics, yet the corrupting effect of communications technology may be even worse.

This book first took shape during the winter of 1971–72, as the result of research begun for my newspaper columns. Then it grew. In the book, I have attempted to create a logical unfolding of ideas, laying out different themes and then weaving them together. The book begins with an overview of my thesis, which is that the old divisions of American politics have in many ways been *reversed* by the Post-Industrial Revolution, and that the old Industrial Revolution-based, North-South party system is in the process of giving way to a new one. In chapter 2 I have tried to document and analyze the Post-Industrial Revolution and the rise of the knowledge industry as a social, economic, and political phenomenon of the same magnitude and importance as the Industrial Revolution and one that reverses the old relationship of the *conservative* elite to the more *liberal* population mass. The following chapter discusses the new pattern of American politics flowing from the post-industrialization that has taken place since the nineteen fifties. A new liberal elite has grown up in the same northeastern bastions of affluence that were Hoover-era standard-bearers of conservatism, and "conservatism" now musters its greatest support in the southern and western areas of historic *populist-radical* proclivities. None of this occurred overnight, and the 1968–72 breakdown of the Democratic coalition was no accident or fluke.

One hundred fifty years ago, the Industrial Revolution fashioned highly organized new parties out of a fluid system. Today's institutionalized system lacks the fluidity for a traditional type of realignment, and the party system is giving way to a politics of communications. I will go into this, and also the fact that between Republicans and Democrats (or some new party or fusion arrangement), the future of American politics is less than clear. But American power and population are moving south and west, racial polarization and tension suggests itself in the cities, and by the nineteen eighties, the average age of the electorate will be a lot higher than it is now, suggesting a movement to the right.

Like all books, this one owes a few debts, notably to the post-industrial socioeconomic analyses of Daniel Bell, the party-disintegration studies of Walter Dean Burnham, the election interviews and theories of Samuel Lubell, and the works of Herman Kahn. The shortcomings in interrelating these trends are, of course, mine.

Washington
November 1974

CONTENTS

PREFACE   v
LIST OF MAPS AND CHARTS   xiii

1 SPINNING THE ELECTORAL COMPASS   1
2 POST-INDUSTRIAL SOCIETY   13
  A. The Knowledge Industry   18
  B. A Mediacracy   24
  C. The New Elite   31
  D. The Dynamics of Liberal Failure   38
  E. The Traditionalist Counterreformation   51
  F. A Redefinition of Ideology   62
  G. Post-Industrial Society Conflict   68
3 NEW PATTERNS IN AMERICAN POLITICS   81
  A. Civil-War Patterns   85
  B. Ethnics and Blacks   95
  C. Evolution, Not Revolution   101
  D. Populism, Culture and Economics   112
  E. The Rise of Ticket Splitting   130
  F. Third Parties and Ideological Trends   138
  G. A New Political Cycle?   145
4 THE DISRAELI ANALOGY   151
  A. Parties in Flux   152
  B. The Role of Party   168
  C. Executive and Legislative Institutionalization   177

5 THE FUTURE OF AMERICAN POLITICS   191
    A. The Party System   192
    B. Post-Industrial Ideology   202
    C. The Demography of Power   208
    D. Centers of Post-Industrial Power   225

NOTES   229
INDEX   237

LIST OF MAPS AND CHARTS

MAP 1 *Basic Party Divisions (1856–1932)*
Most-Republican states

MAP 2 *Basic Party Divisions (1856–1932)*
Most-Democratic states

MAP 3 *New Deal-Era Party Divisions (1932–44)*
Top 15 Republican states in presidential voting

MAP 4 *New Deal-Era Party Divisions (1932–44)*
Top 15 Democratic states in presidential voting

MAP 5 *Top 15 Republican states—1972*

MAP 6 *Top 15 Democratic states—1972*

MAP 7 *Social-Tension Belt*

MAP 8 *Shifting Democratic Presidential Geography*
Top Ten Democratic states—1956
Top Ten Democratic states—1960
Top Ten Democratic states—1964
Top Ten Democratic states—1968
Top Ten Democratic states—1972

MAP 9 *Critical Election Patterns*
Top Ten States of Federalists and Democratic-Republicans—
Top Ten States of Republicans and Democrats—1828
Top Ten States of Republicans and Democrats—1860
Top Ten States of Republicans and Democrats—1896
Top Ten States of Republicans and Democrats—1932
Top Ten States of Republicans and Democrats—1968–72

MAP 10 *Top 18 States in Combined Wealth, Culture, Health-and-*
Security, and Civic-Affairs Criteria (1930)

MAP 11 *Top 18 States in Combined Wealth, Culture, Health-and-*
Security, and Civic-Affairs Criteria (1970)

MAP 12 *Two Dozen Lowest-ranking States Based on 1970 Census*
Data for Wealth and Education, and Miscellaneous Data for
Culture, Health, and Civic Affairs, as Tabulated in Lifestyle
magazine, November 1972
The Bottom Fifteen States in Per-capita Literacy, Media Consump-
tion, Education, Symphony Orchestras, Libraries, and Scientists

MAP 13 *Geography of Protestant Church Membership*

MAP 14 *Right-Wing Splinterism—1968–72*

MAP 15 *The Ideological Division of National Politics*
Most-Liberal States
Most-Conservative States

MAP 16 *The Common Geography of Intraparty Ideology*
A) The Democrats
B) The Republicans

MAP 17 *Areas of Principal 1960–70 Population Growth*
Northeast-upper Midwest-Pacific coast knowledge-industry
belt
Southern-southwestern axis

CHART 1 *U. S. Presidential Cycles of the 19th and 20th Centuries*

CHART 2 *The New American Knowledge Economy*

CHART 3 *The Emergence of the Knowledge Industry, 1940–73*

CHART 4 *The Expanding Empire of HEW*

CHART 5 *The Postwar Rise of the Communications Industry*

CHART 6 *Persons Characterizing Themselves as Conservatives or Liberals, 1963–69*

CHART 7 *Job Picture for 1980—an Official Report*

CHART 8 *Converging Political Attitudes of Parents and Children*

CHART 9 *Ethnic Voting Patterns in 1960–72 Presidential Races*

CHART 10 *Black Population in Selected Cities, 1930–70*

CHART 11 *The Dixie Presidential Shift, 1944–72*

CHART 12 *Academic-Community Realignment*

CHART 13 *Party, by Ethnic Religious Groups, Geneseo City/Township, Illinois (1877)*

CHART 14 *Ticket Splitting—Congressional Districts with Split Election Results: Districts Carried by a Presidential Nominee and U. S. House Nominee of Different Parties, 1920–72*

CHART 15 *Prevailing Presidential Splinter-Party Regimes in U. S. History*

CHART 16 *England: The Chronology of the Industrial Revolution*

CHART 17 *Voter Turnout in Presidential Races, 1852–1972, Indiana and Massachusetts*

CHART 18 *The Evolutionary Political Institutionalization of the Presidency*

CHART 19 *The Institutionalization of the House of Representatives*

CHART 20 *Public Trend Away from Liberal Viewpoint*

CHART 21 *The Changing Demography of U. S. Presidential Elections*

CHART 22 *The Dramatic Shift in New England's Labor Force*

CHART 23 *Southern Population and Economic Trends*

CHART 24 *Relative Difference Among Regions in per-Capita Personal Income in United States*

CHART 25 *The Graying of America*

MEDIACRACY

1

SPINNING THE ELECTORAL COMPASS

FEW PERIODS of American political history have generated as much electoral analysis as the 1968–74 Nixon-Watergate era. Both the Republican and Democratic parties watched their fortunes seesaw: up one year, down the next. Confusion was the rule.

But the ambiguity of *party* circumstances—of Democratic versus Republican prospects—in the mid-seventies is no excuse for the minimal amount of attention that has been paid to basic upheavals in the American polity. Simply put, the revolutionary social and economic changes of the nineteen sixties have also revolutionized the underpinnings of U.S. politics. However hazy the future of our present-day parties, shifts and reversals in the basic context of life in these United States have laid down a new playing field.

To put a little fast flesh on these bare bones, national politics, especially on the presidential level, is simply no longer divided along the familiar lines that prevailed for a century after Lee's surrender at Appomattox and the implementation of the Industrial Revolution. What took place between the 1850s and the 1950s was a political era of its own; its social striations and political coalitions belong to the history books, and not to current thinking. Now there is a new game, with new bases and foul lines to replace the old.

During the previous century, the nation's economic elite was conservative, and liberal-conservative struggles were rooted in that economic context. This book will examine the rise of a "new class" of affluent liberals—and the impact of that rise. A new correlation is arising—among education, wealth, and *liberalism*—to replace the old one—among education, wealth, and *conservatism*. And, on a number of issues, opposition to liberal elitism is strongest among the groups historically in the vanguard of opposition to conservative economic elites. Upheaval has also undermined or reversed many of the loyalties rooted in the industrial era-Civil War orbit of American politics.

It is the contention of this book that despite the confusion of party circumstances, the social and economic shifts briefly touched upon in the previous paragraph are the stuff of a fundamentally changed era, a watershed in American politics. If this is true—if we are experiencing a degree of change like that of the mid-nineteenth century—then the present imprecision and obsolescence of party lines can be expected to yield new alignments based on the new socioeconomic criteria. As a precedent, one can cite the far-reaching and pervasive Industrial Revolution-based upheaval of the British and American party systems between 1830 and 1865.

To a considerable extent, political (and party) evidence of these new forces can be found in 1968–72 voting patterns on the presidential level. But, at the local level, old alignments and loyalties have persisted in a welter of confusion and ticket splitting. This multitiered behavior—an unprecedented degree of ticket splitting—helps camouflage some of the logic in the over-all pattern. Analysts who do not separate presidential and lesser balloting will find less proof to support the notion that U.S. politics is reorienting itself to reflect the post-industrial characteristics described in chapter 2.

Party confusion is logical enough. Such confusion was also widespread, as will be shown, in the early period of the Industrial Revolution. Moreover, the Watergate imbroglio raised further doubt about the future role of the Republican Party. And, at the same time, it spurred analysts to renew speculation about the viability of the New Deal Democratic coalition. Most of its components, from Dixie to blue-collar workers, retain their Democratic label *on the state and municipal level*. But these same elements form a diminishing proportion of the Democratic *presidential* coalition, which is quite different —and much more reflective of the new divisions in American society. Yet, because all these groups continue to call themselves "Democrats," analysts have been loath to find realignment, with "the Democratic Party" still so superficially all-encompassing. "The Watergate syn-

drome" and 1973–74 re-emergence of economic and employment issues reinforced this reluctance.

However, in the wake of the 1972 election, even the cautious
scholars of the Center for Political Studies of the University of
Michigan argued that the party umbrella had become ineffective on a
national basis: profound ideological cleavages divided the left and
right wings of the "Democratic Party," and 42 per cent of all Democrats (conservatives and moderates) had supported Republican presidential nominee Richard Nixon. As a whole, the hostility between
the two wings of the Democratic Party was more pronounced than
the hostility between the two major parties. On one side were the
key blocs of the New Deal coalition: Southerners, ethnics, and
blue-collar workers. Leading the other side were the advocates of the
New Politics (suburban liberals, skilled professionals, collegians)
and their minority-group allies.

To some extent, the 1972 ideological cleavage within the Democratic Party reflected the post-industrial economic cleavage suggested
by David Apter: the "technologically proficient" (professionals and
knowledge technicians) plus the "technologically superfluous" (the
poor and unskilled minorities) versus the "technologically obsolescent" (the Middle American masses of clerks, truck drivers, blue-
collar workers, agricultural smallholders, and other latter-day yeo-
manry).[1] Much of the ideological hostility between groups rests on
these differences in vocations and thus culture and lifestyle, likely
to be an increasingly important phenomenon. The Michigan study
found that with respect to liberal-versus-conservative ideology, "the
differences between the Democrats and Republicans were less extreme than those between the two Democratic factions."[2]

The dynamics of this shift are not clear to those who let themselves
be guided by state and local election results that only partially (and,
at best, slowly) reflect the national factors so omnipresent in the
past two or three presidential elections. Or to those who isolate
election statistics in a cultural vacuum. The Michigan analysts note
that "the past 12 years have witnessed an increased articulation of
the ideological differences between the parties, as well as profound
social and cultural turbulence that has been immediately and widely
transmitted by the mass media," but they do not probe the fundamental nature of the socioeconomic revolution that has caused this
upheaval and in the process made old party lines irrelevant.[3]

A little more breadth of analysis is in order. Politics cannot be divorced from geography, from history, from economics, from sociology. Those who approach election patterns with the single-discipline skills of political science often miss the importance of massive recent change in social and economic patterns. Current-day politics is changing in an epochal way, because it cannot help but reflect these other epochal changes. And when one weighs these shifts, elaborated upon in chapter 2, then the deep-rootedness of some new political divisions becomes apparent. So far, the over-all upheaval has been insufficiently described.

For example, in the closing weeks of the 1972 campaign, two prominent Republican politicians nursed peripheral but highly informative worries. Mississippian Clarke Reed, chairman of the Southern GOP Conference, wanted his own state to chalk up the nation's highest GOP percentage, and the unfortunate Charles Colson, then counsel to Richard Nixon, hoped that his Massachusetts birthplace wouldn't spoil a fifty-state Republican sweep.

As things turned out, Mississippi did chalk up the nation's top Republican presidential percentage on November 8. For the *fourth* straight national election, Jefferson Davis' home state gave the presidential candidate of the Democratic Party his lowest vote percentage. Seventy-eight per cent of those Mississippians voting chose Nixon, while George Wallace's Alabama, proclaimed by its license plates as "the heart of Dixie," came in second. Mississippi and Alabama were one-two on the GOP presidential list in 1964 as well, and, in 1968, they were independent George Wallace's best states. Meanwhile, Massachusetts, among the top Democratic states in every presidential race since 1960, did wind up as the only state to back George McGovern. Nixon aide Colson explained it by saying that Massachusetts had a disproportionate number of kooks.

This cleavage is not likely to maintain its 1964–72 intensity. The great upheavals of U.S. presidential history have always had strong sectional overtones, but these generally moderated once the underlying shift of direction was clearly established—a role that Gerald Ford's administration is likely to repeat. At the same time, however, there is no turning back history, and the basic Massachusetts-Mississippi dichotomy is bound to continue.

By every criterion, Mississippi and Massachusetts could hardly be farther apart. From the Civil War to date, Mississippi has been the most impoverished, least cultured, least educated, and least civic-minded state in the Union. And Massachusetts? Like the rest of New

England, the state ranks high on the national list of wealth, education, culture, and civic awareness. Proper Bostonians are still the butt of anti-establishment jokes, just as William Faulkner's Snopes family (of imaginary Yoknapatawpha County, Mississippi) are used to convey an image of low-income rural crudity. Even in the Watergate furor, Massachusetts was at one end of the spectrum— leading the anti-Nixon clamor—while Mississippi was at the other.

But, in political terms, what has taken place is a historical reversal. Pre-Civil War Massachusetts was the stronghold of abolitionist and free-soil politics, and the seedbed—if not the actual birthplace— of the Republican Party. It produced Abraham Lincoln's largest victory margin in the wartime election of 1864. And in the New Deal election of 1936, it gave the Republican Party a unique success: Massachusetts was the only state to both 1) elect a new Republican U. S. Senator (Henry Cabot Lodge) and 2) send a predominantly Republican delegation to the House of Representatives. Mississippi, like the rest of the Deep South, produced the nation's highest vote percentages for Franklin D. Roosevelt and the Democratic Party during the New Deal years from 1932 to 1944.

As late as the nineteen fifties, and even well into the sixties, civics books in classes across America still portrayed the two major parties in their post-Civil War geography: the Republicans as the party of Yankee New England and the Democrats as the party rooted in the Solid South. Even by that time, it was simply not true any longer. But it *had been* true back in the nineteen thirties: The New Deal coalition—to anyone who pays the slightest attention to either voting returns or history—must be described as having originated and developed within the post-Civil War framework of American politics.

To understand why the old framework is collapsing, and what that collapse (or even reversal) means, it is necessary to appreciate what shaped it in the first place. The Civil War century of American politics is actually just that—a period extending roughly from 1856 to 1956, during which national political alignments passed through three successive stages of industrial-era partisanship.

The early stage of this combat (1856–96) reflects the orbital political division between the Yankees of Greater New England (from Maine west through the Great Lakes to Minnesota and Iowa), who were the major architects and entrepreneurs of mid-nineteenth-century industrialization, and the essentially agricultural Greater South (including much of the border and the southern-settled Ohio

Valley sections of Ohio, Indiana, and Illinois). After the dust of Appomattox settled and military Reconstruction of the South came to an end (1876), the initial GOP edge faded into a stalemate and the two major parties were closely matched until the 1894–96 upheaval. Although rural areas often showed the sharpest political cleavages, between, say, northern-Ohio Yankee Republicans and southern-Ohio Butternut Democrats, or between Wisconsin Yankee and Scandinavian Protestant Republicans and Wisconsin German or Irish Catholic Democrats—nevertheless the crucial and pivotal context of national 1860–96 politics was industrial versus rural. That is, Yankee Republicans committed to the supremacy of an industrial North versus southern Democrats linked to agricultural interests.

But if the 1860–96 political era was shaped by the Yankee-led industrialism, the period from 1896 to 1932 can be said to represent the political triumph and solidification of that industrial impetus and the Republican Party it controlled. By embracing Populism and William Jennings Bryan in 1896, the Democrats tipped the economic and political balance, ending the Civil War stalemate that had prevailed since the end of Reconstruction, and precipitating decisive GOP gains in the industrial states. The Republican states of New England and Pennsylvania became even more loyal, thanks to the heavy GOP shift in urban industrial counties. But more importantly, this same shift transformed such states as New York, New Jersey, Ohio, and Illinois, marginal from 1876 to 1892, into reliable supporters of Republican presidential candidates.

Steel and steam, railroads and Republicanism went together. From 1896 to the 1920s, the Republican Party broadened its reliance on the cultural geography of Greater New England into a supremacy based on control of the industrial North. In the nine presidential elections between 1896 and 1928, the GOP carried the industrial North eight times, and the Democrats carried the region only once: in 1912, when Bull Moose Republican Theodore Roosevelt and regular Republican William Howard Taft split the party vote. Woodrow Wilson, the man elected that year, was the only Democrat to gain the White House between 1896 and 1932. Wilson narrowly won a second term, in 1916, by mobilizing a solid southern and western phalanx of states to overcome Republican Charles Evans Hughes's success throughout most of the industrial North.

The depression of 1929 wrote finis to the entrepreneurial industrial era and ushered in a collective-bargaining-based era, in which the political impetus shifted to *labor*. In the early New Deal years, to be sure, the old McKinley-period alignments were still obvious: In both 1932 and 1936, GOP presidential candidates fared best in New England and the northern industrial states, while FDR's highest ratios came in the agricultural and extractive South and West. And indeed, one can see the same patterns as late as 1948: Republican Thomas E. Dewey did best in the industrial North (winning four of the six New England states plus New York, New Jersey, Pennsylvania, and Michigan), and Harry Truman's best ratios came in the South and West.

Even so, the dynamics of change were hard at work. First, organized labor, nurtured by New Deal policies, was in the process of turning the blue-collar industrial states into prime territory for *Democratic* presidential candidates, and at the same time, this increasing urban and labor bias was eroding party loyalties in the conservative South and Bryanesque agrarian West. Second, another major force was at work in the prosperous industrial states: the growth of the post-industrial service and knowledge sectors of the economy, nurturing a new economic elite politically linked to the Democrats, giving the latter still another demographic base, in states such as Massachusetts, New York, Michigan, and California. Third, depression hard times and the shift in the agricultural economy triggered a mass migration of southern Negroes to the big cities of the industrial North and California. In the decades after World War II, all three of these growth factors—labor, Negroes, the knowledge sector— combined to move the industrial North out of its old Republican industrial era politics into a new orbit. Meanwhile, the tide of national migration and urban growth was shifting the balance of national power to the South and West.

By 1960, there were good reasons to believe that America was on the verge of a new political framework. And as the presidential elections of the sixties ticked by, it became clear that the Civil War, or industrial, century of U.S. political alignments had run its course. Yankee, industrial New England, the most Republican and least Democratic region of the United States through the early-industrial (1856–96), industrial (1896–1932), and labor-New Deal-Fair Deal eras (1932–52), was in the process of becoming the section of the country where Republican presidential candidates commanded the *least* support!

Thus, the extraordinary 1972 Massachusetts-Mississippi convolutions reiterated in the Watergate contretemps really amount to what the British army band played at Yorktown: "The World Turned Upside Down." The Civil War framework of the parties has been turned upside down; the New Deal coalition is finished, although its collapse may not be obvious. And with this shift has come a clouding of the old Republican correlation with wealth and education: New York's archetypally affluent and fashionable East Side of Manhattan supported Hubert Humphrey in 1968 and George McGovern in 1972, and the Harvard Law School, citadel of American professional elitism, backed McGovern six to one in a straw poll. Back in 1936, of course, cartoons in *The New Yorker* showed East Side matrons going down to the Trans-Lux to hiss Roosevelt newsreels, and the Harvard straw polls went solidly Republican during the New Deal.

Despite these obvious reversals, Old Guard politicians and academicians are fighting the idea of realignment and its probable corollary, a new majority—New Left-slanted or right-slanted, deep-rooted or shallow—to replace the spent New Deal coalition. Political analyst Richard Scammon exaggerated in summer 1972 when he proclaimed himself as "fighting a one-man battle against realignment." Many others have also resisted.

Much of the confusion is understandable. Periods of U.S. political realignment have rarely been marked by clarity, public optimism, or voter enthusiasm, and this one is no exception. Since 1960, when presidential election turnout reached 64 per cent, voter participation has drifted down to 62 per cent in 1964, 61 per cent in 1968, and an abysmal 56 per cent in 1972. As usual in such a period, minor parties have been common, most often on the right. Besides George Wallace's ten-million-vote candidacy in 1968, third-party conservatives elected a U.S. senator in New York in 1970, and an independent conservative won in Virginia. American Party candidate John Schmitz scored 1 per cent nationally in 1972, but he gathered a sizable protest vote in Idaho, Alaska, and other western states. When people don't get what they want from the major party, they stay home or turn to splinter candidacies. Since the upheaval of the sixties began, the impetus of U.S. splinter politics has—for the first time in our history—been on the right. Meanwhile, voter turnout has slumped badly.

Heretofore, when the compass of American politics has begun to spin, one of the major parties—or a newly formed major party—

has usually brought it under control by getting on the course desired by the *principal* restive surge of public opinion. Then the other party, in turn, has adjusted to new pressures. Voter turnout surges. Party "responsiveness," that overused word, has often depended on realignment, on the major party's shifting to a power base compatible with new policy direction. As a result, U.S. political history has been characterized by a rather clear succession of cycles, described this way by Professor Walter Dean Burnham:

It has been recognized, at least since V. O. Key's "A Critical Theory of Elections," in 1955, that some elections in our history have been far more important than most in their long range consequences for the political system. Such elections tend to "decide" clusters of substantive issues in a more clear-cut way than do most of the ordinary varieties. . . . There is even a consensus among historians as to when these turning points in electoral politics took place. The first came in 1800 when Thomas Jefferson overthrew the Federalist hegemony established by Washington, Adams and Hamilton. The second came in 1828 and in the years afterwards, with the election of Andrew Jackson and the democratization of the presidency. The third, of course, was the election of Abraham Lincoln in 1860, an election that culminated in a catastrophic polarization of society as a whole and resulted in civil war. The fourth critical election was that of William McKinley in 1896; this brought to a close the "Civil War" party system and inaugurated a political alignment convenient to the dominance of American capitalism over the American political economy. Created in the crucible of the massive depression, this "system of 1896" endured until the collapse of the economy in the second. The election of Franklin Roosevelt in 1932 came last in this series and brought a major realignment of electoral politics and policy making structures into the now familiar "welfare pluralist" mode.[4]

Each of these critical elections began a new political cycle during which one of the major parties was clearly dominant in presidential voting. Some analysts do not recognize 1896 as the beginning of a new cycle, but the majority agree, and the idea of a series of cycles starting respectively in 1800, 1828, 1860, 1896, and 1932 has come to be a hallmark of U.S. politics. Historians examining British party elections can also construct a cyclical pattern, but the U.S. model is unique because of our special historical geography and chronology of settlement. All five cycles can be linked to shifts in population, exhaustion, or institutionalization of the prior regime, the growth of third parties, and the build-up of regional discontents.

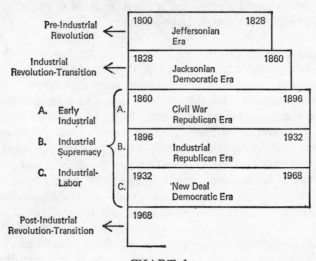

CHART 1
U. S. Presidential Cycles of the 19th and 20th Centuries

As Chart 1 shows, even the numbers proclaim a cyclical theory. Since 1828, when the modern party system more or less began, upheavals have come in 32–36-year intervals. Each critical election put an end to the ideological excess or institutionalized inertia of the previous regime: 1) Jackson's triumph in 1828 smashed the Establishment-dominated "no-party" system that had grown out of James Monroe's "Era of Good Feeling"; 2) Lincoln's election in 1860 ended the incapacity of the Whig-Democrat alignment to face up to North-South divisions, resolution of the slavery issue, and the challenge of the Industrial Revolution; 3) the McKinley breakthrough of 1896 ended the twenty-year stalemate that had prevailed since the mid-seventies, giving industrialism its head and defeating Populism; and 4) FDR's 1932 victory toppled a big-business regime whose credos had helped cause the Great Depression and were unsuitable to national reconstruction.

Prior to these critical elections, as the shortcomings of the regime in power became apparent, third-party movements usually sprang up, identifying the direction from which cyclical upheaval would soon come: The Free-Soil and Abolitionist groups of the 1840s and early 1850s predicted the basic thrust of the new Republican Party and Abraham Lincoln; the Grangers and Populists offered early evidence of the Bryan movement, which would spur realignment (and enthrone industrialism in 1896); and the various socialist candidacies of the World War I era, plus Robert La Follette's 1924 third-party Progressive movement, foreshadowed the basic direction of the New Deal.

Population movement was invariably a factor, creating as it did new political demands, power balances, or social tensions. The opening up of the trans-Appalachian "New West" helped fuel the 1828 victory of Andrew Jackson. Mid-century expansion, and the inability of Congress to continue balancing slave states and free states, was important to the formation of the Republican Party, and the states brought into the Union after the Homestead Act were vital to keeping the GOP in power. The great growth of the northern industrial region was a central factor in launching the new era after 1896, and the political coming of age of the urban immigrant masses during the nineteen twenties laid much of the demographic base of New Deal success.

Scholars enjoy elaborating these phenomena, but it is hardly necessary to structure the minutiae. Suffice it to say that American presidential politics has had a unique logic, a unique and seemingly cyclical structure that responds to certain recurring influences. Using these criteria, one can suggest that the nineteen sixties marked the start of major realignment—a new pattern of U.S. politics shedding the old skin of industrial-era loyalties for a new one as yet imprecisely marked. After all, as of 1968, the typical thirty-six years had passed since the launching of the previous cycle. Liberalism's New Deal-through-Great Society impetus of solving crisis with social programs often served to aggravate the tensions of the nineteen sixties. Dixicrat, States' Rights, and George Wallace's American Party splinter movements had arisen on the right to manifest the anger of southern and blue-collar constituencies breaking away from New Deal loyalties. Moreover, since the New Deal, U.S. population distribution had undergone enormous change: Southern blacks had flooded into major northern cities, creating new tensions with whites;

city after city saw its white middle-class populations empty into the suburbs; and a major white migration had moved from the Northeast and Midwest to the "Sun Belt" of the South and Southwest. In other words, by the late sixties, quite apart from the Massachusetts-Mississippi reversal, U.S. politics once again satisfied most of the historic indices of a new political cycle taking shape.

No single, crashing event has been necessary—like the coming Civil War in 1860 or the Great Depression in 1929—to set these forces in motion. Basic social and economic forces have already done that. Prior to 1972, some political scientists queried the lack of a hammer blow to fatally break the old system. But the events of 1972–74 may have provided that blow. Massive erosion of public confidence, from the Vietnam War and urban riots of the sixties to the Watergate crisis of 1973, has weakened the old party system—in all likelihood, fatally—and pointed to a subsequent orbit of conflict further emphasizing the very cultural animosities apparent in U.S. internal strife. As chapter 2 will describe in detail, much of this conflict can be related to the new lifestyles, values, reactions, and counterreactions that have appeared in the United States with what sociologist Daniel Bell calls "The Coming of Post-Industrial Society." Post-industrialism involves the changeover of the United States from an industrial economy based on the production of goods to the *first* economy in the world resting on the production and consumption of services, knowledge, and technology—and this metamorphosis, in turn, was closely related to the campus and communications revolutions plus the rise of ideology. In the end, Nixon-era strife may turn out to have been most important for its role in collapsing the old party system.

But if a new cycle can be said to have begun in 1968, the question is: Another traditional (32–36-year) party shift, or something quite new? More likely than not, the Post-Industrial Revolution, especially the escalating political centrality of the media, signals a new type of party—and a new, minimal role for parties that will not replicate the deep-rooted industrial-era pattern. Local and presidential voting patterns are becoming disconnected. The changed circumstances of communications-age society are the key.

2

POST-INDUSTRIAL SOCIETY

ECONOMIC UPHEAVAL and political change go together. Only a little more than a century ago, the now-fading industrial era was a source of great political consternation as it first spread its grimy wings in Britain. In 1845, an angry Benjamin Disraeli wrote a novel, *Sybil*, subtitled *The Two Nations*, railing against the way in which the Industrial Revolution, with its upthrust of beer barons and Lancashire cotton-spinning magnates, was shredding the traditional fabric of English society and politics. His point was essentially correct, if too gaudily stated. Disraeli's England, and the rest of Europe in its wake, was embarked upon the most thorough socioeconomic upheaval since the sixteenth–seventeenth-century period of Renaissance, Reformation, and the rise of capitalism. The latter had replaced feudalism with the nation-state; the Industrial Revolution, in turn, transferred political power from a rural-based aristocracy to a broader and urbanized middle class.

The dynamics of the Industrial Revolution are far from irrelevant to American politics of the seventies. Certain occasional, infrequent magnitudes of socioeconomic change—the Renaissance, the Industrial Revolution—have been pervasive enough to throw existing political alignments into obsolescence and disarray. If one accepts the idea of revolutionary transportation and mass production as the key to the mid-nineteenth-century upheaval and a basic pattern lasting through the nineteen fifties, then the impact of the *Post-*

Industrial Revolution—the shift to a media polity and a knowledge economy—represents another such watershed.

In their time, the emerging Industrial Revolution politics of the early-nineteenth century represented a massive change. From the end of the dynastic Wars of the Roses, in 1483, to the Glorious Revolution, of 1688, the Reformation and the rise of capitalism secured a hold on Britain. After the Glorious Revolution ratified the ascendancy of Protestantism and commercialism, parliamentary politics began to institutionalize on a party basis: Tories versus Whigs. It was very much a clash of family against family, and British political historians are wont to wryly note that, as late as 1820, the best explanation of Tory-Whig partisanship often eschewed ideology— or, indeed, issues of any kind—and looked to family loyalties going back to the divisions of 1688. American party politics came out of a kindred caldron: the Revolutionary War. Our early division between Federalists and (Jeffersonian) Democratic-Republicans reflected colonial-era antecedents and disparate attitudes toward how far the social-reform thrust of the American Revolution ought to be carried.

As discussed at greater length in chapter 4, the Industrial Revolution created an entirely new political context. Cleavages dating back to the reign of William and Mary or disputes over royal prerogative became absurd. So did arguments over Hobbes versus Locke. In both Britain and the United States, Tory versus Whig and Federalist versus Democratic-Republican divisions lost their importance. By the 1830s, party nomenclature was in flux. And by the late 1850s, the Industrial Revolution had wiped out old party cleavages and created new ones: Republicans (northern industry) versus Democrats (southern agriculture) in the United States, and Liberals (shopkeepers and urban industry) versus Conservatives (traditional church and gentry) in Britain. Obviously, party divisions can be capsuled in this way only by a dangerous degree of simplification, and things were to become very different in, say, 1939, from what they had been in 1870. Even so, it seems fair to say that the party cleavages prevailing from the mid-nineteenth century through the nineteen fifties owe their basic shape to what might be called "industrial-society politics"—that is, the loyalties shaped by industrialization-related conflicts ranging from the U. S. Civil War to labor-management collective bargaining.

Tensions run high when an advanced society is undergoing the magnitude of change represented by the Industrial Revolution. Political power, the distribution of wealth—everything hangs in the balance. Issues tend to zero in on encouraging versus regulating the practices and socioeconomic pursuits of the new class. In the case of the Industrial Revolution, there was a bad lag—and resultant squalor and oppression—before industrial expansion was far enough evolved to be regulated.

Since World War II, the United States (far more than Britain) has been in the vanguard of a new, post-industrial economic era increasingly built around the sale of services and knowledge rather than manufactured products. The percentage of Americans who still live in the original cities of nineteenth-century industrialism has plummeted; the mill canyons of the Merrimack Valley and others like it have become cemeteries of economic geography. Only a few miles away, Massachusetts' research, think-tank, and high-technology complex along greater Boston's Route 128 has become an early symbol of the new post-industrial socioeconomy. Roughly 35 per cent of the U.S. gross national product is now accounted for by the production, consumption, and dissemination of knowledge. Not guns, railroad engines, ginghams, or calicos: *knowledge*. And, not surprisingly, this massive shift in the locus of American wealth, culture, and power has thrown old political loyalties and alignments into a tizzy. In New York City, the blue-collar workers and bus drivers of Queens keynote conservative animosity toward the liberal post-industrial upper-middle class of midtown Manhattan, a *reversal* of industrial-era ideological combat.

Exact description of this "knowledge industry" is difficult. Some of its component parts are obvious: the huge bureaucracies of government multiplied tenfold since the New Deal era, the colleges and universities now serving 10 million young Americans, the huge communications empires, the network of think-tank and charitable foundations, and the huge corporate giants of knowledge technology —IBM, Xerox, and so forth. The lesser fry include consultants on problems from poverty to banking, professionals—from doctors and lawyers to architects—and many others providing a variety of specialized services. Indirectly, many other forms of "commerce" are involved. Banks, insurance companies, and stock-brokerage houses are becoming more "knowledgified" as the corporate economy itself leans more toward computerization and information systems. Many large corporations are also moving toward the research

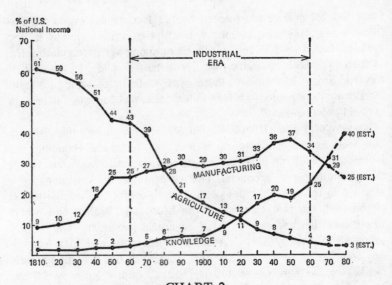

CHART 2
The New American Knowledge Economy

Notes:

1) Included in the manufacturing category (all manufacturing except categories excluded below) are public utilities, mining, and transportation, closely tied to the industrialization of the United States. These additions increase the post-1950 turndown in the manufacturing segment.

2) Data for early years (1810–30) are projections based on changes in agricultural/rural/farm employment/residence output and in value of coal produced and shipping carried.

3) Components of "knowledge" segment figure (capable of precise use only since 1929):

    a) Communications category—all

    b) Manufacturing category—printing, publishing, and allied industries, electrical machinery

    c) Services category—miscellaneous business services

                motion pictures

                amusement, recreation services

                medical, other health services

                legal services

                educational services

                non-profit membership organizations

                miscellaneous professional services

    d) Government, government enterprises category—general federal government

                general state government

N.B. While some of the above categories are not entirely knowledge industry in nature, some other categories not included (for example, finance, insurance, and real estate) have major knowledge-industry components, so the above totals are reasonable.

and the "social awareness" outlook promoted by the knowledge sector.

Like the Industrial Revolution, the Post-Industrial Revolution hardly occurred overnight. It began during the New Deal and World War II, breaking into a run during the nineteen fifties and becoming obvious, in size and importance, during the "social revolution" of the sixties. An approximate graph of the percentage of the GNP accounted for by the production, consumption, and dissemination of knowledge is shown below.

Economic upheaval of this magnitude has, of course, changed American society and culture. In increasing measure, America's new mandarins are not the people who sell manufactured items but the people who shape and market *ideas and information*. The media have become pivotal. Politics have also been affected. Instead of having a vested economic interest in stability, as did previous conservative business establishments, the knowledge sector has a vested interest in change—in the unmooring of convention, in socioeconomic experiments, in the ongoing consumption of new ideas. The coming of the age of the knowledge elite in the sixties was partially the result of—and then dangerous additional fuel for—a decade of social ferment.

The knowledge sector fattened on this surge. Oregon Congresswoman Edith Green, then the ranking Democratic on the House Education and Labor Committee, coined the term "Education-Poverty Industrial Complex" to describe the way in which firms and individuals were reaping huge profits from government-research and social-program spending.[1] In the 1920s and 1930s, historian Charles Beard argued, with some success, that conservative Supreme Court decisions were deifying a Constitution based on the economic self-interest of the Founding Fathers.[2] The evidence furnished by Mrs. Green and others supports a kindred economic interpretation of the liberal interest group's commitment to eliminating the housing, educational, and other roots of unequal opportunity.

Heavily liberal knowledge-sector politics fit every aspect of logic. The intelligentsia's traditional support for liberal credos is bolstered by economic interest in social and research spending plus involvement in the mores of the new affluent knowledge-sector culture. For the first time in memory, liberalism has become the ideology of a privileged sector of the population, and many of the nation's chic residential districts, formerly the strongholds of conservative businessmen, are now strongly liberal—such places as Back Bay, Boston; the East Side of Manhattan; Scarsdale, New York; Shaker Heights, Ohio; suburban San Francisco; and so forth. Educators, consultants, and media executives have changed yesteryear's population of bankers, railroad vice-presidents, and merchants.

As a result, conservative politicians are attacking knowledge-sector liberals, condemning "elitists," "the eastern establishment," and the "Manhattan arrangement" in the style once reserved for railroads, banks, and public utilities. Rural, blue-collar, and middle-class constituencies are unhappy with "elitist" positions on such issues as crime, marijuana, busing, capital punishment, pornography, abortion, and related "Greening of America" issues of social and moral change. Futurist Herman Kahn has said that "growing hostility to this class is one of the most serious things this country faces."[3] On the other side of the ideological coin, Harvard's Samuel Beer believes that "The Media Revolution is as powerful as the industrial revolution was. The word manipulators are on top, and like the 19th Century capitalists everyone considered inferior . . . will wind up running the world."[4] Whichever side of the argument one takes, the evidence is clear that post-industrialism has shaped a new economic, political, and social context for America.

A. THE KNOWLEDGE
INDUSTRY

Post-industrialism reached its critical mass during the nineteen fifties, when the United States became the world's first nation with more white-collar workers than blue-collar workers. Both the New Deal and World War II were vital staging grounds. A mere quarter of a century earlier, when the Democrats came to power in 1933, the idea of a massive U.S. knowledge industry would have been ludicrous. Despite jokes about Roosevelt and his government of Harvard professors, the production, dissemination, and consumption of knowledge was a piddling force. Steel and shipping still had the money; intellectuals were grateful for WPA jobs. Moreover, until the rise of a large, distinct knowledge sector, broadcast networks, major newspapers, and fashionable Ivy League colleges tended to reflect the conservative views of the industrial establishment. Not until the 1950s would government programs, burgeoning communications, research, technology, education, and social work muster the

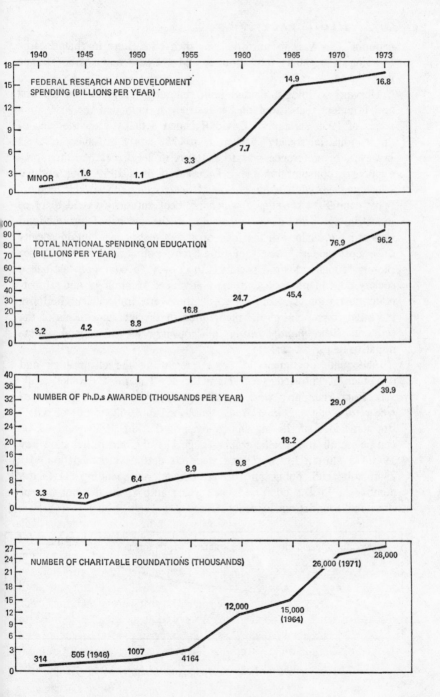

economic prowess to nurture their own elite. Late in that decade, sociologists began to talk about the advent of a new socioeconomic era.

Harvard sociologist Daniel Bell, generally recognized as the first and foremost theorist of post-industrialism, launched the term in a series of 1959 seminars.[1] David Riesman actually used the idea of "post-industrial society" earlier, in a 1958 study of "mass leisure"; however, his reference was to patterns of leisure rather than production or consumption.[2] Ralf Dahrendorf, in a 1959 book entitled *Class and Conflict in an Industrial Society,* hypothesized a coming "post-capitalist" society, in which political authority would displace industrial-era criteria of ownership of the means of production.[3] Others have dealt with the idea of a post-mass-consumption society or a post-modern society. Future-shock popularizer Alvin Toffler prefers "super-industrial society," to convey "a complex, fast-paced society dependent upon extremely advanced technology and a post-materialist value system."[4] Yet, all these are embroidery; Bell has the basic conceptual cloth: recognition of the metamorphosis of the economy from *manufacturing* to *knowledge* as the central, determinative factor.

Inadequate documentation exists regarding the chronology and dynamics of knowledge-sector emergence. The most detailed analysis, Fritz Machlup's work on *The Production and Distribution of Knowledge in the United States,* published in 1962, is out of date.[5] But some idea of the big change-over of the late 1950s and 1960s can be seen in the specific graphs (page 19) of Chart 3 that show key 1940–73 shifts: 1) in federal research and development outlays, 2) in total U.S. public and private educational spending, 3) in the number of Ph.D.s conferred each year, and 4) in the number of charitable foundations incorporated.

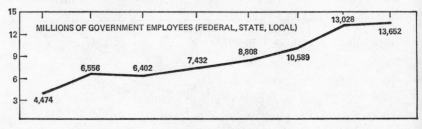

CHART 3
The Emergence of the Knowledge Industry, 1940–73

The importance of these dates and dynamics to political analysis ought to be clear, confirming the essential correlation between the growth of the knowledge sector and a basic, fundamental shift in political loyalties and alignments. As the knowledge sector grew, its first major political impact was felt during the late fifties in the Democratic "reform" movements of Manhattan, Boston, Chicago, and Los Angeles. Spearheaded by liberal middle-class professionals, these clubs were concentrated in the most fashionable urban areas, and their values—forerunners of the New Politics—were quite opposite to those held in the working-class areas that then dominated the Democratic Party. Obviously, changing economics is not the only factor involved, but the correlation between knowledge-sector emergence and the New Politics is clear enough from New England to California. As the one grew, so did the other.

Research and development outlays are central. In the past decade, $150 billion has been spent on the three components of R&D: basic research, applied research, and development. The big surge came after World War II: annual federal R&D expenditures were $250 million in 1940, just under $1 billion in 1948, $3 billion in 1957, $8 billion in 1960, $16 billion annually during the 1967–71 period, and $20 billion in 1974.[6] While federal R&D is the biggest component, it accounts for only 60 per cent of the nation's total research commitment. The 1973 R&D Resources Report of the National Science Foundation fixed that total at $27.3 billion in 1971 and (estimated) $28.9 billion in 1972.

This magnitude of expenditure reshapes a nation. Back in 1940, there were just a handful of R&D companies in the United States, but, by 1969, the National Science Foundation estimated that there were 11,355. The number of non-profit research centers in the country has climbed from thirty-two hundred in 1965 to fifty-three hundred in 1969 and roughly seven thousand today.[7] The biggest build-up has been in New York, New England, California, and the Washington, D.C., area. The Washington mushrooming process is illustrative: In 1950, there were forty-eight private R&D firms in the area; by 1956, there were 107; and in 1967, there were 339 firms with 44,445 employees and a payroll of $360 million a year. Then, from 1967 to 1969, the total number more than doubled once again: by November 1969, there were just about seven hundred firms, with an annual payroll of $585 million. The estimate for 1975 is fifteen hundred firms, with a total payroll of over $1 billion.[8]

The confluence of the civil-rights revolution, the urban crisis, and the Johnson landslide of 1964 gave a tremendous boost to the education, urban-planning, welfare, social-research, and brotherhood vocations. After Lyndon Johnson's 1964 victory, the lopsidedly Democratic Eighty-ninth Congress enacted scores of social programs that had been on the liberal agenda for years. Educational, urban, and housing outlays soared. Enactment of the War Against Poverty soon brought expenditures of $2 billion a year (and—as cynics noted—a hundred firms in the greater Washington area alone that were consulting on problems of poverty).[9]

Meanwhile, government itself was mushrooming. Chart 4 shows the explosive growth of the federal Department of Health, Education and Welfare. In 1946, civilian employment in federal, state, and local government totaled 6.5 million; by 1956, 8 million; by 1966, 11 million. The figure for 1972 was 13.6 million. Much of the growth has been at the state and local level. Labor Department estimates for 1980 project *18 million* civilian federal, state, and local government employees. Bureaucracy has become one of the largest segments of the U.S. economy, hiring more people than the entire durable-goods segment of manufacturing.[10]

As the federal money began to flow into social endeavors, private enterprise began to stir. Corporations began to find educational, job-rehabilitation, and urban efforts profitable. Many of the new conglomerates mushrooming during the sixties led the way. In 1967, Socialist Michael Harrington wrote about the *Social-Industrial Complex* and predicted that remedial sociology and private profits would prove incompatible.[11] As noted before, Congresswoman Edith Green lamented that a new "Education-Poverty Industrial Complex" had grown up around federal spending. And Robert Krueger, president of Planning Research Corporation, estimated the professional services market at $7 billion a year and growing.[12]

Having become a major item of commerce, social concern spread to law and finance. In the bull market of 1965–68, Wall Street investment houses gobbled up securities with names smacking of scientific technology, research, planning, communications, ecology, advanced housing or educational techniques, informational systems, computer hardware and software, anti-pollution technology, and so forth. Blue-chip law firms began to show an interest in poverty,

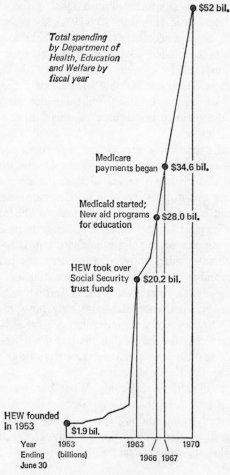

CHART 4
The Expanding Empire of HEW

housing, and consumer law. Fortunes made in these fields created new concentrations of wealth (which showed striking availability to left-liberal presidential candidates in 1968 and 1972). The New York *Times* and other major newspapers hailed "big-business progressives" for supporting Great Society urban and educational programs, and such knowledge-industry behemoths as Xerox and IBM played up-front roles in organizations such as the Urban Coalition.

Meanwhile, foundation power was also burgeoning. In 1950, there had been a thousand charitable foundations in the United States, controlling $5 billion in resources. By 1970, there were twenty-five thousand, with total assets in excess of $20 billion.[13] The Ford Foundation alone controlled $3 billion in assets. University endowment funds quadrupled between 1950 and 1970. With the number of students at higher educational institutions rising from 2 million in 1950 to 8 million in 1970, federal education aid ballooned —and so did the national importance of universities and related research complexes.

Obviously, the knowledge sector of the American economy is hard to define—at least beyond involvement in the production, consumption, and dissemination of knowledge. Planners and architects obviously are part of it; so are people in education, communications, and government bureaucracies. But what about the research chemists at Dow Chemical or the marketing analysts at Standard Oil? While nobody thinks of napalm-manufacturing Dow Chemical as being in the liberal-leaning knowledge industry, the point is that big business is becoming steadily less entrepreneurial and steadily more related to knowledge, research, and information. Urban-affairs specialists at a big insurance company may have much the same outlook as HUD bureaucrats or journalists at Time-Life. Post-industrial theorist Daniel Bell believes that the transition will continue and the "knowledge institute" will replace the corporation as the key organization of the next hundred years.[14]

Statistics are difficult to come by: What can be said with little room for doubt is that an increasingly large, affluent slice of America earns its bread from handling and applying knowledge, and that this new segment of the economy is already a powerful vested interest for social change and liberal politics.

B. A MEDIACRACY

Among the most important trends of the 1970s has been a spreading perception of the pivotal, well-nigh dominant, role the media have come to play in American life. If the Industrial Revolution created a new elite and launched a new, business domination of politics, the knowledge revolution raises the prospect of dominant *media* influence—of mediacracy instead of aristocracy or democracy.

As of the mid-seventies, this possibility is just beginning to be taken seriously. From various perspectives—political science, sociology, economics—theorists are pinpointing the new centrality of the media. Author Joseph Epstein has even argued that the media may play the same role in the post-industrial era that Wall Street played in the earlier period: that of socioeconomic-elite-*cum*-bogeyman:

> The next national villain, if they have not already arrived in that role, figures to be the Media. . . . To break a politician, to make a celebrity, to turn an issue, these are not small things. Wall Street and Madison Avenue had money at their disposal, which gave them power; the Media have the attention of the public at their disposal, which gives them an equivalent if not greater power. . . . Should the country fall into a full depression, who better to hold responsible than the party thought to hold the most power in the nation, and at the moment, that party is thought to be the media.[1]

While most Americans may not perceive the economic nature of the Post-Industrial Revolution, they *have* perceived its impact. A survey taken in early 1974 by *U. S. News & World Report* found a cross section of national leaders ranking television ahead of the White House as the country's number one power center. In this respect, the past two decades have witnessed a vital quantum shift. Economic data make this clear. The media have not simply become more powerful in the old context of things; *their growth has changed the old industrial-era equation.*

By definition, the communications industry must serve as the linchpin of the economy's new knowledge sector. But, through the nineteen fifties, while the industrial era prevailed, the still relatively small and subservient communications industry had no particular ideological coloration of its own. Magazines, broadcasting companies, newspapers, and advertising firms tended to be conservative, like the business community as a whole. This remains true in most parts of the South, Midwest, and Rocky Mountains, where traditional economic forms still dominate.

Then, as the communications industry ballooned during the late fifties and early sixties, along with other knowledge-sector elements, it began to take on a distinctly liberal ideology. The first media affected were those in the fashionable urban areas. Such media as *Time, Life, Newsweek,* the New York *Times,* the Washington *Post,* the Boston *Globe,* the Baltimore *Sun,* the Cowles publications, and the TV networks—many of them on the conservative side in the thirties—started becoming distinctly more liberal than the country as a whole. As the media revolution intensified, so did its ideological impact.

Here one must note that there is no real parallel outside the United States. Other countries have relatively small private-media sectors. Elsewhere, television is generally government controlled and not a massive private enterprise like CBS, NBC, and ABC. The concentration of private-media economic power in the United States —backstopped by other knowledge-sector enterprises, notably education—dwarfs that of any other nation. The United States is as far ahead of the rest of the world in the Post-Industrial Revolution as circa-1850 Britain was in the Industrial Revolution.

Most of the key U.S. media are owned by large communications conglomerates. Newspapers own broadcasting stations. Broadcasting companies own magazines and publishing houses. Since the communications business mushroomed in the sixties, it has begun creating its own culture—or, as Nixon-administration spokesmen argued, adversary culture. Even though most small-town and small-city newspapers remain conservative and Republican, the provincial print media have barely held their own since the fifties. With the rise of the knowledge industry, communications affluence and influence have tended to concentrate in the New York-Washington corridor (and in a few other areas such as Los Angeles and Chicago, where two important media baronies that were once conservative stalwarts—the Los Angeles *Times* and the Chicago *Tribune*—have become increasingly middle-of-the-road). It is this "New York-Washington media axis," with its "Ivy League elitist adversary culture," that triggered conservative animosity.

Chart 5 shows the late-nineteen-fifties and early-nineteen-sixties coming of age of the communications industry. The rise of the New York-Washington media axis is less easy to chart, but here are some statistics. Since 1940, the New York *Times* has increased its circulation 30 per cent in its home city and 150 per cent beyond New York. The New York *Times* news service, purchased by only sixteen North American newspapers in 1956, is sold to about 250 today. The Washington *Post*/Los Angeles *Times* service, started in 1962 with twenty-one subscribers, now has over two hundred. In the years from 1940 to 1968, *Time, Newsweek,* and *U. S. News & World Report* increased their circulation by 585 per cent. Those are the big guns in the print media.

All figures in millions of dollars	1930	1935	1940	1945	1950	1955	1960	1965	1970	1973 (Est.)
Newspaper Receipts	1,073	668	846	1,792	2,375	2,926	4,136	5,156	6,967	8,310
Magazine Receipts	507	300	409	1,019	1,119	1,413	2,132	2,626	3,195	3,655
Radio Station Revenues	—	87	147	299	445	543	597	793	1,137	1,465
TV Station Revenues	—	—	—	0.3	106	745	1,269	1,965	2,808	3,700
Advertising Volume	2,607	1,690	2,088	2,874	5,710	9,194	11,932	15,255	19,600	25,765
Electronic Computer Sales	—	—	—	—	1	105	500	1,400	3,630	4,750

CHART 5

The Postwar Rise of the Communications Industry

Television's growth is bigger still; just a few households had television in the years after World War II—few are without it today. Television has become a multibillion-dollar business, and the three New York-based television networks, via their news and documentary programs, have become the principal arbiters of American opinion. Survey after survey spotlights television as the most influential medium in the United States. One estimate has 90 per cent of U.S. national news coverage originating with UPI, AP, the New York *Times* Syndicate, Time Inc., the Washington *Post* (which owns *Newsweek*), and the television networks.[2]

Since the New York *Times,* the Washington *Post,* and three networks and major newsmagazines are all based in New York and Washington, as are most other opinion magazines (*Harper's Magazine, The New Republic,* etc.), most publishing houses, and many small broadcasting companies, the existence of a cultural-geographic "media axis" seems indisputable. Liberal opinions are virtually *de rigueur* within this milieu, and failure to advance them is professionally crippling. Daniel P. Moynihan errs in harping on elite Ivy League origins. Columnist Robert Novak best capsuled the dynamics this way, in April 1972: "The national media is a melting pot where the journalists, regardless of background, are welded into a homogenous ideological mold, joined to the liberal establishment and alienated from the masses of the country."[3]

This overwhelming left-liberal tilt has been strengthened by the interaction of the major media and the social upheavals of the sixties. Media expert Ben H. Bagdikian, in his book *The Information Machines,* noted that the communications revolution of the 1840s (Morse's telegraph, railroads, steam vessels, etc.) helped stir up Europe's revolutions of 1848, and he argues that "the spasms of change in American society in the mid-Nineteen Sixties are attributable in large part to new methods of communication."[4] Obviously, the media—television in particular—fueled the civil-rights revolution by spreading information, hope, and interracial examples across the South. Television also fanned youthful consciousness of poverty and the contradictions of U.S. society.

Besides spurring upheaval, the media were in turn strongly influenced by it. The fashionable media substantially interacted with other involved and growing segments of the knowledge industry: universities, think-tanks, foundations, social and welfare workers, urban planners, and so forth. The New York-Washington media axis became closely linked, in succession, to the liberal integration, anti-poverty, anti-hunger, anti-war, and ecology causes. Article followed article, in-depth studies abounded, and television documentaries—many later proven partially erroneous and distorted—stirred additional controversy. While the media in Chillicothe or Peoria might be spokesmen for local families, banks, or industries, the New York-and-Washington-based media were emerging as pre-eminent spokesmen for the causes of interest-group liberalism.

Until the Post-Industrial Revolution, the media—indeed the entire knowledge industry—did not represent a power concentration in their own right. Instead, they reflected the politics of other U.S. subcultures. The 1956 edition of C. Wright Mills's book *The Power Elite* makes little mention of the media.[5] But, by the late sixties, the communications industry was the center of a new, knowledge economy six or eight times as rich as it had been in 1956, and capable of sustaining an affluent intelligentsia. Lionel Trilling, Irving Kristol, Daniel P. Moynihan, and others have described major elements of the new class as an "adversary culture" hostile to the prevailing middle-class values of work, patriotism, and traditional morality. Its power lies in the fact that it is not some starving assemblage of garret pamphleteers but an *affluentsia* with substantial control over the knowledge and information functions of an economy and society in which those functions are becoming dominant. This makes concentration of media power—and television power especially—a vital question. Patrick Buchanan, the Nixon-administration aide who most frequently expressed conservative anti-media philosophies, offered this analysis in his 1973 book *The New Majority:*

> The growth of network power, and its adversary posture towards the national government, is something beyond the tradition—something new in American life.
>
> The executives, anchormen and correspondents of the network news would have us believe that they are the direct heirs of John Peter Zenger and Elijah Lovejoy. That is not the case.
>
> These men are not victims of society or government in any sense of the word. They are ranking members of the privileged class, the most prestigious, powerful, wealthy and influential journalists in all history. The corporations in whose studios they labor are not struggling journals; they are communications cartels, media conglomerates holding positions within their industry comparable to that of Ford and General Motors.[6]

Coming years are likely to see the media increasingly at the center of U.S. political conflict: first, because of their ongoing increment of power; second, because of their espousal of adversary-culture views; third, because of the increasing articulation by young conservatives of anti-media politics; and fourth, because media influence is becoming so determinative of the fate of politicians and political ideas. The media are seen replacing party organizations and corporations in influence.

Meanwhile, the law is in flux. In 1973, the Florida Supreme Court acted upon the complaint of one spurned politician in handing down a decision that the Miami *Herald,* having attacked an office seeker, was obliged to give him space to reply. But the U. S. Supreme Court overturned the ruling. On the television front, new dispute has been focused on the Fairness Rule. Indeed, media theoretician Marshall McLuhan asserts that the Communications Revolution has turned politicians, bureaucrats, and experts into mere "servants" of the "new electronic citizenry who create and exchange information as a way of life."[7] In bygone eras, politicians were much less at the mercy of the media. Even if the press was solidly against a President or a governor, it was only one factor in opinion molding. As late as FDR's day, political opinion was largely a product of courthouses and clubhouses, rallies, torchlight parades, Tammany picnics, turkeys at Christmastime, jobs for the needy, and the rest of the "old politics." Per McLuhan, the Communications Revolution has changed this: politicians and political ideas are now largely merchandized via the media, and if the people are to have a full choice, the media cannot be allowed to decide who and what should be advanced or suppressed.

Media focus on the supposed guarantees of the First Amendment may be missing the overriding factor: the massive metamorphosis of socioeconomic power in the 180 years since the ratification of the Bill of Rights. Via the knowledge revolution, the weak, halfpenny press of the eighteenth century has become one of the most influential forces in the nation. John Peter Zenger's ideas were subject to the whims of the government; now many politicians argue that *they* are subject to the whims of the media.

Returning to the idea that the media represent an emerging new concentration of power akin to the railroads, trusts, and monopolies of the late-nineteenth century, a similar legal debate may also be beginning: how to square the rights of the public with the rights of the media. Bear in mind that, one hundred years ago, railroads, utilities, and trusts were *also* claiming the protection of the Bill of Rights. Then it was not the First Amendment at issue but the Fourteenth, under which a person's or a corporation's right to "due process" was deemed infringed by legislation applying unprecedented limitations on practices and rates. For years, the courts overextended the protections of the Bill of Rights, but, ultimately, the balance of public interest was perceived, and regulation triumphed. Thus, the Bill of Rights is hardly a static legal concept. If the Fourteenth Amendment could mean something different in 1938—in recognition of changing circumstances—from what it did in 1888, then perhaps the First Amendment may undergo a shifting interpretation of its own to reflect the new status of the communications industry. The media may be forced into the status of utilities regulated to provide access. Marshall McLuhan's speculation in this direction—that the idea of "a right to global 'coverage' has taken the place of the older right of each individual to express his opinion"—may very well prophesy a major post-industrial-society political battleground.[8]

C. THE NEW ELITE

As we know from studies by Vilfredo Pareto and others on the "circulation of elites," that circulation is less than precise; national elites do not change like the guard at Buckingham Palace. Thus, emphasis on the new elite in American sociopolitics mostly rests on a decisive shift in *importance*. A lot of Americans are still making high incomes in manufacturing; and a lot of affluent citizens are conservatives—perhaps a majority. Even so, the Post-Industrial Revolution has created a new knowledge elite heavily liberal in politics. Given the increasingly communications-based nature of our society, their influence is enormous and rapidly overshadowing that of the manufacturing sector. Attacks on the new mandarins—the "eastern establishment"—refers to this element and their allies, and not to some fusty Louis Auchincloss or J. P. Marquand-style Ancien Regimists still holding out on Beacon Hill or Park Avenue.

Before describing and locating the new class, it may be useful to show what makes it so different. American cultural and political history has been a procession of elites, from Tidewater Virginia tobacco planters and Federalist merchants to the "malefactors of great wealth" whom Franklin Roosevelt damned so effectively. Until now, however, these elites have been essentially conservative: agricultural or industrial upper classes dedicated to minimizing income taxation, government restriction of business, and the cost of labor. To be sure, they were not always opposed to government activism. Programs such as Alexander Hamilton's systemization of debt, Nicholas Biddle's Bank of the United States, Henry Clay's American System of internal improvements, and the huge post-Civil War system of land grants to railroads characterized activism of a sort enthusiastically *favored* by conservative economic elites. What they usually did not like was legislation aimed at raising the wages of the masses or redistributing income to the poor by means of assistance programs.

Although the extent varied, opposition to change generally went hand in hand with economic affluence. Sometimes, as in the early days of the Industrial Revolution, entrepreneurs wanted limited social upheaval that would open up a society of third earls and fourth marquesses to the *arrivisme* of first beer barons. This was nineteenth-century liberalism; a demand not for equality but for *access*. It was not a demand for changing the system so much as for getting into it. Most of all, nineteenth-century liberalism was not interested in transferring wealth to low-income groups or in providing social services based on their needs. No such market existed. To nineteenth-century elites, whether they styled themselves conservative or liberal, low-income groups were generally an economic threat rather than an economic opportunity. To elites whose affluence came from agriculture, manufacturing, shipping, and finance, social change usually *cost money*—higher taxes, higher wages, shorter hours—instead of *generating profits*.

Agricultural and industrial societies always had their unhappy intellectuals—lawyers, clerks, teachers, radical journalists—men whose profits lay in ideas rather than things, and who were thus in the vanguard of upheavals and demands for reform. But the intelligentsia was always a small subclass, influential at times when it could channel public unrest, otherwise subordinate. The Post-Industrial Revolution has changed this. The economy of the late-twentieth-century United States is a marketplace of ideas and advanced technology. Sociologists have replaced carpenters, communicators have replaced coachmen, analysts blacksmiths, computer programmers wheelwrights. About 25 per cent of U.S. jobs are filled by people who deal in information, knowledge, research, or communications, and an increasing number of the best positions go to managers and theoreticians who deal in ideas and methods. They approach society from a new vantage point. Their capital is movable, not fixed. Progressively less of the U.S. gross national product comes from extractive or manufacturing industries, and even there, research has become the key. Change does not threaten the affluent intelligentsia of the Post-Industrial Society the way it threatened the landowners and industrialists of the New Deal. On the contrary, change is as essential to the knowledge sector as inventory turnover is to a merchant or a manufacturer. Change keeps up demand for the product (research, news, theory, and technology). Post-industrialism, a knowledge elite, and accelerated social change appear to go hand in hand.

Previous economic elites necessarily emphasized tradition and traditional institutions: family, church, monarchy. Much of Europe remains that way, with the Anglican and Catholic religions being bulwarks of conservative politics in provincial Britain, France, and West Germany. Support for the monarchy, the church, and the family all nurture political traditionalism among low-income Europeans, with the result that upper-income elites promote and preserve these institutions. Studies of British voting show clearly that Anglican (Established) Church membership and enthusiasm for the Crown correlate strongly with the propensity of 30–40 per cent of the British working class to back Conservative rather than Labour Party candidates. Conservative American elites have long appealed to low-income traditionalists with intangibles such as free enterprise, our constitutional government, and the American way. Until recently, the central facet of low-income objection to conservative politics was *economic*. A small middle-class minority of intelligentsia might oppose conservative traditionalism on cultural grounds ranging from social justice to anti-clericalism, but the bulk of the ballots against conservative elites were cast on economic grounds— and traditionalism won many more votes for conservatism in low-income ranks than it lost among the free-thinking middle classes.

Post-industrialism is turning this pattern on its proverbial ear. The new knowledge elite does not preserve and protect existing traditions and institutions. On the contrary, far more than previous new classes, the knowledge elite has sought to modify or replace traditional institutions with new relationships and power centers. Secondly, in the United States the great mass of population is now in the middle-income bracket, and it resents the new elite's nihilism as well as its demand for tax dollars to support or increase programs seen as benefiting the elite/ghetto social engineering symbiosis. These relationships are at the root of a politics very different from that of the industrial (or New Deal) era. Turnabout No. 1: The new elite often attacks the traditional institutions most strongly supported by the non-elite. Turnabout No. 2: Non-elite economic opposition to the new elite reflects *opposition* to high taxation and welfare spending rather than the traditional popular desire for more outlays. Turnabout No. 3: There is unprecedentedly little income-level distinction between the new elite and their foes. Plumbers and professors do not have the same income disparities that prevailed between millowners and millworkers or nobles and swineherds. Cultural and social issues are displacing direct economic hostilities.

Nothing is more central to the controversiality of the new class than its 1963–72 attempt to sidestep existing outlooks and institutions and reprogram American society. Conceiving themselves unfettered by the past, the new elite thought that *society* could be unfettered—and old restraints cast aside. Aided by the revolution in oral contraceptives, moral standards were thrown off, from King's Road in London's Chelsea to San Francisco's North Beach. What had been promiscuity became openness, naturalness, and freedom. Youthful naïveté became goodness; war and the military became intolerably evil; divisions of class and ethnicity were ignored amid new blueprints of busing, rent subsidies, and proclamations of a new brotherhood and social malleability; criminality was downplayed amid talk of unequal opportunity; poverty was declared conquerable, and everyone was labeled educable—environment, not heredity, being the key; drugs were tolerated and even encouraged, if not as another vista of life, at least as another expression of freedom. Obviously, this compilation is debatable; none of these attitudes have ever been universally shared by the emerging knowledge elite. Suffice it to say that the above *does* represent a general catalogue of outlooks propagated by the intelligentsia of the sixties, themes that became controversial under their auspices.

Polls indicate that many of these positions are negatively regarded by the 60–70 per cent of Americans who support traditional institutions (family, church, neighborhood, police, the military) and who practice traditional lifestyles (the Protestant ethic, closed-door sex, flag-waving, and some hypocrisy rather than "letting it all hang out"). Futurist Herman Kahn expects the conflict between traditional America and the new class to play a major, probably dominant role in the politics of the next decade or two. "The upper-middle class—the group running the media, educators, city planners, some students—all are basically out of touch with reality. It's a very specific illness of a very specific group, less than ten percent of the country. . . . The average American is extremely concerned about the future of the country. He also feels that something is going wrong, but what's going wrong is the upper-middle class . . . Americans are bothered by a credibility gap. Not the gap between the hippies and the President, not the gap between Spiro Agnew and the press, but between the average American and the prestige newspapers and the documentary on television. That's where the credibility gap is. There's an enormous hostility towards the upper-middle class. People like Wallace talk about the guy with a briefcase, the professor with the pointy head."[1] In short, this is the new elite-*cum*-bogeyman—the people who have replaced yesterday's mill-owners and railroad barons as the focal point of popular indigestion.

Kahn's numbers vary. At different times, he has described the upper-middle class as anywhere from 10–20 per cent of the country. But, even on campus, he does not see a majority: "Of the 8 to 8½ million young people in academia today, only 300,000 belong to the counterculture. There are another 2 or 3 million who go along, but the average college kid is still quite square."[2] Arrayed against the upper-middle class, Kahn sees a "square" majority of 60–70 per cent of the population, more or less consisting of the lower-middle class, the middle class, and the traditional upper class.

Although Kahn does not specifically link the upper-middle class to the coming of the Post-Industrial Society first heralded by Daniel Bell, the vocations he singles out—the media, educators, city planners—are at the core of the new knowledge mandarinate. In fact, the influence of the new class extends far beyond knowledge-sector employment to dominate the basic fashion in areas where the Post-Industrial Revolution is farthest advanced. In June 1972, a writer for *The New Republic,* one of the most influential elite journals, noted *without any sense of sociological surprise* that support for the left-liberal George McGovern was virtually obligatory in fashionable Manhattan circles.[3] Cafe-society types and coupon clippers, a bit nonplused by his economics, were kept in line by social chic. And that chic, as Tom Wolfe so bitingly described it in 1971, is liberal to left.

Historically, social and political elitism in the United States has followed clear geographic lines. Since the beginning of the republic, the politics of education and wealth has tended to concentrate along the northeastern seaboard, and in the richest localities (see Map 9 pp. 114–16). It was true in the time of Jefferson, of Jackson, of Bryan, and of Franklin D. Roosevelt. All these men fought elites based in New York, Boston, and their exclusive environs. As the United States filled in its boundaries, an *additional* pattern became clear: the general tendency of elite northeastern politics to pull substantial strength in the Great Lakes and Pacific-coast states, and to generate its strongest opposition in the poorest states of the South, Great Plains, and Rocky Mountains.

In geography, at least, the new elite follows the footsteps of the old, having burgeoned in the communications and education centers of the Northeast, notably in the Boston-New York-Washington corridor, and in areas of the Great Lakes and along the Pacific coast. During the 1972 presidential campaign, George McGovern's brain trust drew heavily from these knowledge-sector concentrations. In explaining the heavy representation of Boston-area academicians, one McGovern aide said, "Whenever you talk about task forces advising candidates, the main sources of brain power or cerebral energy are in New England or on the West Coast."[4] As for media and communications, that axis (as earlier noted) runs between New York and Washington. Between them, knowledge-sector expansion has changed the social demography of some of the nation's most fashionable residential areas from San Francisco to Manhattan. This is the telltale metamorphosis. Conservative bankers, manufacturers, and financiers have been replaced by liberal planners, consultants, and communication executives. Affluent Scarsdale, in Westchester County, once the archetype of bridge-playing suburban matrons, is now the archetype of the new liberal chic. Areas that were citadels of conservative elitism in 1936 are now strongholds of liberal fashion, so there is no mistaking the political geography of a new national elite.

But knowledge-sector vocations *in themselves* are not a reliable ideological indicator. From Cape Canaveral, Florida, to Arizona, and to Southern California, many of the aerospace and military research and technology centers built up during the sixties are conservative strongholds notwithstanding their high ratios of college graduates and research vocations. The important distinction appears to lie between that segment of the knowledge sector *essentially engaged in social and human resources endeavors*—academicians, urban planners, journalists, social-welfare experts—and *those whose expertise is spent in the direction of military and aerospace research, product marketing, and industrial technology.* The first group dominates the post-industrial climate of the Northeast, the Great Lakes, and the Pacific Northwest, where educational and social concern have long been strongest; the second is important in the "Sun Belt" of the South and Southwest, with its greater tradition of militarism, individualism versus community-mindedness, and racial tensions between whites and non-whites. Obviously, the distinction, like so many others that have been attempted, is not precise and clear. Yet the fact that post-industrialism goes in these two very different directions is important, because it presumably sketches a major component of post-industrial political conflict. Only certain elements of the college-educated middle class are part of the new liberal elite. Attempts by public-opinion expert Louis Harris and others to classify all young people and college-educated persons in a "change coalition" cannot survive more-particularized examination.

Further embellishment is also in order on the rootlessness of the new elite(s), be they northeastern knowledge sector or Sun Belt technological. The change orientation, the anti-traditionalism, of the liberal elite has already drawn comment. But it should also be noted that the traditionalism and institutionalism of the conservative technology group are plastic, the ersatz heritage of "Disney World" and "Six Flags over Texas." With most of its population and urban-suburban sprawl filled by post-World War I migrations, the Sun Belt may be the most conservative section of the country, but it has the *least* tradition: one or two generations back to the bulldozer. There is none of the genuine, ordered, hierarchical conservatism of Oxfordshire, Normandy, Württemberg—or even the rural East.

Secondly, although they may be affluent, the groups coming to the fore in the post-industrial era are not like past cultural-economic elites. For one thing, they do not have the same distinction of income. Prior elites—less than 1 per cent of the nation, with another 10–15 per cent in the middle classes—could live far above the rest of the country in style and manner, thanks to the low-priced labor of the rest of the work force. Put this together with the substantially hereditary nature of class and income, and one finds an element of the population secure in its privilege, position, and lifestyle—the basis of a genuine conservative elite. Today only a tiny fraction of the top 15 per cent of Americans can live in privileged, leisured, and secure fashion. The cost and availability of servants are not even discussed in most upper-middle-class households. Changing wage and vocational patterns make it impossible for most of those in the 85th–99th income-tax percentiles to live too far apart from, say, those in the 45th–60th percentiles. The minimal lifestyle difference between eighteen and thirty-six thousand dollars a year is undoubtedly a factor in growing interest among youth in the quality and fulfillment of life. But it is also suggestive that the days of a genuine economic elite are over. If, as Daniel Bell suggests, knowledge is in the process of replacing capital as the currency of vocational success, then the trend is to a meritocratic elite, with minimal roots in security or tradition, little sense of family and place, and small ability to serve the societal anchor function of past Western elites.

Critics of the thesis that post-industrialism has created a new liberal American elite can still cite data showing correlations between wealth and Republicanism or income level and conservatism. In a national sample, such correlations would exist. And most of the country's largest fortunes, being rooted in bygone economic eras, are admittedly Republican and conservative. At the same time, the old correlation between income and conservatism/Republicanism is clearly on the decline. The most affluent young people tend to be the most liberal, and whereas conservative wealth predominates in Texas, Idaho, and the Carolinas, liberalism predominates in the most affluent post-industrial areas—from California to New York City and New England. Even though this largely upper-middle-class population group has less money than the old families of the industrial era, it is reasonable to label it as the "new elite" because of its position astride the basic dynamic of national socioeconomic change.

D. THE DYNAMICS OF
LIBERAL FAILURE

Although the nineteen sixties closed on a note of despair, of riot scars at home and napalm scars in Southeast Asia, it had begun as a decade of optimism. Looking back in the early seventies, Walter Lippmann recalled ". . . a period of American imperialism and American inflation. Inflation of promises, inflation of hopes, the Great Society, American supremacy—all that had to be deflated because it was beyond our power and beyond the nature of things."[1]

Therein lay the trap: a decade couched in the optimism of a new, just-coming-to-power generation of educators, sociologists, planners, and communicators. Moreover, the nineteen sixties were anything but a chronological fluke. Their buoyancy could not break through during the Eisenhower fifties, Indian summer of industrial-era Republicanism, and, by the seventies, the larger dreams of 1966 or 1967 had more or less been lost in painful cynicism. As previously suggested, the sixties were one of history's rare confluences: as in the Industrial Revolution, the overlap of a new economic and technological era and the feckless spirit of social adventure and problem-solving thereby set in motion.

It is useful to recall the America that entered the sixties proclaiming, in John Kennedy's words, a "New Frontier." Two new states had just come into the Union: Hawaii and Alaska—proof enough that America was still expanding toward a Manifest Destiny in the Pacific. Slowly escalating intervention in Indochina bespoke Washington's faith that the limits of American power had not yet been reached. Lyndon Johnson showed his New Deal roots when he spoke of making Asia safe for democracy and bringing TVA to the Mekong. And the Texas President showed his frontier mentality when he spoke of "nailing that coonskin to the wall."

At home, the New Frontier was urban and racial. Because civil-rights laws were succeeding in striking down discrimination, emboldened planners thought that additional legislation could promote equality and restructure society—and the anti-Goldwater landslide had provided a heavily liberal Eighty-ninth Congress (1965–66) to enact such proposals. Again, New Deal origins were revealed in the faith that legislation could rebuild society. Such techniques had worked under Franklin Roosevelt, but the problem lay in the very real difference of the challenges. Selective socioeconomic assistance to non-whites was a major departure from the New Deal's across-the-board economic assistance to farmers, home buyers, workers, and so forth. Lyndon Johnson surpassed John Kennedy, invoking dreams of his Pedernales boyhood and proclaiming the "Great Society." Instead of a New Frontier, it was to be the *last frontier*— the mixing and equalizing of America, the ultimate consummation of the idea of the melting pot.

Underpinning all of this was a new belief in mankind, not dominant in the still-segregated thirties: the idea that ethnicity and class were fading phenomena that could increasingly be overcome by social technology. This idealized view of the perfectibility of man was a combined outgrowth of a) the dominant U.S. social tradition, b) the tradition and earlier success of New Deal liberalism, c) the youthful optimism inherent in the mushrooming college population, and d) the self-interested economics and doctrines of the post-industrial new class just beginning to make itself felt in the United States and to a lesser extent in Britain and Europe. Last (and hardly least), the civil-rights revolution raised the unique challenge of assimilating a large non-white population. Sociologist Amitai Etzioni, director of the Center for Policy Research, has described the mood and premise:

> Imbedded in the programs of the federal, state and city governments and embraced almost instinctively by many citizens, especially liberal ones, is the assumption that, if you go out there and get the message across—persuade, propagandize, explain, campaign—people will change, that human beings are, ultimately, quite pliable.[2]

Such is not the psychology of the nineteen seventies. Despite the fact that minorities have made sizable economic strides in the decade since the Great Society began, even the officials who blue-printed the many federal programs admit that they were largely ineffective. Prosperity worked, not the Great Society.* As of the mid-seventies, Jean Jacques Rousseau's belief that man could be perfected by perfecting his environment once again appears to have miscarried. To an extent, as indicated, the Great Society was the fatal overextension of the American frontier quest: Manifest Destiny at home and abroad. Because the end of "frontierism" and the failure of the melting pot coincided with the onset of America's decline abroad, some liberals argue that war in Asia drained away funds with which the domestic Great Society could have succeeded. But it is also possible to argue that the Asian and urban frontiers were both failure-prone outgrowths of a common ideological drive. After all, the parent New Deal and Fair Deal had successfully encompassed domestic social expansion *and* welfare imperialism in their time. By the time of the Great Society, each impetus had been carried too far by conceptual overexpansion and undercut by internal conflict within the old coalition. As the sixties came to a close, there was a split between the knowledge sector and the New Politics ele-

---

* In this section, the term Great Society is used in a limited sense to connote only the 1964–68 themes that emphasized social engineering, i.e., the War on Poverty, rent subsidies, welfarism, compensatory education, racial balancing, and so forth. Medicare and Social Security increases do not fall into this category.

ment, with its domestic program interests, and the national-security-minded, southern, and labor-based Old Guard.

An increasing number of scholars are taking a negative view of the New Frontier and Great Society eras. The war in Indochina can only be described as among the most ignominious applications of power in recent history, launched by Ivy Leaguers, university deans, and foundation executives—McGeorge Bundy, Dean Rusk, Walt Rostow, Robert McNamara, et al.—as the first computer-programmed conflict of the Cold War and then scuttled as the new economic interests and humanist ideology of the knowledge sector took over liberal political reins. Meanwhile, domestic Great Society programming failed as knowledge-sector theorists miscalculated the reprogrammability of U.S. social patterns. Both failures—defeat in a long-drawn-out war and acceleration of rising expectations and social unrest at home—have added to the political tensions of the seventies.

Clear historical precedents can be found for the misplaced optimism of the Great Society. If the knowledge sector got carried away with the idea that its expertise could overcome human nature and solve society's problems, the industrialists of the mid-nineteenth century had similar notions, and so did the business philosophers of corporate America during the Roaring Twenties. When innovative techniques and methods are getting started, especially in technological break-through periods, there is a tendency to see the world as an entirely new place, with old restraints and inabilities suspended to a greater extent than they actually are.

The utopianism of the circa-1965 knowledge sector bears strong resemblance to the social reform and ideas of progress voiced in the mid-nineteenth century by the intellectuals of the two areas most affected by the Industrial Revolution: Unitarians and Transcendentalist New England and liberal England. Here is Massachusetts' Ralph Waldo Emerson: "Machinery and transcendentalism agree well . . . stagecoach and railroad are bursting the old legislation like green withes. . . . Our civilization and these ideas are reducing the earth to a brain. See how by telegraph and steam the earth is anthropologized."[3] Across the Atlantic, England's Poet Laureate, Alfred Lord Tennyson, put comparable enthusiasm into verse:

For I dipped into the future, far as human eye could see
Saw the vision of the world, and all the wonder that would be

Saw the heavens fill with commerce, argosies of magic sails
Pilots of the purple twilight, dropping down with costly bales

Til the wardrum throbbed no longer, and the battle flags were furled

In the Parliament of Man, the Federation of the World.[4]

Wide-eyed homage to the Industrial Revolution may have reached its zenith at the great Crystal Palace exhibition of 1851. Opening the vast acreage of demonstration textile machinery and steam engines, Britain's Prince Consort proclaimed that "we are living at a period of the most wonderful transition, which tends rapidly to accomplish that great end to which indeed all history points—the realization of the unity of mankind."[5] Such was the idea of progress unleashed by the Industrial Revolution—the belief that steam and rails were tools for the creation of a brave new world. In a somewhat lesser vein, the ballyhoo years of the nineteen twenties—which saw the coming of age of automobiles and radio—were another time when business expertise and expansion were regarded as the vehicle of unlimited social progress. President Coolidge said that "the business of America is business"; prosperity became a religion; and Bruce Barton—in the best-selling U.S. non-fiction book of 1925 and 1926, *The Man Nobody Knows*—hailed Jesus as a great sales executive and "the Founder" of modern business.

Whether in 1850, 1925, or 1965, the idea of progress has rested on more than philosophy. Economics are central. Typically, the interests advancing the theme of progress are also those profiting from the euphoric glow. The knowledge sector profited from the proliferation of Great Society social programs—in the short term, at least— just as nineteenth-century industrial and railroad barons profited from Social Darwinism, and the watered stock and pyramided holding companies fattened on the loose ballyhoo-years climate that saw business leading America to the millennium. The impetus and the excess were similar.

Few scholars have cared to pursue analysis of the self-interest underlying measures advocated by the educational-poverty-industrial complex in the name of social advance. One can usefully begin by recognizing, as Professor Theodore Caplow has pointed out, that the Great Society programs of the sixties—from the war against poverty to rent subsidies—represented a major departure from the methods of the New Deal: "Nearly everything that had been learned, under the New Deal and later, about how to accomplish social improvement was sedulously disregarded. The New Deal had, for example, experimented with both direct and indirect subsidies and discovered the general superiority of direct subsidies for effecting income transfers without harmful side effects. The War on Poverty shied away from direct subsidies but distributed indirect subsidies on a scale previously unseen. . . . The New Deal's experience with federally financed social services was consistently unfavorable. The War on Poverty established so extensive a network of social services that every urban slum became a cockpit of innumerable overlapping and uncoordinated agencies charged with re-educating, retraining and reorganizing the poor."[6] Mr. Caplow's point is an essential ladder to the next level of analysis: that the Great Society adopted an indirect subsidy/services strategy for very logical reasons. First, that it was not sufficient to give the poor money, because the real concern was race and racism—so that low-income blacks must be organized, educated, trained, residentially dispersed, and otherwise integrated into white society. To do this, the money must go to planners and experts who would provide housing, education, and rehabilitation services and compel the rearrangement of society. Second, as the knowledge-sector expansion and social concern of the sixties caught hold, there was an ever-increasing array of bureaucrats, foundations, planning groups, and business concerns that developed a major economic stake in, and lobbied for, the services/indirect-subsidies approach. Indeed, a substantial part of the mammoth new outlays went for promotion, conferences, public relations, and other advertisements for the idea that social justice required steadily larger program and research outlays. Chart 4 shows the incredible expansion of the Department of Health, Education and Welfare. Yet, at no time did any television network produce a documentary decrying the hundreds of public-relations aides involved in "the selling of HEW" to match their controversial exposé of Pentagon self-salesmanship.

Massive expansion of federal spending on indirect subsidies/services aimed at the poor was as much of a subsidy to the emerging knowledge and services economy as tariff and railroad land-grant legislation was to post-Civil War industrialism. Various studies of Great Society programs have shown how little money—often 10–25 per cent—actually made its way through the maze of bureaucratic, consultant, and business-contractor overhead into the hands of the poor. Arguably another of history's recurrent examples of political power applied to advance the interests of an ascending economic group convinced that it represents *the* new force for achievement in society.

The economic motivation and profit given to the knowledge sector by the Great Society is immense. In Representative Edith Green's words: "Both education and poverty have become what Wall Street would call growth industries. We're seeing the replacement of the military-industrial complex with the education-poverty-industrial complex."[7] Numerous major corporations have spun off subsidiaries to pick up poverty and education contracts. Irving Kristol has detailed the motivation of welfare workers to recruit relief recipients to swell the rolls and increase the *raison d'être* of social services.[8] *Fortune* magazine, in a 1972 article entitled "Housing Subsidies Are a Grand Delusion," acknowledged that the new subsidies given to builders to put up housing of a sort designed to achieve a social and racial mix were extravagant and wasteful—in order to tempt private enterprise into an otherwise uneconomic field—and principally a source of cash and tax benefits to opportunistic builders. Moreover, "a whole profession of consultants has arisen to help baffled mayors, legislators and project sponsors find their way through the regulatory thickets."[9] Bernard J. Frieden, director of the Harvard-M.I.T. Joint Center for Urban Studies, has estimated that "between one-fifth and one-half of the total federal subsidy does not reach the residents but goes for federal and local administration expenses and for tax benefits to investors."[10] Research has been a similar grab bag for the new upper-middle class, as demonstrated in the earlier analysis of the expansion of universities, think-tanks, and research-and-development installations. If welfare and housing subsidies have gone only partially to the poor, education and research expenditures have gone almost entirely to the new post-industrial class.

Useful documentation of this income impact has been provided by economist Peter Henle in the Labor Department's *Monthly Labor Review*. After a study of individual earnings during the period 1958–70, he found that the principal economic beneficiaries of the nineteen sixties were not the poor but the elite. As Henle put it:

> Over the 12-year span covered by this study, there has been a slow but persistent trend towards inequality in the distribution of earnings and in the distribution of wages and salaries. . . . If the impact of fringe benefits could have been included in the calculations, the trend would undoubtedly have been even

more pronounced. . . . The occupational and industrial groups with higher earnings (professional and technical, managerial, professional services, finance and insurance) grew most rapidly, thus contributing to earnings inequality.[11]

In his book *Coping: On the Practice of Government,* Daniel P. Moynihan has traced the redistributionist effects of spending on public school education, showing how the principal beneficiaries are teachers, counselors, and administrators, all higher-salaried groups than the public at large. Noting that teachers receive about 68 per cent of the operating expenditures of public elementary and secondary schools, Moynihan observes that "over the past two decades, teachers' pay has increased at a rate roughly twice that of wages in the private economy." In 1973, their average annual salary was $9,210—$1,300 higher than the average salary of taxpayers in private industry. Moynihan concludes: "Without abusing probabilities (or asserting the existence of detailed evidence), it may be said that increasing educational expenditures will have the short-run effect of increasing income inequality."[12]

The Great Society's helter-skelter approach—a mixture of When-I-was-a-boy-on-the-Pedernales New Deal optimism, poor planning, recklessly distributed cash, and knowledge-sector avarice—produced the inevitable mediocre results. The United States simply did not have the experiential base for success. As the decade of the sixties opened, the United States was spending just 7 per cent of its gross national product on social welfare, in contrast to 12–14 per cent for the nations of Western Europe and Scandinavia. As Robert L. Heilbroner has pointed out, we lack the working-class-oriented, social-democratic tradition that has been responsible for bringing so much of the welfare state to so much of Europe. The combination of affluence, the psychology of the frontier, and immigrants in pursuit of the American dream created a much different mystique from that prevailing in the finite, established, hierarchical societies of Europe. To quote Heilbroner directly: "The rampage of Social Darwinism in late Nineteenth Century America, with its long-abiding legacy of anti-welfare attitudes in the Twentieth, cannot be divorced from the myth (and the reality) of the frontier or the facts of economic life itself. The result was a peculiarly American anaesthetizing of the public's social conscience which, coupled with its profound suspicions of government 'from above,' led towards a mixed indifference and impotence with regard to social neglect."[13]

Thus, when the United States did begin to move into the social-welfare field, the activity came too fast, too avariciously—in the let's-get-going spirit of the old frontier rather than in the long tradition (but also awareness of class, and class limitations) of European social democracy. Some of the result was foreseen by U. S. Socialist Party Chairman Michael Harrington. In a 1967 discussion of "The Social-Industrial Complex," he expressed fear that the involvement —and dominance—of private enterprise in "social concern" would lead to a warping of programs to suit the needs of the entrepreneurs rather than of the poor and the broader community interest.[14] Let knowledge and social concern become business, and profit motivation would sway and distort decision making. The interaction of the Post-Industrial Revolution and its emerging knowledge sector, with the social challenge and programming of the sixties, was fatal. Much of the first great surge of American social-welfare activity was misspent—on naïve, rosy-hued ideas of progress that served specific economic interests rather than society as a whole.

This verdict would be unfair, despite the widespread profiteering, if the many programs had worked. Generally speaking, they did not. A few of the direct schemes more in the New Deal tradition succeeded: expanded Social Security and (probably) Medicare. Economic growth also aided poor people. But the efforts of the sixties in welfare, education, and housing have been disastrous and counterproductive, creating many new problems and playing an important role in changing U.S. political alignments.

Among the most persuasive analysts of the Great Society welfare mentality have been Irving Kristol and Nathan Glazer. First, the context: After 1964, under the auspices of the War on Poverty and kindred programs, roughly a hundred thousand community-action agency workers began *recruiting* people for welfare—telling the poor about welfare availability, pushing for higher benefits and looser requirements, organizing recipients, leading sit-ins, scorning low-income rehabilitation as the imposition of middle-class values, and, most of all, discouraging welfare recipients from taking "dead-end" or "inferior" jobs. Not surprisingly, welfare ranks mushroomed, in New York City trebling, from four hundred thousand to 1.2 million by 1972. But hopes of reprogramming the poor were not realized. Large sums of money poured into social casework produced no appreciable family upgrading. Kristol leaned heavily on a New York study entitled "The Multi-Problem Dilemma," in which social-work experts were forced to admit that fifty families given intensive supervision and rehabilitation showed no meaningful improvement over fifty families given only the usual welfare treatment. Other studies produced similar admissions. Far more important, welfare families as a group—intensively supervised or not—were falling apart under the pernicious influence of welfarism. Kristol described it this way: "Something appears to have gone wrong: a liberal and compassionate policy has bred all sorts of unanticipated and perverse consequences. One such perverse consequence, and surely the most important, is the disorganization and demoralization of the Negro family. It used to be thought that a generous welfare program, liberally administered, would help poor families stick together. We now find that as many black families are breaking up *after* they get on welfare as before they got on; and that in general, the prospect of welfare does nothing to hold a family together. Mr. [Daniel P.] Moynihan was percipient in emphasizing, back in 1965, that there was a connection between family disorganization and the influx of poor black, female-headed families to welfare. What we can now see is that the existence of a liberal welfare program might itself have been responsible, to a significant extent, for this family disorganization."[15]

The extraordinary thing is that much the same thing had happened before—in early-nineteenth-century England, at the beginning of the Industrial Revolution. In 1795, English authorities launched what came to be known as the Speenhamland system, assuring the poor a guaranteed income by means of subsidies in aid of wages (calculated on a scale dependent on the price of bread). Historian Robert Webb offers this typical description of the impact of Speenhamland: "The plan permitted the payment of outdoor relief, cash allowances in lieu of or supplementary to wages, to bring family income up to a minimum subsistence level. The practice encouraged farmers to pay low wages; administration was often lax; payments rose with the number of children, whether illegitimate or legitimate; and, as a result, the forty years after its inception brought a disastrous decline in the responsibility and morale of the poor. Promiscuity, normal in the rural life of the time, was encouraged as illegitimate children became financial advantages."[16]

Also, and hardly coincidental, the well-intentioned English rationale of Speenhamland bears striking resemblance to the psychological dynamics of circa-1965 U.S. concern. The French philosopher

Alexis de Tocqueville discussed the curious problem—to wit, why did prosperous England have so many more "paupers" than impoverished Spain or Portugal?—in a penetrating 1835 work entitled "An Essay on Pauperism." It is ironic, he observed, that: "In a country where the majority is ill-clothed, ill-housed, ill-fed, who thinks of giving clean clothes, healthy food, comfortable quarters to the poor? The majority of the English, having these things, regard their absence as a frightful misfortune; society believes itself bound to come to the aid of those who lack them. In England, the average standard of living a man can hope for is higher than in any other country in the world. This greatly facilitates the extension of pauperism in that kingdom."[17] The timing of Speenhamland assistance is important; it did not come in Hogarth's mid-eighteenth century, when polite society was content to leave the London poor clutching at penny gin bottles; it began when the Industrial Revolution was beginning the advance that put England economically out in front of the world. However, the English learned from the experience, disowning their altruism about the time De Tocqueville described it, and replacing it with the harsh poor-law amendments of 1834, which enabled the country to create a labor market and carry the Industrial Revolution to its full heights.

Education is another field where knowledge-sector goals of the perfectibility of the poor seem to have miscarried. Harvard's Christopher Jencks created something of a storm with his 1972 book entitled *Inequality: A Re-assessment of the Effect of Family and Schooling in America*.[18] His major points: that compensatory programs, racial balance, per-pupil spending ratios, and the like make little difference to the quality of education a pupil receives or to his later achievement in life. The principal determinant of education, he argues, is the caliber of the entering children, mostly a matter of family, intelligence, and social class. To Jencks, the Great Society variety of social engineering was ineffective. Equalization of opportunity is impossible without substantially eliminating economic and social inequality through income redistribution. However, Jencks favors spending a lot of money on ghetto education and extras because it is a way of raising the standard of living of the children in question (i.e., income redistribution). Other experts continue to see compensatory education in a more hopeful light than Jencks, but there is no doubt that his studies and others signal a new skepticism.

New research into genetics and heredity leans in the same direction. Arthur Jensen and Richard Herrnstein have been pilloried by large elements of the academic community for studies emphasizing the hereditary nature of intelligence—and the inability of social engineering to surmount biology. Herrnstein, who had just completed a three-year term as head of Harvard's psychology department, set off a furor with a September 1972 article speculating that "biological stratification" already taking place was creating a "hereditary meritocracy." With intelligence being largely (85 per cent) a matter of heredity and with intelligence being the increasingly pivotal currency of vocational success in a knowledge society, Herrnstein saw a dim future for the low-income, low-IQ poor. Unemployability, he speculated, could come to "run in the genes of a family just as certainly as bad teeth do now." In an interview with the New York *Times,* he acknowledged that his conclusions, if true, amount to a death sentence for the ideal of egalitarianism. Edward Banfield has been convincingly negative in analyzing the success and prospects of liberal urban programs and in seeing as dim a future as Herrnstein.*

In the meantime, the new sociology and the cost of education have produced a considerable public backlash. On one hand, unrealizable ghetto expectations have been kindled; on the other hand, middle-income voters have grown angry at 1) the way their neighborhood school districts are being shuffled to provide for a racial and economic mix and 2) the way their taxes are climbing to pay for it all. Until 1965, when the Great Society began to burgeon, school taxes typically used to pass by 4-to-1 and 5-to-1 majorities. By the late sixties, an unprecedented ratio of tax-increase referendums were being rejected for the two reasons above. In 1973, Dr. Sidney

---

* In many ways Banfield, Kristol, Herrnstein, Jensen, Glazer, and company are to mid-1970s reform what men like Roscoe Pound, Thorstein Veblen, Franz Boas, John P. Altgeld, and Charles Beard were to turn-of-the-century reform. Back in those days, the dominant ideology was Conservative Darwinism—belief that existing social arrangements and institutions represented the survival of the fittest and should not be tampered with. To crack this viewpoint, which dominated fashionable universities, churches, and newspapers, these men promoted the influence of environmental change: ethnic traits were not hereditary but changed with environment (Boas), law changed with judges (Pound), environment and poverty were the roots of crime (Altgeld), economics represented self-interest (Veblen), and the U. S. Constitution embodied eighteenth-century self-interest (Beard). Over the past seventy years, these ideas have been extended so far—to busing, social engineering, judge-made law, refusal to recognize heredity's influence—that they have become an Establishment dogma, like Conservative Darwinism was in its time.

Marland, Assistant Secretary for Education in the U. S. Department of Health, Education and Welfare, lamented: "There is manifest in this country—to my knowledge, for the first time in our history—an active loss of enchantment with our schools. . . . For the first time, Americans in significant numbers are questioning the purpose of education, the competence of educators and the usefulness of the system."[19] Public resentment-*cum*-backlash has been especially emphatic in areas such as greater Detroit, where the courts have ordered a multiplicity of metropolitan-busing and low-income-housing-distribution schemes.

Housing and urban planning offer another set of failures. Martin Anderson's study *The Federal Bulldozer* made clear early how urban renewal was destroying low-income (often black) housing in the central city to open up space for commercial redevelopment and the downtown apartment buildings favored by young professionals (often knowledge-sector liberals).[20] Early-1974 data on the failure of the Section 235 and 236 programs—subsidy schemes to help the poor purchase or rent middle-income housing—paint a colossal portrait of failure: twenty-eight thousand repossessed houses in cities such as Detroit, St. Louis, Chicago, and Philadelphia, at a cost to the government of hundreds of millions of dollars; entire blocks and neighborhoods turned to slum, and then to boarded-up, vandalized wastelands.[21] James G. Banks, Washington, D.C., housing-authority director, is quoted as saying that "what we have done under the subsidy programs has created an environment that promotes social disorder."[22] *Fortune* magazine made this summation: "Many Section 236 projects are in trouble because Congress misjudged human nature. To stay on a sound financial footing, such projects require a range of incomes among their tenants, some getting full subsidy and a substantial number receiving little or none. But FHA has found that too many tenants move out if their incomes rise instead of paying more rent for the same unit. . . ."[23] George Sternlieb, director of the Center for Urban Studies at Rutgers University, describes Sections 235 and 236 as "a Frankenstein Monster" and warns that 236 "may foist the worst waves of slums on the country since the first anti-slum ordinances were adopted in the 19th Century."[24]

The fact is that U.S. residential sentiments have balked planners' hopes. A small upper-middle-class minority may like new towns like Reston, Virginia, urban-renewal downtown brownstones, or high-rise apartments convenient to central-city cultural amenities, but the great majority of the people like small towns, suburbs, or neighborhoods with a piece of land and a sense of community. Survey after survey shows this. The uproar against low-income housing in Forest Hills, New York, suggests that the Jewish middle class, hitherto minimally concerned with territory and neighborhood, opposes residential experimentation with the same vehemence as gentile neighborhoods and suburbs hitherto involved.

In welfare, education, housing, and urban planning, the failure of Rousseauistic judgments of human nature has been compounded —and the negative consequences multiplied—by the extent to which Great Society programs were enlarged and shaped to suit economic interests. Often, the poor were only secondary beneficiaries of spending tailored to the theories and pocketbook of the new class. Without this coincidence of the "civil-rights revolution" with the emergence of the knowledge sector and its confidence in a new progress, there would have been less far-fetched theorizing and less reckless, large-scale financial outlay—as well as less urban disintegration and less backlash. One can even argue that the knowledge sector has cut as reckless a socioeconomic swathe as the early railroad barons and factory owners of the industrial era.

E. THE TRADITIONALIST COUNTERREFORMATION

By the beginning of the nineteen seventies, the outline of a traditionalist resurgence was apparent, but its depth and dynamics were less clear. Some analysts, such as Richard Scammon and Ben Wattenberg, postulated a superficial "social issue" reaction that found the public angry about drugs, campus demonstrations, and soft-on-crime attitudes while satisfied with basic Great Society programs.[1] Others, such as Walter Lippmann, posited a deeper reaction against the basic Rousseauistic philosophy of taxing the great bulk of the population to support social engineering on behalf of the few. Still others found a substantial racial base for voter reaction against crime and programs—from busing to welfare—seen by many as unduly favoring or helping blacks.

In-depth analysis would seem to support a mixture of the Rousseauistic and racial factors, with only a thin overlay of unconnected, separate public reaction to the drug and campus-demonstration issues (albeit the latter are often very prominently featured in voter-poll responses). Certain ingredients of urban collapse—notably the rise in crime—can be linked to liberal policies which fed both on urban welfare programs *and* on the tendency of liberals to excuse anti-social behavior with the same arguments of economic, educational, and residential deprivation that were used to promote basic Great Society programs. Most importantly, the urban deterioration and soaring crime of the sixties seem to have been much, much worse in the United States than anywhere else, either in Western Europe, Canada, or Australia. Futurist Herman Kahn has commented on the hardly coincidental fact that the United States was alone among the major Western nations in unsafe streets: "Since World War II, all developed countries have had a sharp increase in safety on the streets. The only developed country in the world where it is unsafe to walk the streets at night is the United States of America. I really mean that. Nobody would be surprised at a young girl walking around Paris at three in the morning. The most obvious characteristic of cities around the world is that they are safe day and night. Except here."[2]

But aside from a certain permissivism-based increment, U.S. liberal policies cannot be held responsible for the category of problems lumped together as the youth revolution: college unrest, pornography, drugs, hippies, and the like. They are a limited international phenomenon, intriguingly catalogued and analyzed by—again—Herman Kahn:

"When I talk about Zone 1, I mean Scandinavia, Atlantic Germany, the Netherlands, the Flemish part of Belgium, England (but not Ireland), Canada, the U.S., New Zealand, Australia. Along with Zone 6 (Switzerland and Austria primarily), these are the only places in the world that have ever had stable democracy. These are the areas of the world that used to be, if you'll excuse the word, manic Protestant and are becoming manic atheist. Zones 1 and 6 have the highest standard of living in the world, the greatest technology in the world. It's also the only part of the world with a middle-class drug culture. . . . It's the only part of the world where you have counterculture. It's the only part of the world where you have public pornography. It's the home of the multi-national corporation and the breakdown of the family. . . ."[3]

Elements of Kahn's categorization may be disputable, but his cultural geography makes an important political point: the hippie-drug-pornography-youth scene grew up not only in the United States but in countries such as Germany, Australia, and Britain that had *conservative* governments during much of the period in question. Which suggests that the behavior involved is more a function of modern post-industrial society in general than of any specific circumstances of U.S. politics, albeit our large college population, unique Vietnam malaise, and large knowledge sector all aggravated the situation. Besides, polls suggest that public reaction against hippies, student unrest, and drugs is more cultural than political. Except for a few highly political contexts (such as California in 1966), Democrats and Republicans *shared* a negative reaction and showed little disposition to vote as if one party favored hippies, drugs, and campus riots while the other opposed them. On the national level, the major exception was the 1972 election, in which George McGovern was tied to these attitudes by the GOP's slogan that he was the "triple-A candidate—acid, amnesty and abortion." But, for the most part, the electorate has not translated its attitudes on these matters into preferring one party over the other. Voter realignment can be much more productively correlated with reaction to Great Society-type programs dealing with welfare, schools, taxes, and neighborhoods, where there is a very substantial difference between the major parties.

Confronted with the moral, racial, and social upheaval of the nineteen sixties, the bulk of the American people—with varying speed and intensity—seem to have turned against the new cultural climate. It ·is important to consider the reaction on two levels: 1) cultural, where the pattern is relatively clear; and 2) political, where the nature and direction of public protest is somewhat more confused in its partisan implications.

Religion has been one of the more important staging grounds of the counterreformation. During the late-nineteen sixties, clergy in the more fashionable denominations and metropolitan areas had followed the trends of the campus and of the communications industry by growing steadily more liberal and taking up the cudgel for social activism. (Here again, one can relate church attitudes to the larger culture: the early stages of the Industrial Revolution nurtured a new religious social activism in Britain and New England, and in the nineteen twenties, many churchmen followed Coolidge Era fashion—when business and sales were the new credo—by portraying Jesus as the world's first business executive and top salesman instead of the circa-1968 portrait of Jesus as the first social activist.)

But such clerical activism miscarried with many Americans and pushed quite a few in the opposite direction. In 1973, Professor Will Herberg argued that "the noise you hear coming out of churches is from the leaders. . . . What they're doing is pushing church membership more and more towards conservatism." Several recent studies document this shift. National Council of Churches official Dean Kelley, in a 1972 book entitled *Why Conservative Churches Are Growing,* suggests that people want religion rather than social activism from churches, and that the trend is away from activist denominations and toward the fundamentalist churches; Unitarians, Episcopalians, Congregationalists, Methodists have been losing members; the big gains have been going to Mormons, Southern Baptist, Missouri Synod Lutherans, Jehovah's Witnesses, Pentecostals, Orthodox Jews and so forth.[4]

Some observers paint a broader-brush view of the religious reaction to the upheaval of the nineteen sixties. Christopher Booker, a young Englishman who participated in the British satire-and-cynicism bubble as a scriptwriter for TW3 (the television show "This Was the Week That Was"), labeled the driving force of the sixties as a "Cult of the New," led—per the title of his 1969 book—by *The Neophiliacs.*[5] To Booker, the late-sixties return to tradition was another of mankind's five-stage fantasy cycles by which dreams of a liberated society burst into a return to reality—and religion (both to explain the flaw in man's condition and to provide the means whereby he can come to terms with it).

Herman Kahn sees the return to religious and cultural tradition in even larger terms: He says "67% of America is square and getting squarer. . . . The biggest movement in America in the 70's is the counter-reformation. Religions such as the Baptists, Church of Christ, Pentecostals, Jehovah Witnesses and the Jesus freaks are all on the same rise. I want to emphasize this because the United States is the only Western country that seems to be going through this counter-reformation on a large scale."[6] Kahn's distinction seems vital: religion is not surging in Britain, Sweden, or other advanced European countries, where a reaction might be expected. The United States has a much higher ratio of church members and churchgoers. Kahn draws an analogy between U.S. circumstances and the Catholic Counter Reformation of the mid-sixteenth century. And while Kahn does not do so, one can amplify the analogy by comparing the con-

temporary United States and sixteenth-century Spain, spiritual linchpin of the Counter Reformation.

Virtually every historian agrees that Spain was the driving
force behind the Council of Trent and the Counter Reformation, and
the circumstances of mid-sixteenth-century Spain correspond in
several important ways to those of the present-day United States.
Much more than religion was involved in the Spanish-led Counter
Reformation. In 1545, besides being the leading world power, Spain
was a nation that had gone through fifty years of racial and cultural
turmoil. To no small extent, the Counter Reformation was a quest for
certainty, stability, and assurance.

Just as the past thirty-five years saw the United States go to war,
emerge as the world's foremost power, construct a world empire of
sorts, and then experience an agonizing social and cultural revolution,
so the years between 1492 and 1545 were extraordinary ones for
Spain. In 1492, the same year that Christopher Columbus launched
the colonization of the New World, Spain had just finished unifying
itself as a nation: the Moors were thrown out of the Iberian Penin-
sula's southern provinces, and Andalusia was added to the León and
Castile of Ferdinand and Isabella. Within a half century, Spain had
taken over not only most of the Caribbean, Mexico, and Central and
South America, but Italy, parts of North Africa, and the Low Countries. This nation, not even united until 1492, became a greater
empire—at least in geographic spread—than Rome!

Meanwhile, at home, Spain was Europe's only multiracial society.
After the reconquest of Spain from the Moors was completed,
hundreds of thousands of non-white North Africans remained, and
many Spaniards feared their presence. At roughly the same time,
Spain's large Jewish group was forced to convert to Christianity or
face expulsion. In 1654, there were fifteen hundred Negro slaves in
Cadiz, and other sizable black populations were found elsewhere in
Spain.[7]

While such degree of multiracialism, unparalleled elsewhere in
Western Europe, was a factor in Spain's notable Renaissance cultural achievements, it was also a source of social ferment, disquiet,
and eventual reaction. Martin Luther was not the only trigger of the
Counter Reformation; one can also see a spur in the unique Spanish
domestic situation. As Spain pushed its religious crusade, national
leaders also cracked down on intellectual diversity, and the alien
Moors were finally expelled.

Massive national change and social tension helped push Spain toward a policy of reaction to tradition and conformity, and today, Herman Kahn sees a similar impetus in the American counterreformation: "Religion, tradition, authority . . . a high degree of loyalty to the country, the city, a secret society, perhaps." Like Spain, we may be reacting against years of turmoil. "Think of the 1960s," Kahn says, "as the period of the Reformation. Remember that historically, after the Protestant Reformation, you had the Catholic Counter-Reformation. That is what we are having today—the middle-class Counter-Reformation."[8]

Resurgent ethnicity is obviously another major component of the seeming counterreformation. Numerous scholars have remarked on the ethnic re-emergence: Father Andrew Greeley (*Why Can't They Be Like Us?*—1971), Michael Novak (*The Rise of the Unmeltable Ethnics*—1972), Peter Binzen (*Whitetown, U.S.A.*—1970), and others.[9] Frequent reference is made to the possibility that the ethnics are asserting their own identity in response to the black power/black identity syndrome. This seems unlikely, because blacks can hardly be the reason for a parallel emergence of a) French consciousness in Canada and b) multiethnic assertion in such varied European nations as Britain, Belgium, France, Switzerland, Spain, and Austria. Rather than posit a local black-reaction explanation for U.S. ethnicity (presumably one factor, though), it seems more useful to probe several common U.S. and European patterns.

First, *not all* ethnic minorities are involved. In Europe, the German-speaking populations of Italy and France seem *less* irredentist now than previously; likewise, the political activity of Finland's Swedish minority seems to be ebbing. Most members of Switzerland's three ethnic streams—French, German, and Italian—seem content, except for a small minority of Jura Mountains separatists. In contrast to the affluent Germans of France and Italy and the commercially influential Swedish element of Finland, the restive minorities of Europe are mostly those with *no irredentist links*—no political homeland—and until now little cultural/political focus: Scots, Welsh, Bretons, Walloons, Corsicans, Basques—all the submerged ethnic elements of Western Europe. *This is the principal focus of current European ethnic self-assertion, and it is probably largely a result of the Communications Revolution—a composite of a new search for identity and a sense of exclusion from the dominant national culture.*

There is a similar pattern in the United States. Obvious resurgent ethnicity seems concentrated among those groups sprung from outside the dominant Zone 1 culture identified by Kahn (i.e., Britain, Scandinavia, the Netherlands, Germany, Canada, Australia). Besides blacks and Chicanos, the U.S. ethnic groups constituting Michael Novak's rising unmeltables are Greeks, Italians, Poles, and other Slavic and Mediterranean groups—the late migration (and also that least inclined to the new culture and morality of the upper-middle class).*

It is a matter of no small importance *which* WASP culture has provoked the reaction: the old milieu of millowners and wing collars, or the new elite with its purple sunglasses, permissive morality, and mockery of family and community. The latter outlook is not only ascendant but more fundamentally at odds with Slavic and Mediterranean culture; however, there are definite cultural and political crosscurrents.

Within the Slavic and Mediterranean groups, the ethnic resurgence of the late sixties is extraordinary. From the Portuguese and Atlantic islander (Azores) settlements of southeast Massachusetts to the Polish neighborhoods of the industrial Great Lakes, new folk festivals and ethnic-heritage studies keep appearing. Because of the emphasis on family, neighborhood, community, and heritage, the ethnic reassertion can safely be said to represent cultural traditionalism. It also represents a repudiation of the notion of the melting pot—of the idea that everyone is assimilating and that social planners can program or engineer as they like, disregarding ethnic and community factors.

On the part of working-class and middle-class U.S. WASPs, the ethnic resurgence appears to have something of a parallel in several notable cultural expressions: the mushrooming of Country and Western radio stations and record sales, plus the surge of related interest in antiques, Americana, and country living. The major growth of Country and Western music closely follows the chronology of nineteen-sixties upheaval. In 1960, there were eighty fulltime country radio stations; by 1965, there were 208, and 650 by 1970.[10] Big-city pop stations began switching to country—and profiting. Television began running more "country" shows. By late 1969, a major tide was apparent. Merle Haggard's "Okie from Muskogee" rose to the top of the

* One activist singles out Poles, Italians, Greeks, and Slavs, whose initials form the categorical acronym "pigs."

hit parade attacking marijuana and draft-card burners. In early 1970, an interesting article in *The Nation* entitled "Singing to Silent America" said:

> Current conditions and events have always been an inspiration for Country and Western songs. In the 1920's, there were songs about specific floods and railroad accidents; today there are songs about airline hijacking and mining disasters. Country songs have also interpreted conditions and events. In World War Two, the repertory was strongly patriotic; in the 1930's it mirrored the frustration of the depression. Today, the themes of country music unmistakeably mirror the fears and reactions of silent America. . . . Music trade publications in recent months have talked of a "musical backlash" on "top 40" popular radio stations. Records by black artists are not getting much play these days on such stations, a major reason being that the white station managers feel that their predominantly white audiences are made uncomfortable by the musical "soul" sound of the ghetto. . . . The themes appearing in country music are another such signal. Those who can see the advantage of being an "Okie from Muskogee" are not just the long-time clients of country music—those who drive trucks, work the mines and farms—but factory hands, mortgage payers, salesmen and commuters. Songs like *Okie* are a comforting musical antidote to student protest, black militancy and serious debate on the war.[11]

Most Country and Western recording stars echoed the 1968 and 1972 politics of their musical constituency by supporting George Wallace and/or Richard Nixon. But it would be wrong to compartmentalize the "country" craze as entirely conservative; singers such as Kris Kristofferson and John Denver ("Take Me Home, Country Road") indicate the liberal, ecology side of re-emergent interest in rural community and countryside.

Along with the religious fundamentalist, ethnic, and country-music trends—all grist for the evidentiary mill of Herman Kahn's counterreformation—other, lesser trends indicate the same direction: growing membership in "Middle American" fraternal organizations such as the Elks; booming middlebrow-Americana amusements such as "Six Flags over Texas," Disney World, and the like; and, of course, the fifties nostalgia so widespread by the early nineteen seventies.

Resurgent nationalism was also apparent. While Middle America did not care for the Vietnam War per se, cultural reaction against demonstrators, draft-card burners, and advocates of unilateral withdrawal created a patriotic backlash of suport for the idea of "peace with honor" in Vietnam, refusal to accept surrender, and opposition to amnesty. As knowledge-sector liberals pushed policies that ignored the average American's patriotic and national mystique, analyst Samuel Lubell found Richard Nixon able to wrap up his 1972 victory by taking bold measures to mine North Vietnamese waters outside Haiphong.[12] Here again, traditional mores were in evidence. While cultural traditionalism and political conservatism are by no means the same thing, the ferment of the sixties also caused a substantial increase in the number of persons categorizing themselves as conservatives. Chart 6 shows the movement in the nation and in the bellwether state of California:

CHART 6
Persons Categorizing Themselves as
Conservatives or Liberals, 1963–69

	U.S. 1963	(Gallup) 1969	California 1964	(Field) 1969
Liberal	49%	33%	28%	24%
Conservative	46%	51%	32%	42%
Middle of the road			30%	27%
No opinion/don't know	5%	16%	10%	7%

The liberal decline and the conservative rise are both obvious. The reasons are also fairly clear. First, the average American's distaste for and reaction against the liberal-run upheaval of the sixties. Second, the changing definition of liberal versus conservative. Issues of 1963–64 such as Medicare, Social Security, and the principle of federal aid to education were moot by 1969; and liberalism was ceasing to be an *economic* credo (of the liberal "have nots" against the conservative "haves") and becoming a *social* credo (pitting the values and lifestyle of the new class against the greater traditionalism of the majority of Americans). More on these changing positions of liberalism and conservatism shortly.

In partisan political terms, the traditionalist resurgence was also clear by the late sixties. As noted, Lyndon Johnson's great landslide victory of 1964 also brought into office an overwhelmingly Democratic Congress, which promptly passed or expanded controversial programs from the War on Poverty to experimental housing and education schemes. By 1966, reaction against this approach was writ large in the off-year Congressional election results: Republican gains came in those parts of the country where public hostility toward these liberal programs was greatest, notably in the West, the South, and border and middle-class-northern areas. But, by and large, the implications of this regionalism were lost on the media and most political analysts. Despite talk about the war in Vietnam being the decisive issue, the fact was that Democratic losses came in the areas *most supportive* of the war, while the Democrats held up best in the liberal anti-war areas: New England, New York, the Pacific Northwest. In the liberal suburbs around New York City, for example, the Democrats held six of the seven suburban GOP seats they had picked up in 1964.

Clear enough in 1966, the anti-Great Society geography showed up again in 1968 support for Richard Nixon and George Wallace. Lumped together, votes for these two candidates, totaling 57 per cent, ran highest in the South, the Rockies, the Great Plains, and other areas (such as Indiana) that were hostile to the new eastern-establishment liberalism.

Yet the *partisan* impetus of the counterreformation blurred after the Nixon administration took office. With extraordinarily little appreciation of 1966–68 victory dynamics, the new GOP regime was not able to offer the electorate in-depth reassurance on the pivotal issues. Instead of opposing the welfare, busing, and artificial-integration syndrome, the Administration appeared to *embrace* it with such 1969–70 measures and actions as 1) the Family Assistance Plan (guaranteed annual income); 2) continuation of programs such as the War on Poverty, Model Cities, and rent subsidies; 3) Department of Health, Education and Welfare support for busing and other kindred school-integration approaches; and 4) Housing and Urban Development Secretary George Romney's attempts to force minority housing quotas on such blue-collar suburbs as Warren, Michigan.

Conservatives were dismayed. Besides evidencing lack of a coherent domestic-policy perception, postures like this put the Nixon administration at odds with the basic 1966–68 thrust of GOP gains.

Thus, the Nixon administration confronted the electorate in 1970 without any real cutting edge. The so-called "social issue," pilfered from Democratic analysts Richard Scammon and Benjamin Wattenberg, was a superficial hodgepodge of crime-, riot-, and drug-issue emphases designed to be used *defensively* by liberal Democrats who were not free to attack the basic failures of 1965–69. Consequently, when the Nixon administration chose to mount a harsh and superficial campaign against crime, campus unrest, and radicalism instead of attacking the fundamental perceptions and programs of the Great Society, the off-year elections of 1970 saw the GOP fail to continue the strides of 1966 and 1968. Liberal Democrats could hardly be blamed for drug usage, campus unrest, peace demonstrations, pornography, and other problems prevalent not only in the United States but in Canada, Britain, and parts of Western Europe. And what U.S. liberals *could* be blamed for—specific programs and sociology—the Nixon administration itself seems not to have understood.

Confusing to Administration policy makers and analysts alike, the 1970 results underscored the blurred partisanship of counterreformation. The Republicans lost in the West and failed to make headway in the South, and their only real gains came in northeastern areas—New York and Connecticut, for example—where the Democrats swung far to the left and nominated New Politics practitioners, who provided an early glimpse of George McGovern's fate.

The election of 1972 confirmed the cultural trend, but left its partisan implications confused. George McGovern's landslide defeat marked an unmistakable rejection of the social-programming thrust of the sixties. Walter Lippmann declared: "What happened in the Nixon-McGovern election is what happened in all elections of advanced modern industrial societies when the basic policy of the Jacobin or Rousseauistic philosophy is repudiated. By that I mean the belief that man is essentially good and can be made perfect by making the environment perfect, and that the environment can be made perfect by taxing the mass of the people to spend money for improving it."[13]

Be this as it may, there was no clear party mandate. Walter Dean Burnham offered a useful analysis that whereas Teddy Roosevelt could have created a new, positive coalition, Richard Nixon's domestic style could not push beyond a negative repudiation of

McGovern. Neither the President nor the Republican Party proved able to translate the popular mood into a new philosophy.

Indeed, the basic shortcomings of the Nixon administration—from myopic managerialism to the Watergate mentality—suggest that neither existing party structure really lends itself to articulation of the philosophic themes of the counterreformation. Much as in the circumstances of the Industrial Revolution that required political parties to reshuffle before they could construct current ideologies, the U.S. parties of the mid-seventies are not effective vehicles for ideological controversy.

F. A REDEFINITION OF IDEOLOGY

Changing issues and socioeconomic divisions justify increasing speculation about the obsolescence of "liberal" and "conservative" as the basic cleavages of Anglo-American political ideology. Both terms arose out of the unique circumstances of the French Revolution and the Industrial Revolution, when middle-class ideas and concerns surged forward to displace the old politics of aristocratic cliques and factions. Granted that the two names represent a long-time division of political behavior, the actual appellations themselves are very much products of a particular era and may not be able to serve very usefully in a new one.*

Late-eighteenth-century Europe, not Britain or America, produced the term "liberal." In France, the supporters of the popular movement called themselves *libéraux,* and in Spain the term was *liberales.*[1] George Washington used the word "liberal" to connote moral and re-

---

* "Words are witnesses which often speak louder than documents. Let us consider a few English words which were invented, or gained their modern meanings, substantially in the period of sixty years with which this volume deals. They are such words as 'industry,' 'industrialist,' 'factory,' 'middle class,' 'working class,' 'capitalism,' and 'socialism.' They include 'aristocracy' as well as 'railway,' 'liberal' and 'conservative' as political terms, 'nationality,' 'scientist,' and 'engineer,' 'proletariat' and (economic) 'crisis.' 'Utilitarian' and 'statistics,' 'sociology,' and several other names of modern sciences, 'journalism' and 'ideology,' are all coinages or adaptations of this period. So are 'strike' and 'pauperism.' . . . To imagine the modern world without these words (i.e., without the things and concepts for which they provide names) is to measure the profundity of the revolution which broke out between 1789 and 1848 and forms the greatest transformation in human history since the remote times when man invented agriculture and metallurgy, writing, the city and the state." E. J. Hobsbawm, *The Age of Revolution, 1789–1848* (1962), p. 17.

ligious broad-mindedness, but it did not gain political currency at the time. Use of the word "liberal" began in British politics as a Tory slur during the 1820s, sounding as it did simultaneously Continental, disloyal, and agnostic. King George IV, writing to a friend in 1825, said that the name put him in mind of the 1790s.[2] The essence of the early-nineteenth-century liberalism was emphasis on individualism and opportunity, and opposition to a closed society of hereditary privilege. As such, British liberalism was closely identified with (and nurtured by) the emerging urban middle classes and industrial entrepreneurs. In the United States, where the term was not in use, Jeffersonian Democracy—a pre-industrial philosophy—opposed aristocracy and hereditary privilege but deplored urbanization and industrialization.

"Conservative" came into the British political lexicon at about the same time as "liberal." However, the original derivation of the term, once again, was French: from the words *Sénat conservateur* in the French Constitution of 1795.[3] George Canning used the term in its present sense in 1824, and by January 1831, John Wilson Croker, a Tory strategist, was writing in *The Quarterly Review:* "We have always been conscientiously attached to what is called Tory, and might with more propriety be called the Conservative Party. . . ."[4] He thought the appellations Whig and Tory should be dropped because the struggle was no "longer between two political parties for the ministry, but between the mob and the government . . . the conservative and subversive principles." After the passage of the Reform Bill of 1832, Tory leader Sir Robert Peel observed: "I presume the chief object of that party which is called Conservative . . . will be to resist Radicalism, to prevent those further encroachments of democratic influence which will be attempted (probably successfully attempted) as the natural consequence of the triumph already achieved."[5]

Although the basic lines of division were apparent by the 1830s —liberals favoring change and social fluidity, conservatives seeking to curb same—a generation passed before those names made sense. During the 1850s, the oxymoronic terms "liberal-conservative" and "conservative-liberal" came into use, and many Tories disliked the name "conservative" because of its association with Peel and repeal of the Corn Laws, so dear to the hearts of the landed interests. As late as 1868, Disraeli could say that his Tory-Conservative government intended to follow a "truly liberal policy."[6] The purpose of these comments is not to elaborate on the uncertainty and instability of the parties—more on that in chapter 4—but merely to point out that the two ideological terms were still confused.

So too in the United States. For a while, in the 1830s, there was talk that the Whig Party, itself newly formed from the wreckage of John Quincy Adams' National Republican Party, would rename itself the Conservative Party. But that did not happen. In 1837, a Pennsylvania newspaper, speaking of the possibility of a change in the name of the opposition from Whig to "Conservative" suggested instead that they use the cognomen "Fast and Loose."[7]

More importantly, it is useful to underscore the chronology: The political terms "liberal" and "conservative" emerged with the Industrial Revolution and the power of the middle class. This roughly coincided with the Reform Act of 1832, which greatly expanded the British electorate (and which itself reflected the impact of steam and rail: the expanded vistas of rail travel rendered absurd the parliamentary representation of "rotten boroughs" but not cities). Ideological and party names remained confused—on both sides of the Atlantic—during the 1830–65 period, when the Industrial Revolution was having its greatest economic and philosophic impact. As society stabilized, so did nomenclature. The first ministries of Benjamin Disraeli (1868) and William Gladstone (1868) are generally regarded as marking the beginning of clear Liberal-Conservative division.

Conservatism, by this point, could generally be defined as standing for the existing order of things, and cleaving, where possible, to traditional practices and procedures. Liberalism, in contrast, stood for the interests of men and ideas. As time passed, the beneficiaries of liberalism changed—from the individualists in the nineteenth century to the working classes aided by the depression-era New Deal. But the central tenet of liberalism was always one of individual opportunity, competitive merit, and anti-elitism. Even though these ideas were attenuated by Fair Deal and New Frontier economic welfare legislation, the basic principle was not contradicted: individual opportunity was being promoted against an economic elite.

The new knowledge-sector U.S. liberalism of the sixties changed this. Before long, liberalism was being promoted *by,* not *against,* an elite, and the goal was not individual opportunity but group equality. This represents a watershed upheaval, and it came about in a number of ways. First and most obvious, the advent of post-industrial society, in which the elite represented the institutionalization of liberal economic interests and philosophic ideas of equality. Second, the economically and sociologically spurred metamorphosis of liberalism from a credo of equal opportunity to one that attempted to impose actual equality. Here, two interests were at work: 1) economic—liberalism's new multibillion-dollar social engineering industry; and 2) ideology—liberalism's difficulty in admitting that there comes a point where equality of opportunity has been substantially realized, and actual equality—thanks to human differences—is still remote. The confluence of the two was deadly: Liberalism has become an economic elite dedicated to promulgating artificial social relationships, just the outlook against which French *libéraux* had mobilized two centuries earlier.

Several commentators have developed this point. University of California (Berkeley) Professor Paul Seabury argued in 1972 that devices such as quotas contradicted central beliefs: "Beaumarchais' point in *The Marriage of Figaro* was that exclusionary practices in the 18th Century aristocratic France were repugnant precisely because they had nothing to do with a person's individual qualities and skills but everything to do with his arbitrarily assigned status. Is the situation any different where reverse discrimination is concerned? The gravity of the current situation in America can be seen in the fact that what began several years ago as a method of alleviating the black man's condition has since spread like wildfire to other groups and categories—ethnic, sexual or chronological— each claiming the right to preferential treatment."[8]

Sociologists Peter and Brigitte Berger describe much the same problem in their theme of "The Assault on Class." Liberal policies such as crosstown busing, obligatory distribution of low-income housing into suburbia, and racial quotas in college faculties and other employment represent a metamorphosis of the attempt to correct injustice and lack of opportunity into an assault on the class system itself. Such an approach is mistaken, they argue, because the class system is too big a reality in America: people want to enjoy (and want their children to enjoy) the residential and educational prerogatives of their economic achievement. Class-conscious behavior —i.e., middle-class flight from a subsidized or bused lower-class influx—can be curbed only by a degree of compulsion (like East Germany's forbiddance of *Republikflucht,* or fleeing to the West) that is simply out of the question. In ideological terms, such liberal insistence on manipulative programs represents a new outlook: an immensely significant progression from *proscriptive* to *prescriptive* political and legal positions. Instead of discrimination and artificial preferences being prohibited, liberalism is seeking to prescribe community social patterns. The focus is no longer on safeguarding individuals but on furthering collectivities. "The injury to the individual, regrettable though it may be, is legitimated in terms of this or that collective destiny. Concern for the rights and welfare of the individual, regardless of his or her group membership, has been one of the great moral themes of modern liberalism. It is deeply ironic that a moral impetus rooted in this same liberalism should now be in the process of giving birth to an ethic of collectivities that is profoundly illiberal in its implications. . . . These tendencies have even deeper roots in American history. The demon racism has quite logically replaced the demon rum, and the new Prohibition requires an extension of police powers at least equal to those required by the old."[9]

Both Seabury and the Bergers see liberalism becoming a creed that seeks to arbitrate and ascribe social patterns, rather than working to block such ascription as of yore. Yet neither analysis jumps the final hurdle: recognition that liberalism is increasingly the ideology of a new knowledge-society economic elite and thus has logically become a vehicle for 1) trying to advance elite economic interests and 2) trying to *dictate* (rather than loosen) social patterns. Once one accepts that liberalism is becoming the credo of a new economic elite, the illiberality—in historic terms—of its actions follows logically enough. The fact that it is nominally trying to help low-income persons against middle-class society lends a patina of "liberalism," but the key is the attitude of the liberal elite toward yesterday's *Lumpenproleteriat,* now become the *Lumpenbourgeoisie.* Whereas, only a generation ago, liberal intellectuals decorated the walls of federal buildings with WPA murals showing heroic steelworkers, policemen, loggers, and tobacco farmers, members of the new "liberal" knowledge elite are now prone to savage these same people as rednecks, ethnic clods, Archie Bunkers, and the like.

Only elites have typically described the masses this way, and the point is not whether the attitude is right or wrong; it is simply not liberal in the 1780–1960 sense of the word. Liberalism cannot operate as the credo of an elite. Now that it has become such, small wonder that the terminology lends itself more to confusion than clarification.

At the other end of the spectrum, the name "conservative" has little more justification or continuing utility. To live up to its function of *conserving,* conservatism must be the ideology of a tradition-minded economic elite. But since the Post-Industrial Revolution, the U.S. elite has become more and more liberal- and change-minded, leaving the job of conserving the "old values" increasingly to the less affluent angered by the programs and moral values of the new upper-middle-class knowledge sector.

The result is several forms of "conservatism": first, the pseudo-conservatism or rightwing Populism of the *Lumpenbourgeoisie,* which seeks to overturn many of the programs and institutions of the liberal establishment; second, a business orientation that takes the earlier conservative line toward certain economic matters—favoring doctors, coal companies, wheat exporters, and so forth—while remaining fundamentally ignorant of the new issues and cleavages triggered by the Post-Industrial Revolution; third, the genteel conservatism of certain intellectuals, which deals in warmed-over Von Hapsburgs and the like to create an artificial milieu where conservatism is still a Fifth Avenue brougham rather than a Queens pickup truck. None of these represent a functioning post-industrial conservatism: the first for obvious reasons; the second and third because they do not relate to the issues and interests of the ascendant American elite. Indeed, one can argue that "conservatism" simply cannot operate in a post-industrial economy, because the elite is committed to change—turnover in knowledge, research, and society—and the popular element is inclined to restrain or eject the elite.

Such is the case for terminological obsolescence. As noted in Professor Hobsbawn's statement at the beginning of this subchapter, "conservatism" and "liberalism," along with many other of our everyday political words, are the products of the era of the Industrial Revolution. There is no reason why they would be useful beyond it. Both past great upheavals of what is called "modern" world history, first the period of the Renaissance-Reformation and then the era of the French and Industrial revolutions, have created new ideological and political contexts. The battlefields and denominators of one era were not those of the next. Another such ideosemantic watershed is at hand in the nineteen seventies.

G. POST-INDUSTRIAL
SOCIETY CONFLICT

There can be no doubt about the permanence of the Post-Industrial Revolution. By 1980, the production, consumption, and dissemination of knowledge is expected to account for at least 40 per cent of the gross national product, up from 35 per cent in 1970. Seven out of ten employed or self-employed persons in the United States will be providing *services* for others (including information), while only three out of ten will be producing actual *goods*.

Future economic growth is expected to occur almost entirely in the knowledge-and-services sector. Estimates put together by the U. S. Labor Department in 1970 predicted an increase of 15.5 million civilian jobs during the seventies. Of these new jobs, nearly 85 per cent will be in services, government, communications, and trade. Chart 7 shows the breakdown.

Post-industrial theorist Daniel Bell suggests that "by the end of the century, the proportion of factory workers in the labor force may be as small as the proportion of farmers today."[1] Professor Victor Fuchs, author of *The Service Economy,* sees a future where "the large corporation is likely to be overshadowed by the hospitals, universities, research institutes, government agencies and professional organizations that are the hallmark of a service economy."[2] The question is only one of degree; few serious observers dispute the trend.

Relative affluence and post-industrialism are projected to go hand in hand. Already, only 9 per cent of white American families are below the poverty line and almost two thirds have incomes over ten thousand dollars a year. By 1980, according to the National Planning Association, "the number of households with incomes in excess of $15,000 will have grown from almost 8 million now to 24 million, about half the total."[3] Much of this new wealth will flow into the consumption of services and knowledge. These vocational and consumption trends must clearly bolster the new class, reinforcing the centrality of social-issue and lifestyle politics as opposed to the direct economic-issue politics of the industrial era. Economics will remain a central underlying political determinant, but, taxation aside, *direct* economic issues—minimum wages, collective bargaining, unemployment, and the like—will be much less important than they were during the industrial era.

JOB PICTURE FOR 1980—AN OFFICIAL REPORT

MORE WORKERS will have jobs in these fields:

	Employment in 1969	Employment expected in 1980	INCREASE, 1969-80
Services, miscellaneous	13,412,000	18,097,000	4,685,000
State and local government	9,446,000	13,662,000	4,216,000
Trade	17,274,000	20,282,000	3,008,000
Manufacturing	20,545,000	22,133,000	1,588,000
Construction	4,208,000	5,427,000	1,219,000
Finance, insurance, real estate	3,896,000	4,593,000	697,000
Household help	2,322,000	2,770,000	448,000
Federal Government	2,758,000	2,970,000	212,000
Transportation	2,935,000	3,086,000	151,000
Communications, utilities	1,698,000	1,840,000	142,000

FEWER WORKERS will have jobs in these fields:

	Employment in 1969	Employment expected in 1980	DECREASE, 1969-80
Agriculture	3,932,000	3,156,000	−776,000
Mining	654,000	584,000	−70,000

U.S. News, November 2, 1970   Source: U.S. Dept. of Labor

CHART 7
Job Picture for 1980—an Official Report

Beyond these economic generalities, there is much less agreement on where American society is heading. Charles Reich's overinflated *Greening of America* thesis uses post-industrial affluence as a launching pad for the notion that many of the young are shedding yesterday's materialism for a new humanism. Others, even though they do not go as far as Reich, agree in seeing a new generation with greatly different values. Ranged in opposition are those who see the young as just another short-term rebellious wave like others before them, and those who limit the greening phenomenon to only a minority of young people and see the dominant tide going the other way.

Herman Kahn thinks that young America, even in the post-industrial era, is still predominantly traditional: "There are about 9 million young people in college, and I'd say that substantially more than two-thirds are there to climb the economic ladder."[4] He differentiates the "upper-middle class graduate [who] while still oriented to achievement is not interested in advancement. He wants to do something 'important' or 'significant,' but he doesn't really care whether he's going to make $15,000 or $20,000 or $25,000 a year."

This mentality and its derivation has been quite accurately capsuled by Paul Goodman: "The shagginess and chosen poverty of student communities have nuances that may be tremendously important to the future. We must remember that these are the young of the affluent society, used to a high standard of living and confident that if and when they want, they can fit in and make good money. Having suffered little pressure of insecurity, they have little need to climb, just as, coming from respectable homes, they feel no disgrace about sitting a few nights in jail."[5] Stretching the point a bit, these are Reich's "Greens," but are they taking over? Against them, sociologists Peter and Brigitte Berger have hypothesized the "Blues"—the lower-middle-class youngsters from Wichita, South Philadelphia, and piney-woods Georgia, the Baptists, Lutherans, and Catholics, the kids from St. Aloysius and Texas A&M who didn't grow bored with filet mignon and country clubs because they never had them.[6] To the Bergers, the "Greens" are largely a class phenomenon rather than a metamorphosis of human nature, and if the children of the upper-middle class no longer want to run General Motors or the Pentagon, then the children of Levittown, Little Italy, and Yoknapatawpha County will be glad to assume control.

In a related vein, Seymour Lipset sees youthful attitudes divided by class polarity: "What has happened is that increasing numbers of white young people in the South and in many working-class districts of the North have been exposed in recent years to repeated discussion of the supposed threats to their schools and communities posed by integration. They have been reared in homes and neighborhoods where anti-Negro sentiments became increasingly common. Hence, while the upper-class scions of liberal parents were being radicalized to the left by civil rights and Vietnam war issues, a sizable segment of Southern and Northern workingclass youth were being radicalized to the right. The consequences of such polarization can be seen in the very different behavior of the two groups in the 1968 election."[7]

While Kahn, Lipset, and the Bergers emphasize the certainty of class divisions, other studies have increasingly scotched the notion of an entire "new" generation differing in basic values. First of all, some rather innovative studies—for example, analyzing the language and themes of *The Great Gatsby,* by F. Scott Fitzgerald—suggest that the youth of the sixties are much like the youth of the twenties (now the grandparental mainstays of U.S. conservatism). Arizona Professor Lee Nash, who went through *Gatsby* using line-by-line content analysis for alienation indicators provided by social scientists Melvin Seeman, Kenneth Keniston, and Dwight Dean, argued this parallel: "The old contempt for Coolidge and Babbitry appeared scarcely related to riotous protests against Nixon and Du-pont. Yet the irreverence, the Bohemian tendencies and especially the alienation of many youths in both the Twenties and Sixties were remarkably of a sort."[8] The post-World War I era, Nash alleges, witnessed the introduction of key forces in modern society that stimulated modern alienation: assembly-line technology, sales/advertising, installment buying, movies, records, radio. Technology kindled hopes but failed to realize the high ideals of Progressivism or even to maintain prosperity. According to Nash, "The Sixties decade was an intensified version of these economic and social phenomena, with the addition of television, moonshots and atomic weaponry. Parallels are obvious in recent youthful disillusionment with leaders who have presided over the Vietnam War, environmental injuries and economic decline." More to the point, if Gatsby's generation became the Nixon vote of 1960–72, the youth of the sixties are likely to follow a kindred course.

Other research confirms that the youth of the mid-sixties, instead of consummating a new direction in liberated thinking, have on the average showed a trend back toward 1) conservatism and 2) parallelism with their parents' views. In 1965, M. Kent Jennings of the University of Michigan and Richard G. Niemi of the University of Rochester polled basic attitudes of seventeen hundred high school seniors and their parents. Eight years later, when the same people were polled again, both young people (in their mid-twenties) and parents showed a strong conservative trend on issues of integration, and cynicism toward federal spending.[9] Interestingly, the younger group showed the much stronger conservative trend, forsaking collegiate liberalism and drawing close to the attitudes of their parents. Differences are more between classes than age groups. Chart 8 shows the shift.

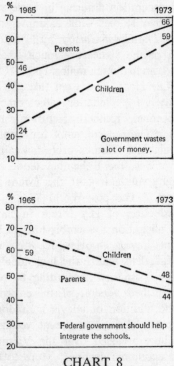

CHART 8
Converging Political Attitudes of Parents and Children

Synthesizing these arguments, the truth would seem to be that while post-industrialism has not made over human nature (any more than did the Enlightenment or the Industrial Revolution), changing culture and economics *have* "greened" the outlook of a substantial minority of the population—especially among the affluent young. At the same time, their emergence has stimulated a broader countertrend. Per Herman Kahn's 1973 estimates:

"Sixty-seven percent of America is quite square and getting squarer. . . . It's the biggest thing going in America today and it will either dominate or heavily influence the next decade or two . . . [yet] the Counter-Revolution will not slow down the growth of the 'single class,' but it may slow down its acceleration. . . . There are basic forces in our culture that move it in the direction of a secular humanism and there are less basic counteracting forces in our culture that are acting against this movement. I believe the more basic forces are the ones moving in the direction of secular humanism. So I believe the Counter-Reformation is a relatively temporary phenomenon. I think it can't last more than two decades—maybe it will last only five years."[10]

Kahn looks for considerable counterreformation success, via a synthesis of old values and new, but also for a continuing tension: The counterreformation "will not pick up the prestige universities, Bohemia or many transcendental ethnics" (i.e., Yankees, Reform Jews, Quakers, Unitarians, etc.—the core groups of the knowledge-sector elite).

Youthful liberalism cannot hope to maintain the central role it has played in advancing the new culture. First of all, the flush of the sixties has faded among most youth. Secondly, the burgeoning of the campus population, which both encouraged and reflected the explosion of the knowledge sector, reflected the coming of age of the postwar boom babies. That population surge passed its elementary school zenith in the early sixties, its high school zenith in the mid-sixties, and its college maximum in the early seventies; the mid-seventies mark its heyday at the polls. Eighteen-to-twenty-four-year-old voters will be eligible to cast about 19 per cent of the total U.S. vote in 1976. From there on, it is downhill. As Chart 25 shows, the population will be aging after 1976, and the youth vote will be progressively less important. A synthesis suggests itself: 1) the youth-surge-*cum*-culture has peaked with the counterreformation it helped provoke, and both are likely to give way to a synthesis by the late seventies; also 2) a quite substantial part of the population will nevertheless be permanently affected by the new values and ideas churned during the sixties and early seventies.

Certain basic post-industrial categories of conflict seem probable: 1) social perfectibility and the "Idea of Progress," 2) lifestyle and morality, 3) economics and productivity, 4) bureaucracy and government regulation, 5) nationalism and the U.S. world role, and 6) media power.

The idea of progress is seemingly in retreat, definitely among centrist Democrats and even among many liberals. An increasing number of sociologists are being heard from on the limits of social policy. Yet the pressures are still there: low-income black populations taking over central cities, the notion that such populations must be elevated and dispersed, the vested interests of the knowledge-sector and welfare establishment. Race-conscious social engineering is bound to remain a political issue. Race itself is likely to be a central denominator—if not an overt theme—of U.S. political division.

Lifestyle and morality are the issue sectors that should witness the greatest easing of tradition. By 1985, 50 per cent of American families are projected to earn over fifteen thousand dollars a year. Futurists expect them to use this affluence for a more leisured life, often merely reinforcing existing class predilections, but frequently adjusting their value structure in the process. Given the ballooning of the affluent upper-middle-class knowledge sector, even conservative sociologists predict that hedonism will increase and that a "liberal" trend will prevail with regard to marijuana, abortion, sex, and marital relations. Herman Kahn expects a synthesis between traditional values and the "Greening" syndrome, the synthesis turning out "pretty much like the traditional society, but modified by increasing tolerance" in lifestyle matters.[11] The limits of behavioral change have been pretty well probed: There is little likelihood of young people escalating to incest, hard drugs, sodomy, et cetera. But over the next decade or two, considerable controversy is likely to focus on legal questions of marijuana, drugs, abortion, and sexual freedom.

By 1985, some argue, economic motivations may be less important to the average American because of increased income and a growing margin for leisure spending. Herman Kahn is of this school: "As you get near the end of the century, you'll find increasingly more families that are more or less satisfied with their income."[12] Daniel Bell sees the "economic mode" of thought, which prevailed during the industrial era, giving way to a post-industrial "sociologizing mode," which subordinates economic growth and increased consumption to broader, communal non-economic goals that may entail reductions in output and loss of efficiency.

Perhaps, but both Kahn and Bell pay relatively little attention to the economic assertiveness of the less affluent white and (especially) non-whites. Theories relying on spreading economic satisfaction must be taken with a large grain of salt. Post-industrialism is on safer ground predicting a change in forms of economic organization:

Corporations and labor unions are likely to lose relative strength as the knowledge sector strengthens non-corporate (and non-labor) institutions. As a result, corporate and labor-union power can be expected to continue yielding to public regulation. Meanwhile, several economic issues seem bound to escalate. One is the question of productivity and the New Politics-*cum*-knowledge-sector idea of subordinating economic growth to environment and lifestyle quality. Too many Americans are still interested in economic growth, and although the "sociologizing mode" Bell postulates may be a wave of the future, any shift from the still-prevalent "economic mode" will be a major issue in itself. Fuel production and manufacturing remain central to the U.S. living standard. Productivity (economic mode) versus environmentalism (sociologizing mode) may pose a major friction, varying with the acuteness of energy and natural-resource shortages. In this connection, British historian Arnold Toynbee has raised the gloomy possibility of reduced supplies and vastly increased prices of vital minerals—engineered by Asian, African, and Latin American producer nations—which would have the effect of turning the industrial nations of Western Europe and North America into "siege economies" suffering ongoing economic recession, social malaise, and expanding government authoritarianism.[13] At the very least, the fuel and commodity problem must be considered as an offset to post-industrial-affluence hypotheses.

Taxation is a second economic issue that seems sure to grow in importance as more persons move into middle brackets and feel a tax burden that public spending never before imposed on them. By the early-nineteen seventies, anti-tax sentiment was clearly surging in the tax-and-welfare-state-conditioned Scandinavian countries, and U.S. traditions are much less receptive to taxation psychologies. Samuel Lubell has described one such U.S. reaction as the "mechanization of the Southern Baptists," by which he means that many poor white Southerners who have left the farms for middle-class urbanized areas now espouse a fiercely individualistic opposition to federal spending and social programs.[14] The same can be said of many ethnics and blue-collar workers. However, despite general hostility to new taxation, there *are* new program sectors—from health insurance to nursing homes—that the working-classes-turned-lower-middle-classes do support. What they object to are the social programs favored by the knowledge sector for the bilateral benefit of the new class and the urban-rural welfare class.

Inflation is the third predictable economic issue. The post-industrial knowledge-and-services economy, while less prone than industrialism to massive unemployment fluctuation, is especially prey to inflation. Expanding governmental and services employment is a relentless generator of price increases; witness the huge rise that has occurred since the speed-up of post-industrialism in the mid-sixties. Like taxation, ongoing inflation has redistributive overtones between socioeconomic classes. Indeed, modern history's great periods of economic upheaval, while ultimately generating more wealth, have also been eras of great inflation—helping some economic classes and hurting others. For this reason, economic breakthrough eras have generally seen *more* economic-issue tension, not less (even though the character of the struggle has invariably shifted to new issues).

Looking back over the past five hundred years, the two major pre-twentieth-century surges of inflation occurred more or less simultaneously with 1) the Reformation, rise of capitalism, and Counter Reformation (1520–1620) and 2) the French Revolution and early Industrial Revolution (1775–1815). Another fair-sized surge occurred in the middle of the nineteenth century (1848–73) as the Industrial Revolution went into high gear. In each case, inflation fueled the emergence of the era's new class. As described by the New Cambridge Modern History (which entitles its appropriate volume "The Counter-Reformation and Price Revolution, 1559–1610"), Western Europe's massive (500 per cent) sixteenth-century price inflation—rooted in vastly expanded gold and silver supplies from America, plus increased trade, credit, and commodity demand—played a key role in building trading and financial fortunes at the expense of the feudal aristocracy.[15] Inflation during the French and the early Industrial revolutions also contributed to shifting power—a redistribution of income toward bankers, merchants, and industrialists. Often, the common people paid the price with a *reduced* standard of living as price increases outran wage gains—and this contributed to a politics of high economic-issue content. Recent U.S. inflation has the same conflict potential.

All of which suggests that economic issues should continue to be central. In post-industrial circumstances, the traditionalist (or, as David Apter says, the "technologically obsolescent") electorate will be on one side—favoring productivity versus sociology, opposing more taxation, reacting most strongly to public spending and inflation—while the New Politics coalition (of the "technologically proficient" and the "technologically superfluous") will favor the subordination of the corporation, growth of the public sector, more taxation, and heavy education/housing/welfare outlays.

While these issues are perhaps better described as "socioeconomic" than purely "economic," they do not suggest the *end* of economic issues so much as the emergence of a *new level* of economic issue to partly displace industrial-era conflicts over employment, job opportunity, minimum wages, collective bargaining, and all the other right-to-earn-a-living ingredients of 1860–1960 political strife. Obviously, the watershed is not precisely marked, and in many areas the old issues dominate or cut deeply. But the national transition is well under way.

As post-industrialism advances, sociologists expect that more and more basically economic issues will be resolved through governmental decision rather than in the marketplace: Pensions, health benefits, housing assistance, day-care services, credit, food costs, and so forth will increasingly flow from political rather than market action. Vocational, regional, and other interest groups will have to fight their economic battles in the political arena. If Bell and the others are right, then government is on its way to becoming the prime distributive and redistributive mechanism. Industrial-era, free-market-oriented conservatives balk at this prospect; their reorientation will be another battleground.

Bureaucracy is unpopular among most Americans, albeit for various reasons. Yet the basic thrust of post-industrialism—a growing complexity, which obliges government arbitration and regulation—seems bound to keep the size of government growing. Recent projections by the Industrial Conference Board predicted the number of non-educational employees in state and local government growing from 4.3 million in 1970 to 7.9 million in 1990.[16] Libertarian-to-anarchic instincts are widespread on both the left and the right intellectual fringes of U.S. politics, but they are not strong in the middle. Limiting bureaucracy per se is usually not the real crux of anti-bureaucratic issues: Typically, voters are unhappy about the cost or the sociology of the programs involved, and the true objection is to high taxes or to social engineering (among conservatives) or police power (on the left). Most post-industrial theorists seem to take increased government regulation as a matter of course; the question is, by and for whom?

Ebbing martial and nationalistic fervor is an element of the post-industrial trend. True in the United States, it is also true in Britain, Canada, Western Europe, and Australasia—Herman Kahn's Zone 1, referred to some pages ago. Yet, although the direction of movement is apparent, the scope is ambiguous. Patriotism and militarism turned out to be major *pro-traditionalist* factors in the 1972 election, catching New Politics practitioners off guard with the obvious importance that most Americans still attached to honor, the flag, victory, "no surrender," and related virtues, despite the eleven-year agony of Vietnam. Knowledge-sector de-emphasis of nationalism and military preparedness is bound to be unpopular with the traditionalist electorate.

Debate over the media—especially the issues of access and power —will be a central aspect of post-industrialism. The traditional Populist constituencies of the South and West are clearly up in arms.

Taxation, inflation, sex, war, and government regulation: Even in a new context, these are hardly new issues, which may serve to underscore a basic point. For centuries, theorists have been speculating that this or that invention or bit of progress would change mankind. Saint-Simon, Comte, Spencer, and other archpriests of industrialism predicted a radical difference between the emergent spirit of the industrial era and the landholding militarism that it was replacing. Out of technology would come rationality and productivity as the basis for increasing wealth for everybody in lieu of the old way of seizing and plundering wealth from others. Life would become peaceful, and producers would rule.

Only part of this dream has come true. Industrialism *has* meant more wealth and rationality—highwaymen and White Companies are no longer plundering. But martial and acquisitive spirits, far from being eliminated, have been elevated from looting one's neighbor to saturation-bombing rival nations. The idea that post-industrial society will impose a "sociologizing mode" may be similarly inaccurate.

In large measure, post-industrial conflict seems to reflect the economic, philosophic, and cultural cleavage between the New Politics/ knowledge sector and the traditionalist element. Tension between advocates of the "sociologizing mode" and the "economic mode" runs high. The potential for authoritarianism is considerable: first, because of the escalating size and scope of decision making that must be handled by government; second, because of the nature of media and communications power. On one hand, the new class seems out of kilter with the beliefs of the majority. And on the other hand, the traditionalist coalition seems to lack the technical and intellectual capacity to turn things around within the political, administrative, and communications framework established by liberal forces in basic control of Washington since the New Deal.

During the nineteenth and early-twentieth centuries, as Samuel Lubell has underscored, new U.S. political coalitions, while invariably pursuing a few polarizing issues, have been able to promote an essential unification theme of moving the country forward. The principal exception came in 1860, when no unifying coalition was possible and civil war proved unavoidable. Looking at the dimensions and polarizations of post-industrial conflicts, it is once again difficult to see a unifying coalition in any of the political groupings of the seventies.

3

NEW PATTERNS IN AMERICAN POLITICS

IT IS never really correct to talk about new patterns in American politics. The presidential alignments of 1972 reached back to those of previous years, just as the upheavals of 1860 and 1932 had also reached back. But post-1968 analyses emphasizing these shifts and their roots ran afoul of academic reticence. First, the closeness of the 1968 election induced many experts to play down its importance, in effect disinterpreting it. One frequent approach was to doubt any major trends and to discount obvious shifts—Southern, Yankee, or ethnic—as merely products of eroding tradition rather than realignment based on any new dynamic. Next came Watergate, and the seeming breakup of the Republican "new majority" only a few months after the Democrats' 1972 McGovern debacle had given the GOP real cause for optimism. Then the resignation of Richard Nixon and the coming to power of Gerald Ford spurred controversy as to whether the presidential Republican Party would continue to draw its greatest strength in the South and West.

These are good reasons for ambiguity. In 1968, the Wallace vote had yet to make its GOP presidential decision of 1972, so Dixie was still hanging fire. Then, in 1972 (and especially beginning in 1973), the Watergate furor began to destroy the Nixon administration and seemed also to be destroying the new political dynamics implicit in the 1972 election. And, in 1974, Gerald Ford began his administration with a clear commitment to increase GOP strength in the party's old northeastern-midwestern core area.

From the start, most analysts have failed to realize the genesis and impact of the Great Society, while only a handful of sociologists were conversant with the massive change already riding on the back of post-industrial economics. Thus, theses suggesting realignment along these lines ran into heavy flak from *status quo* defenders. Richard Scammon and Ben Wattenberg wrote in *The Real Majority* that the New Deal coalition still prevailed. In a revision of his work *Presidential Elections,* Professor Nelson Polsby said that there was simply no basis for assigning the bulk of the 1968 Wallace vote to the GOP. Analysts Mark Levy and Michael Kramer, in their book *The Ethnic Factor,* admitted that yesterday's Democratic ethnic majorities were shrinking but they saw no major shift except in a few typical cockpits of racial turmoil. Most observers saw the South slipping out of the Democratic presidential grasp, but even that possibility was challenged after the 1970 elections by hypothesis of a liberal "new South" and anti-Nixon denunciation like that contained in *The Southern Strategy,* by Atlanta journalists Reg Murphy and Jack Spalding. Based on University of Michigan Survey Research Center data showing Democrats remaining far ahead of Republicans in voter identification, scholars generally opposed the notion of any substantial shift in party loyalties. The Nixon administration was also reticent, shunning identification with the idea of a new southern, western, and ethnic conservative realignment. Until 1972, support for the idea of major realignment occurred largely among spokesmen for the New Right and the New Left. Most centrists, it seems fair to say, did not understand what was happening.

But Richard Nixon's devastating 1972 defeat of George McGovern stirred speculation anew by tapping *exactly* those trend groups— southern, Wallaceite, Catholic—indicated in realignment projections. Even so, Democratic retention of control of Congress provided a basis for contrary interpretation. The Watergate explosion gave them further cheer. Partly for this reason, old-line Democrats such as those sponsoring the "Committee for a Democratic Majority" argued that the New Deal coalition, or at least something closely resembling it, was a viable constituency for post-1972 presidential victory. However, such calculations disregard both historic precedents and the *evolutionary* nature of the "aberrant" 1972 Democratic constituency. Major upheavals like that of 1964–72 do not simply blow over, restoring the *status quo ante*. When a political party scraps tradition, selecting an unusual—and unsuccessful—presidential nominee, such action has *always* been indicative of a changing dynamic that either gives the aberrant party a new majority or throws it into a period of chaos. After such an episode, no party has ever succeeded in putting the old coalition back together again. This point is central, and worth elaboration.

On four occasions, the defeat of "new coalition" major-party presidential candidates has served to indicate the shape of the majority about to emerge. Andrew Jackson's 1824 defeat turned to victory in 1828. In 1856, when the new Republican Party put itself on the side of Free Soil and northern sectionalism, its presidential nominee, John C. Frémont, lost to Democrat James Buchanan. But, four years later, much the same support base sufficed to elect Abraham Lincoln in a four-way race, provoking civil war and throwing American politics into an entirely new orbit. A similar thing happened in 1928, when the Democrats chose the first Catholic presidential nominee, Governor Alfred E. Smith of New York. Although Smith lost, the voting pattern he laid down—Democratic landslides in urban Catholic areas, including some hitherto Republican—formed an essential ingredient of the Roosevelt coalition in 1932 and subsequent elections. More recently, supporters of Barry Goldwater postulated that the Arizona Republican could establish a new conservative coalition based in the South and West. While Goldwater's own 1964 presidential candidacy failed badly, Richard Nixon put the southern-western coalition over the top in 1968 and 1972. A further note: Each of these new-coalition elections saw the emergent party, even in defeat, capture some states hitherto pillars of the old coalition. Likewise, the incumbent party's ability to survive the first bout—in 1824, 1856, 1928, or 1964—drew primarily on an *established* coalition.

The other group of aberrant nominations features the *unsuccessful* side of realignment. When the Democrats opted for William Jennings Bryan in 1896, his unsuccessful candidacy split the Democratic Party but failed to shape a coalition victorious four or eight years later. On the contrary, Bryan ran in 1900 and lost, and once again—more fruitlessly than ever—in 1908. Aided by the Prairie Populist's 1896 and 1900 failures, old-guard Democrats were able to capture the 1904 nomination, and their choice, conservative New York Judge Alton Parker, swung the party back in the direction of standpat conservatism. Parker's defeat proved worse than those of 1896 and 1900, so that the Democrats turned to Bryan again in 1908. With new forces in motion, reconstitution of the old base was impossible. Being on the wrong side of realignment threw the party into a sort of political schizophrenia. Time and again after 1896, the Democrats chose presidential nominees who were either too radical or too conservative to mobilize the party support base that had given the Democratic presidential nominee a plurality of the popular vote in four of the five elections from 1876 through 1892.* In the two decades before 1896, Democrats controlled Congress for twelve years and outpolled the GOP for the presidency, but Bryan/industrial-Republican polarization had created forces around which the Democrats could no longer mobilize their pre-1896 coalition. Thus, from 1896 until the election of FDR in 1932, the Democrats were able to eject the Republicans from the White House only once—in 1912—because of the Bull Moose split in GOP ranks.

Aside from these several circumstances, the two major parties have invariably nominated presidential candidates basically attuned to the party's existing constituency. Thus it seems fair to say that the parties do not turn to Frémonts, Bryans, Smiths, Goldwaters, or McGoverns lightly. And when they do, to paraphrase Thomas Wolfe, they can't go home again. To describe these upheavals as political "revolutions" is to risk considerable exaggeration. As later portions of this chapter will show, the transitions in question have been more evolutionary than revolutionary. Indeed, to understand these changes it is vital to appreciate their evolutionary nature. Palace revolutions can be undone overnight, whether in Guatemalan or U.S. party politics; *evolutionary* upheavals cannot.

New-coalition elections rest on constituency evolution, and these changes themselves depend much more on minor erosions than on sudden huge shifts in old loyalties. Usually a pervasive new issue has emerged that makes the allegiance dynamics of the old coalition obsolete. Under such circumstances, traditional loyalties do not merely erode, they begin to regroup around new denominators, albeit slowly. There is strong evidence of this in 1960–72 presidential election patterns. A new, generally negative coalition took shape in the old Jefferson-Jackson-Bryan states. It may not have the longevity or potential for positive achievement that yesterday's coalitions had. In more than a few ways, the old party patterns have been *reversing.*

* 1876, 1884, 1888, and 1892.

A. CIVIL-WAR PATTERNS

In some measure, current presidential politics pivot on much the same set of factors that launched the Civil War and its attendant party system: an interrelated trinity of morality, money, and race. Historians have fought over whether the Republicans began as a party of selfless anti-slavery, one of northern-industrial assertion, or one fulfilling a complex regional desire to smash the power of the South. Probably all three outlooks were involved. Beyond New England, the circa-1860 Yankee was counted adept at turning his economic interests into moral and philosophic truths.

Civil War-period cleavages are worth rechecking because they spotlight two U.S. cultural streams that live on today: the community-minded, moralistic North and the individualistic society of the South. Pre-war Dixie never cared much about public schools and the other community-minded institutions of the North. Slavery brought this disparity to a boil. Southerners viewed Yankee abolitionism as hypocrisy while factory workers toiled for a pittance as "wage-slaves" in New England textile mills. To a surprising extent, the polar oppositions of 1860 continue in the nineteen seventies: New England is still one of the richest U.S. regions, and the South, although prospering, remains the poorest; New England is still known for its preoccupation with education, culture, and civic awareness, and Dixie is still known for its cultural apathy and Okie-from-Muskogee individualism; the South is the most military section of the country, New England the least; fashionable New Englanders still lead the nation in advocating this or that preference for blacks while ignoring local (mostly Catholic) poor whites, and Dixie culture is still steeped in racial cleavage. Predictably, these differences play an important role in current U.S. politics.

All of which would make for considerable continuity—and this is the compelling turnabout—save that the events of the past twenty-five years have *substantially reversed* the roles of the parties. The rise of the knowledge industry has created a new, liberal, and largely Democratic moral-righteousness elite based in the Northeast. And despite the confusion implicit in the Nixon-Watergate-Ford transition, the Republican Party has been shifting onto the historic anti-elitist base of U.S. politics.

In one sense, Civil War politics have been reversing, but, in another, they haven't. Here's the vital distinction: The *poles* of U.S.

opinion on the morality-money-race syndrome—i.e., the white South and the fashionable upper-class cultural leadership of New York and New England—have been reversing Civil War-influenced cleavages in their presidential voting patterns; yet patterns in rural areas of border states such as Missouri or in local or Congressional elections lag substantially and still show clear evidence of the old Civil War Republican/Democratic framework. Ticket splitting adds to the time lag.

It's easy to illustrate the reversing poles of U.S. cutural and racial politics. A century ago, Massachusetts was the seedbed of the Republican Party, the breeding ground of abolitionism, the parade ground of northern war opinion. But, in 1972, Massachusetts first gave left-liberal Democratic candidate George McGovern his biggest primary victory and then became the only state among fifty to vote for him. Massachusetts remains the nation's leading exponent of morality politics via such causes as racial balance, disarmament, peace, environmentalism, etc.

The Beacon Hill, Boston, of Oliver Wendell Holmes, William Lloyd Garrison, Wendell Phillips, and Senator Charles Sumner chose George McGovern in 1972; South Carolina—where Charlestonians fired the first Civil War guns at Fort Sumter—went strongly Republican, as might be expected from the seat of U. S. Senator Strom Thurmond and the Nixon "southern strategy."

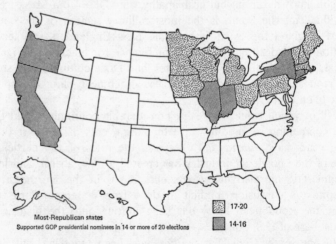

17-20

14-16

Most-Republican states
Supported GOP presidential nominees in 14 or more of 20 elections

MAP 1
Basic Party Divisions (1856–1932)

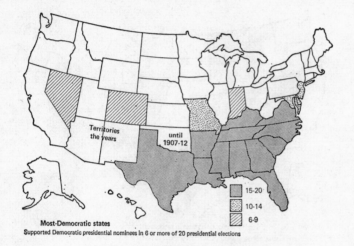

Territories
the years

until
1907-12

15-20

10-14

6-9

Most-Democratic states
Supported Democratic presidential nominees in 6 or more of 20 presidential elections

MAP 2
Basic Party Divisions (1856–1932)

Top 15 Republican states in presidential voting
Ranked by number of elections that state appeared in the list of the top 15 GOP states

MAP 3
New Deal-Era Party Divisions (1932–44)

Top 15 Democratic states in presidential voting
Ranked by number of elections that state appeared in the list of top 15 Democratic states

MAP 4
New Deal-Era Party Divisions (1932–44)

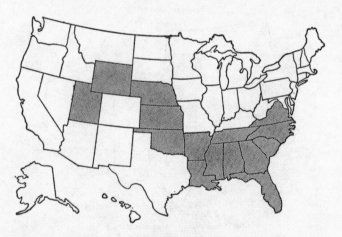

MAP 5
Top 15 Republican states—1972

MAP 6
Top 15 Democratic states—1972

In the presidential elections of 1964, 1968, and 1972, New England was the *most* Democratic region of the country and the South was the *least* Democratic, a shift that coincides with the knowledge economy, the civil-rights revolution, and the emergence of the race issue as a major national factor in politics. Maps 1–6 illustrate the reversal of Civil War loyalties that seems to be taking place. Map 1 shows that the states that were most staunch in their Republicanism during the years from 1856 to 1932. By and large, they represent Yankee America: New England and the New England-settled states that captained the northern cause during the Civil War. Map 3 shows that New Deal-era GOP strength continued to come from the old Civil War axis of the Northeast and Middle West. Map 5 shows the very different 1972 pattern of Republican support. Meanwhile, the Democrats have shed *their* Civil War pattern (shown in Map 2) and the similar 1932–44 pattern (Map 4) and shifted instead to a 1972 base of strength (Map 6) strongly reminiscent of the post-Civil War Republican axis.

As the maps make clear, the Civil War had a dominant effect on the U.S. party system that prevailed from Appomattox until World War II. Indeed, the North-South, Union-Confederate cleavage was even sharper than simple state-by-state maps can show. Counties in border states, such as Ohio, Indiana, Kentucky, Illinois, and Missouri tended to be Democratic if settled from the South, Republican if settled from the North. Highland areas in the Appalachians and the Ozarks were pro-Union in the Civil War and Republican thereafter; such lowland areas as the "little Dixie" sections of Kentucky and Missouri were heavily Democratic.

If Civil War partisanships were coming totally unraveled, these loyalties would be reversing, but they are not; thus a few caveats are in order. Within the states, some traditional patterns linger on. In New England, for example, the best Nixon areas in the 1972 election were the old rural GOP strongholds: the townships and shire towns— from Chelsea, Orange County, Vermont, to down-East Maine— where stalwart Republicanism traces itself back to the eighteen fifties and the Civil War battles commemorated on the century-old marble obelisks and GAR statues. The same is true of upstate New York and rural Michigan. Those old Republican rural counties which have not been given a new sociocultural twist by universities, art and resort colonies, or affluent suburban inroads cast solid 1972 Nixon plurali- ties. Thus, although rural Yankee Republicanism has been eroding, it is not yet turning as sharply as the 1964 vote suggested might happen in the face of a Republican "southern strategy." Small-town and rural conservatism will probably maintain itself in the North for reasons of lifestyle and socioeconomic affinity with the rest of the apparent conservative coalition. Interestingly, the best Nixon counties in New England were among the poorest economically. Fashionable areas are in the vanguard of the past decade's Democratic trend.

Below the Mason-Dixon line, rural Democratic tradition appears to have run its course as far as presidential elections are concerned. Across the Deep South, from Charleston to Natchez, only 10–20 per cent of the white voters supported Lyndon Johnson in 1964; only 10 per cent supported Hubert Humphrey in 1968; and fewer still chose George McGovern in 1972. Democratic presidential strength in the Deep South is overwhelmingly black, and the few counties that produced McGovern majorities were black-dominated—e.g., Greene and Macon in Alabama, Holmes and Jefferson in Mississippi. Local presidential politics is taking on a black-white coloration just as it did in Reconstruction days before ascendant whites imposed require- ments (poll taxes, literacy tests, and so forth) to drive blacks off the voter rolls. This time, it is the national Democratic Party that has been identified with the blacks, while the national Republican Party is seen as less friendly to blacks, as well as to school busing, welfare, and other programs seen linked to black pressures.

If Deep South whites have been as vehemently opposed to the national Democratic Party of the nineteen seventies as their forebears were to the national Republican Party of the eighteen seventies, some of the old pattern can also be found in the border states. Here the Civil War cleavages were more indirect than in New England or the cotton states, and party loyalties persist with less regard for new vicissitudes in the issues that shaped them. This is why talk of "reversal" must be qualified.

For example, the only Missouri county to vote for George McGovern was Monroe County, in the heart of "Little Dixie." I visited there in the summer of 1972, anxious to see how border psychologies were bearing up, just after the South Dakotan's nomination. Southern influence does not leap out at the visitor to Monroe County, except in the names. Missouri's "Little Dixie" was settled from Virginia, Tennessee, and Kentucky right after the War of 1812, and local names evoke the Jeffersonian and pro-French politics of the period: the county is named for Virginian President James Monroe; the county seat for the French capital, Paris; the local hotel for Thomas Jefferson.

A Missouri WPA guide yields more knowledge of Monroe County's settlement patterns than conversation with county voters. Not one mentioned southern antecedents or raised the changing relationship of the South and the two major parties. Nor did any have praise for George McGovern. Pressed for November voting intentions, the average Monroe County dweller simply said: "I'm a Democrat and always have been." In contrast, the white electorates of Charleston, Richmond, and Montgomery, far more attuned to changing racial politics, had long since abandoned a national Democratic Party that had shed its historic relationship with the South. Monroe County typifies the several laggard streams in U.S. politics. Its leaning toward the South in the Civil War, albeit culturally mandatory, was politically reluctant; Monroe County did not support the Democratic nominees in 1856 and 1860 but, rather, the Whig and Constitutional Union candidates, seekers after compromise solutions that were no longer possible. Democratic politics came to Monroe County by Civil War cultural fallout, as it were, and they are ebbing the same way— slowly, by cultural fallout.

As yet of little consequence below the presidential level, shifting partisanships of this sort will be a major factor in American politics for decades to come. The 1968 election raised hell with remaining

Democratic presidential loyalties below the Mason-Dixon line, and the 1972 election reduced them even further. Hubert Humphrey carried a goodly number of predominantly white sub-Mason-Dixon-line counties: two dozen in West Virginia; two score in Kentucky; two dozen in Missouri; a handful in Virginia, Tennessee, and Arkansas; two dozen in Oklahoma; and a hundred-odd in Texas. While this was a poor showing for a Democratic presidential nominee, George McGovern sank much, much lower. Across the length and breadth of the eleven states of the old Confederacy plus Maryland, West Virginia, Kentucky, Missouri, and Oklahoma, McGovern managed to carry only a dozen largely white counties. Most of them are border-state backwaters. Just one county in West Virginia (a state that voted for Hubert Humphrey!) chalked up a McGovern victory: Logan County, a machine stronghold and depressed coal-mining area that HHH had carried 3–1. McGovern barely won Logan. In Kentucky, McGovern narrowly carried Breathitt, Floyd, and several other counties, all poor highland mining areas. Monroe County was the only one in Missouri to back the South Dakotan. Every single county in Oklahoma voted for the Republican presidential candidate, for the first time in history. And, in Texas, Democratic success was confined to a half dozen Chicano counties and poor-white Cottle County (hitherto 4–1 Democratic).

If there is any common bond between the handful of southern white counties that McGovern carried, it is a mixture of lopsided Democratic tradition, cultural backwater status, and remoteness from the collective social issue that shaped the political upheaval of the nineteen sixties. There is little left to show of the Democratic tradition that guided the South through three generations of post-Appomattox presidential campaigns.

Perhaps the best way to indicate how important Civil War loyalties remained in southern presidential politics as late as 1960—and how totally those old cleavages have been wiped out—is to describe a "spectrum color" map I made of the 1960 national election results. By putting counties that were over 70 per cent Republican in black, over 60 per cent Republican in dark blue, over 50 per cent in light blue, over 40 per cent in green, over 30 per cent in yellow, and over 20 per cent in red, I found that the geography of rural partisanship stood out very clearly indeed. Republican blacks and dark blues spread from the rural North down into the highest southern mountain regions. The peaks of the Great Smokies and Ozarks—pro-

North during the Civil War—were just as Republican as upstate New York. Except for a few heavily Democratic urban counties, the rest of the North and West comes out light blue or green. Yellow and red rural counties (20–40 per cent Republican) begin below the Mason-Dixon line. The northernmost yellow and red clusters were the "Little Dixie" areas of bluegrass Kentucky and northeast Missouri. Yellow and red-colored counties were commonplace in southside Virginia, eastern North Carolina, Piedmont South Carolina, most of Georgia, northern "cracker" Florida, southern Alabama, most of Mississippi, southern (Cajun) Louisiana, southeast Oklahoma, central and Rio Grande Texas, and southeast Arkansas. With some notable exceptions, these are the old slaveowning areas of their respective states. John F. Kennedy appointed segregationist federal judges in the Deep South for a good reason.

Four years later, as the civil-rights revolution picked up steam, the Republicans nominated Barry Goldwater, and the segregation-minded Deep South swung behind him. Goldwater's candidacy was the first giant step toward wiping out and even reversing the Civil War pattern. Race-conscious sections of South Carolina, Georgia, Alabama, Mississippi, Louisiana, and other states went heavily Republican for the first time. On a spectrum map of the 1964 election, rural New England would have showed Democratic yellow while the crescent from Charleston to Vicksburg would have been black (over 70 per cent Republican). But the more moderate Democratic Civil War strongholds of the outer South and border turned in their usual reds and yellows. (For example, Monroe County, Missouri, gave Lyndon Johnson a 4–1 lead over Goldwater.)

Mapping the 1968 elections in these colors would have been a frustrating task. Once again, the GOP would see yellow and red sweeping across most of the lowland South. Only the bustling new Dixie metropolitan areas and the old Civil War mountain counties turned in the blacks and blues of Republican majorities. Most of the traditionally Democratic South preferred Third Party candidate George Wallace. North of the Mason-Dixon line, GOP nominee Nixon recovered most (but not all) of the rural Yankee and suburban Republican electorate lost to the Democrats in 1964. From the GOP standpoint, a county-by-county map of 1968 results would have looked like a variation on the usual post-Civil War pattern. Yet this would have been a misleading picture, because a map of the Democratic vote—*excluding the Wallace voters*—would have shown the

Civil War pattern blurred to an unprecedented degree. Debate over what the 1968 election meant—over whether there was or was not a new political alignment—pivoted on interpretations of the Wallace factor.

In 1972, the Wallace vote went Republican and swept the southern rural Democratic reds and yellows off the map. For the first time in over a century, no Civil War legacy is readily visible in the voting pattern, even in states such as Missouri and Kentucky. The rural and small-town North emerges as a sea of black and dark blue. So does the rural and small-town South. Few and far between, counties backing McGovern usually satisfy one of these criteria: 1) large central-city population; 2) large labor-union-member concentration; 3) predominantly black population; and 4) large academic and/or collegian population. Except in Minnesota and South Dakota, hardly any white small-town or rural counties supported McGovern. *Thus, the 1972 presidential election is the first since the 1840–52 period without any substantial Civil War legacy in the rural voting pattern.*

From this, one could posit that the Civil War pattern has been wiped out, not reversed. However, the signs are that the old set of issues—race, lifestyle, money, and morality—is developing a new cleavage with potential for increased sectional overtones. Here are the reasons. Despite the solid 1972 Nixon showings in rural New England and upstate New York, the presidential Republican Party has been losing strength in recent years, and the 2–1 majorities of 1972 are well below those scored by Eisenhower. In turn, from 1964 to 1972, the Democrats were unable to win more than a handful of white presidential votes in many rural southern counties, nor is there any likelihood that this will change appreciably. If one were to make a chart of the two hundred counties giving Richard Nixon his highest vote percentages in 1972, four fifths of them would be below the Mason-Dixon line, heavily concentrated in places like the Florida-Georgia-Alabama-Mississippi piney woods, the Oklahoma-Texas plains, and the Appalachian highlands. Local Nixon pluralities in these counties ranged between 5–1 and 10–1. Secondly, the fashionable urban and suburban areas of the Northeast have been moving *away* from the GOP, whereas below the Mason-Dixon line, such districts have been turning more Republican (lopsidedly so) in presidential elections. Lastly, the largest Republican gains showed a pronounced tendency to cluster in areas of racial tension—whether Brooklyn, New York; Lake County (Gary), Indiana; or the South—

while the Democratic coalition is seemingly moving onto the New England-upper Midwest-Pacific Northwest base least troubled by racial problems and hence (like the same coalition in Civil War days) freer to embrace or profit from minority causes. While there is a real question whether the effective realignment of Civil War loyalties can occur within the existing party framework, there are reasons to think that the late-twentieth-century cleavages in presidential politics will bear considerable relation to those of the Lincoln era. At the same time, because of ticket splitting, local politics and party cleavages will be confused rather than reflective of presidential alignments.

B. ETHNICS AND BLACKS

Ever since Irish Catholic upholsterer William Mooney founded Tammany Hall, in 1789, northern Catholics have usually been presidential-election allies of southern and western forces opposing the politics of the prevailing northeastern establishment. In 1828, Catholics went heavily for Andrew Jackson. New York City's loyally Democratic Catholics, mostly Irish, rioted in 1863 in protest against GOP war policies and the Union army draft, and they also managed to attack Brooks Brothers—then, as now, the fashionable clothiers. When William Jennings Bryan sounded his silver trumpet in 1896, the establishment gnashed its teeth, and Bryan's only substantial northeastern support came from predominantly Democratic Catholics (themselves none too enthusiastic). And, beginning with Al Smith's abortive 1928 White House race, industrial-state Catholics marshaled to form the northern wing of FDR's southern-and-western-based New Deal *entente*.

From 1968 to 1972, there was political speculation that the Catholic, or ethnic, vote was once again lining up with the South and the West, this time under Republican colors. In 1972, Nixon-administration bids for Catholic support received so much attention that one New York Democratic leader, Matthew Troy of Queens County, accused the President of having "done everything but serve mass." Fashionable liberal journals helped shape a similar impression with their incessant portraiture of fascist hardhats, Polish backlashers, and Irish cops.

Prior to 1972, ethnic Republicanism was often overstated by these and similar references. The Catholic GOP trend was only that: *a trend,* not any kind of majority (except in New York City). Unfortunately, treatises leaping to point this out fell into the reverse trap of not perceiving the basic *trend* pattern. One such, *The Ethnic Factor* (1972), by Mark Levy and Michael Kramer, used NBC election-precinct data to show that outside of a few urban areas marked by racial tensions, ethnic support for GOP 1960–68 presidential candidates usually fell in the 20–30 per cent range. Levy and Kramer tended to dismiss the pattern in such tense cities as New York, Newark, Gary, Cleveland, and Detroit as aberrations. Unfortunately, this approach lacked perception of social dynamics. There was no awareness of the forces that would shortly nominate Democratic presidential nominee George McGovern, and no appreciation that in a realignment based on cultural clashes, *the first signs would come in just those cities beginning to exhibit them.* For example, New York City, as an early vortex of establishment-versus-anti-establishment confrontation, has often been in the vanguard of Catholic political shifts that took many more years to "trickle down" to the mill towns of New England or the iron-range cities of Lake Superior.

According to George Gallup, the Republican share of the Catholic vote for President was 22 per cent in 1960, 24 per cent in 1964, and 33 per cent in 1968. No separate figures are published for New York City, but reasonable estimates for Catholics (excluding Puerto Ricans) would be as follows: 1960—45–50 per cent; 1964—40–45 per cent; 1968—55–60 per cent. Then, in 1972, when the GOP presidential share of the Catholic vote climbed to 53 per cent nationally, it appears to have reached 75–85 per cent in the angry "Middle American" Irish and Italian neighborhoods at the end of New York City's subway lines.

Across most of the northern United States, the urban majority of Catholics still see a conservative local Republican establishment made up of Protestant businessmen and a Democratic Party still in Catholic hands. Certainly this is the case in New England and the upper Midwest. But it is not true in New York City. In the capital of the U.S. knowledge/communications industry, Catholics have lost some of their long-time hold on the Democratic Party to middle-class liberal professionals and minority-group members (Jews, Negroes, and Puerto Ricans). As a result, the party no longer represents the cultural and ideological values of Al Smith's old Catholic sidewalks of New York (or kindred suburbia). When the Democrats nominated four Jews and a Negro to their five-man statewide ticket in 1970, New York City Catholics went at least three-to-one Republican. Although the pattern faded in the confusion of 1974, as of the nineteen seventies, the East Side of Manhattan, the city's GOP stronghold from the New Deal era through the mid-fifties, is the citadel of affluent Democratic New Politics liberalism, and the once staunchly Democratic Italo-Irish assembly districts are the most Republican sections of New York City.

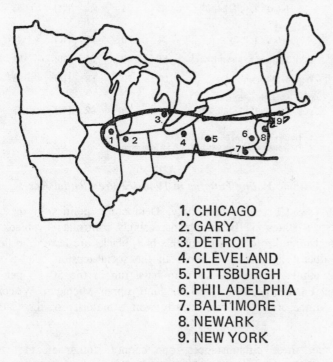

1. CHICAGO
2. GARY
3. DETROIT
4. CLEVELAND
5. PITTSBURGH
6. PHILADELPHIA
7. BALTIMORE
8. NEWARK
9. NEW YORK

MAP 7
Social-Tension Belt

Catholic Democratic loyalties also appear to be weakening in the old industrial "social tension" belt (see Map 7), from the Connecticut and New Jersey environs of New York City west through Pennsylvania (with a jump down to Baltimore) and into the Great Lakes cities of Cleveland, Detroit, and Gary. First of all, black populations are reaching the 40 per cent or higher level in many

Ethnic Voting Patterns in 1960-72 Presidential Races

Democratic Share of the Total Vote for President

	1960	1964	1968[2]		1972
Newark (North Ward)	68%	65%	48%	(16%)	45%
South Philadelphia (Wards 1, 2, 26, 39, 48)	75	64	48	(12)	39
East Baltimore (Wards 1, 6, 7, 24, 26)	72	71	46	(21)	33
Cleveland (Wards 1, 2, 3)	64	73	50	(18)	47
Gary South of Calumet River[1]	67	66	31	(26)	27
Warren, Michigan	69	78	58	(16)	36
West Side Chicago (Wards 12, 13, 15, 23)	66	58	42	(15)	35

1. District 6, precincts 90—123
2. Percentage of vote for George Wallace is in parenthesis.

CHART 9
Ethnic Voting Patterns in 1960–72 Presidential Races

cities (see Chart 10). Secondly, Democratic politics in these big industrial states are becoming increasingly controlled by black and affluent-liberal forces. North of this belt, blacks are fewer and limousine liberalism is less common. In the social-tension belt, Nixon's 1972 ethnic percentages seem to have run in the 50–60 per cent range. Farther north, in New England, upper Michigan, Wisconsin, and Minnesota, McGovern clearly won a majority of the Catholic vote.

Under these circumstances, one cannot slough off the steady 1960–72 Democratic slippage in such places as New York, Newark, Gary, and Cleveland (see Chart 9). Enough cities are being affected to give the ethnic trend real meaning. Even in Italian South Philadelphia, where racial tensions are less obvious than in Newark and Gary, Samuel Lubell has charted 1960–72 GOP presidential increment: among 131 precincts, only one backed Richard Nixon in 1960; then twelve went for Barry Goldwater in 1964; forty-five picked Nixon in 1968; and an overwhelming majority backed Nixon in 1972.

Black Population in Selected Cities, 1930-70

	1930	1950	1970
New York	5%	10%	21%
Newark	9	17	54
Philadelphia	11	18	34
Baltimore	18	24	46
Cleveland	8	16	38
Detroit	8	16	44
Gary	18	29	53
Chicago	7	14	33
St. Louis	11	18	41
Memphis	38	37	39
New Orleans	28	32	45
Atlanta	33	37	51
Richmond	29	32	42

CHART 10
Black Population in Selected Cities, 1930–70

Ethnic disenchantment with the presidential Democratic Party has three obvious roots. The first is economic: Many of yesterday's economic liberals of the New Deal and Fair Deal era have now moved up to lower-middle- or middle-class status themselves and no longer identify with governmental programming for the poor. Secondly, ethnics—especially those of eastern or southern European antecedents and Catholic or Orthodox religion—are high on the list of Americans hostile to the upper-middle-class "Greening of America" predilection for anti-family values (free love, women's lib, easy divorce, and the like), abortion, social experiments, and anti-nationalism. Thirdly, ethnics in many urban areas are locked in municipal and socioeconomic competition with blacks, and from New York to Michigan, ethnic backlash has been an increasing source of jeopardy for recent Democratic presidential candidates.

Cultural geography is a vital factor. In remote areas such as the mill towns of upper New England or the mining centers of the Mesabi Range, white ethnic voters are overwhelmingly Democratic, and pressures eroding those loyalties are minimal. Industrial-era contexts still prevail. To be sure, there was little enthusiasm over any of George McGovern's social programs and positions, but although the Democratic vote among Maine's French Canadians or Minnesota's Slavs dropped by 10–15 per cent, it was still in the 60–70 per cent range—even for the controversial South Dakotan. In these areas, it's not CBS executive vice-presidents but Republican timber and mining executives who own the local limousines. At the same time, there are hardly any blacks to agitate ethnic hostilities. In contrast, the ethnic neighborhoods of New York, Cleveland, greater Detroit, and Gary seethe with Irish, Italian, Hungarian, and Polish hostility toward black and affluent liberal members of the "new class," one or both of these groups being present in large and influential numbers. Consequently, although many of these ethnic voters remain Democrats in contests where social or racial issues are not focused, they have been increasingly hostile to Democratic presidential candidates espousing the interests of blacks and the new class. McGovern won only 25–40 per cent of the ethnic vote in the cockpits of the social-tension belt.

What is more, the social-tension belt has been *expanding* rather than contracting in the years since the early nineteen sixties. In the 1964 presidential election, only a few northern social-issue backlash areas stood out: Gary, sections of Detroit and Newark, and a few locales of New York, Philadelphia, Cleveland, and Chicago. By 1974, Newark, Gary, Detroit, and East St. Louis had black mayors, and so had Cleveland from 1967 to 1971. Racial polarization prevailed in all these mayoralty races, with blacks voting for their man and 80–95 per cent of the whites going the other way. Harvard Professor Thomas Pettigrew, analyzing the 1973 municipal returns, purports to see grounds for optimism. But this cannot be said of the critical cities where blacks make up 40 per cent or more of the population. Forty per cent is sometimes said to be the tipping point for residential neighborhoods, and that may also be true of urban mayoralty psychologies. Where non-whites are only a small minority, white voters seem more willing to elect a black mayor or U. S. Senator: e.g., in Los Angeles or Massachusetts. However, once the non-white population approaches a majority, then election of a black mayor has invariably been accompanied by tension and polarization of voting blocs. Political observers look for blacks to seek the Baltimore and St. Louis mayoralties before the decade is out, and Chicago and Philadelphia (33 per cent black in 1970) may not be far behind.

Since the New Deal began, in 1933, black migration to the major cities of the North has changed the urban demography that made the Roosevelt coalition possible. Besides establishing a basic rivalry with white ethnic populations, the huge black influx has been a central factor in the expansion of educational, welfare, and social research— and is thereby a linchpin of the new class and their value systems. Not surprisingly, industrial-era (and usually organized-labor-based) ethnic loyalties to the national Democratic Party have been ebbing under these pressures. At the same time, the Republican Party— with its own roots in old-line American business—has not been able to translate this ethnic disaffection into broad-based GOP sentiment. The party context of black/ethnic-white urban rivalry is still unclear.

C. EVOLUTION, NOT
REVOLUTION

George S. McGovern was not nominated in 1972 by a flukish, momentary upheaval in Democratic Party thinking. Not at all. On the contrary, his selection was the evolutionary product of a geographic and socioeconomic party shift reaching back several decades. Between the time Franklin D. Roosevelt took power, in March 1933, and the dreary day in January 1969 when Lyndon Johnson laid that power down, the Democratic Party, in control of the government for twenty-eight of the thirty-six years, changed the country enormously, and in the process metamorphosed its own base of power.

This is unusual in itself. During previous U.S. political cycles, the party in office has typically continued to reflect more or less the same constituency that voted it into office (e.g., the Republicans between 1860 and 1932). Even the Jacksonian coalition (1828–60) did not so much change constituencies as have its original *national* base destroyed by the advent of sectionalism and Civil War. What has happened to both major U.S. parties over the past two decades seems unique. First, the Democrats:

1. The Democratic Evolution   Franklin D. Roosevelt took office well aware of his party's southern tilt. John N. "Cactus Jack" Garner of Texas was Vice-President; Alabama's William P. Bankhead was Speaker of the House; and Joseph Robinson of Arkansas led the Democratic Senate majority. In 1938, when FDR was looking for a new Senate leader, the contest pitted his man, Alben Barkley of Kentucky, against Pat Harrison of Mississippi.

Despite all the talk about the New Deal coalition being alive and well in the nineteen seventies, the fact remains that the New Deal coalition—in *all four* of the Roosevelt elections—was centered on the South. That was where FDR received his highest election support ratios, and without the support of the "greater South"—the old Confederacy, plus Maryland, Kentucky, Missouri, Delaware, Oklahoma, West Virginia, Arizona, and New Mexico—Roosevelt would have failed to win Electoral College majorities in both 1940 and 1944. Map 4 makes clear just how fully the "New Deal" coalition continued to rely on the Greater South. And this was logical enough: Many of the economic policies of the early New Deal, from TVA to agricultural subsidies, suited the needs and tastes of the South, then as now one of the poorest sections of the country.

At the same time as southern votes were still central to the Roosevelt administration, whether at the polls or in Congress, there is no doubt that the Democratic *thrust* was shifting to the North. Following the trail blazed by Al Smith in 1928, the New Deal rallied lopsided support in Catholic blue-collar precincts. Such was the urban, labor, and economic bias of the New Deal that rural Democratic strength slipped away, first in dribs and drabs, and then in larger numbers (partly because of rural German isolationism in 1940 and 1944). Compare Roosevelt's fairly narrow 1940 and 1944 popular victories with Woodrow Wilson's 1916 success; the key to FDR's electoral-vote landslides lay in the new adherence of the industrial North.

Party metamorphosis was under way. Below the Mason-Dixon line, pressure on southern Democratic loyalties was already writ large in the 1944 Supreme Court rejection of the "white primary," key to local white ability to use the one-party system to suppress blacks. By 1948, the Deep South was angry enough to bolt the party for the States' Rights splinter candidacy of South Carolina Governor Strom Thurmond. Come November, Thurmond won Louisiana, Mississippi, Alabama, and South Carolina. It was the Deep South's first bolt since the Civil War.

Even so, Truman's farmer-labor support constituted something of a "last hurrah" for the old Democratic coalition. The outer South, border, farm belt, and Rocky Mountains went strongly Democratic as Harry S Truman—himself a son of the border and nephew of a Confederate army veteran—called the Republicans "bloodsuckers with offices in Wall Street," who treated the South and the West "like colonies." Truman survived not only the Dixiecrat revolt, but the break-off of the far left of the Democratic Party under former Vice-President Henry Wallace. For the moment, the pressures building on both wings reinforced the middle. Nineteen forty-eight marks the last time that the Democratic Party was successfully able to mobilize what Walter Dean Burnham has called the "Bryanite-colonial" coalition of the South and West against the northeastern financial-industrial axis.

As the Democratic Party transformed itself during the fifties, evolution got blurry. In 1952 and 1956, the party got ahead of itself by nominating a representative of the emerging egghead sector: Adlai E. Stevenson. But Stevenson was twice decisively defeated. He could not appeal very successfully to the party's industrial or agricultural-era constituencies—Bryanite or AFL-CIO blue-collar —and the knowledge-sector shock troops who won the 1972 nomination for George McGovern were not yet a major demographic factor in national politics. Southern movement away from the Democrats was taking shape. Even though Stevenson managed to hold onto the Deep South, both elections saw Eisenhower chalk up the first GOP victories in the outer South since Herbert Hoover.

But so closely did Eisenhower's victories resemble the GOP landslides of the nineteen twenties, when the Republicans had swept the North and West and made tentative inroads into the South, that some observers thought that the old-pre-Depression Republican pattern was asserting itself again. But, in point of fact, the fifties were a period of hiatus during which basic realignment worked its ways quietly and profoundly. Republicanism was digging its roots into the South, and the Democrats were pushing into northern Republican territory previously beyond the pale because of Civil War tradition. During the fifties, at least twenty Congressional districts were lost that had stayed Republican throughout the entire New Deal. One was the at-large seat in Vermont, in GOP hands since the 1850s. Obvious Democratic trends were at work in Maine, Michigan, Pennsylvania, Oregon, Minnesota, and the Dakotas.

Nineteen sixty saw the Democratic Party move to recapture its lost (to Eisenhower) Catholic votes and to bolster the party position below the Mason-Dixon line. The result: the nomination of Catholic John F. Kennedy for President and Texas' Lyndon B. Johnson for Vice-President. The strategy worked, and the ticket won a narrow victory. But careful reading of the results showed that the Democratic coalition was definitely in the throes of realignment. As Map 8 shows, nine of the ten best Democratic states of 1956 had been southern. Loyalties were eroding, but still substantial. By 1960, the map of the Democrats' top ten states shows an odd mix of northeastern and southern states, a clear sign of loyalties and coalitions in transition. Kennedy's victory marked the first time that New England, seedbed of the GOP a century earlier, was the *strongest* Democratic region in the country!

Top ten Democratic states—1956

Top ten Democratic states—1960

Top ten Democratic states—1964

Top ten Democratic states—1968

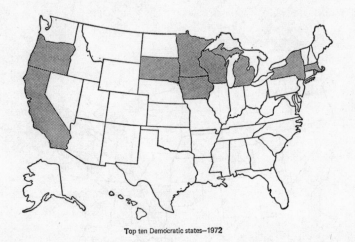

Top ten Democratic states—1972

MAP 8
Shifting Democratic Presidential Geography

No sooner had Kennedy entered the White House than the civil-rights revolution began to move into high gear, and with it the alienation of the South from the national Democratic Party. As the civil-rights drive accelerated, so did Dixie discontent. GOP gains in the South were marked in the 1962 Congressional elections, and Alabama Governor George Wallace, leaping into the headlines with attempts to stall desegregation, readied himself to run in the 1964 Democratic presidential primaries. Ultimately he did so, with considerable effect in Indiana, Wisconsin, and Maryland, but the assassination of John Kennedy cooled the nation's temper and created a climate of moderation for the 1964 election.

Save for the Republicans' nomination of Barry Goldwater, the Democrats could have expected considerable middle-of-the-road and conservative disaffection in 1964. However, with voters perceiving Goldwater as a pro-southern extremist, Lyndon Johnson won in a landslide, and with a constituency that bore more relation to the Civil War *Republican* coalition than to the Democratic coalition of that period. The Deep South swung to Goldwater, while Maine and Vermont—the only two states to go Republican in 1936—were among the top ten *Democratic* states. Such fashionable suburban and downtown areas as New York's Westchester County and the East Side of Manhattan also swung Democratic. For the second straight election,

New England was the nation's most Democratic region. As Samuel Lubell has noted, Johnson won 460 New England townships that had not voted for a Democratic president since, at the latest, 1896.[1]

The Great Society coalition, launched in 1964, was a far cry from the New Deal coalition. Angrily opposed by the Deep South, its roots were in the Northeast, the Pacific coast, affluent suburban areas, and black urban slums. With the aid of a host of new liberal Democratic congressmen from New England, New York, the upper Midwest, and the Pacific coast, the Johnson administration promptly unleashed a massive program of educational, housing, and social-welfare legislation. All this had the effect of moving the Democratic Party off the "Bryanite-colonial" axis and onto the new post-industrial axis. In the 1966 Congressional elections, the Democrats lost heavily in the South, Midwest, border, farm belt, and Rocky Mountain "colonial" axis, but they held many of their seats first won in 1964 in traditionally Republican sections of New England, suburban New York, and the Pacific Northwest. These areas were more responsive to Great Society policies.

Capsule histories such as this tend to be dry, and thus, to an extent, self-defeating. However, the point—and an essential one— is to show that the Democratic Party did not turn to the 1972 McGovern electorate by flukish accident but was, rather, drawn there slowly, in evolutionary fashion, by the civil-rights revolution and the socioeconomic emergence of the knowledge industry. By the mid-nineteen sixties, the affluent northern and Pacific states were definitely taking shape as the Democratic constituency of the future, and the South was definitely trending out of the national party.

Great Society programs—and the Great Society's Vietnam War —nurtured the transition by simultaneously stirring up a social-program backlash among conservatives, and then antagonizing the new affluent liberal constituency of the new class by continuing the war far beyond its 1965–66 peak of general acceptability. Thus, by 1968, both the right wing of the Democratic Party (the Wallaceites) and the left wing (the McCarthyites and Kennedyites) were up in arms. McCarthy won primaries in the New Politics strongholds of New England, the upper Midwest, and the Pacific coast. August 1968 saw the long arm of the LBJ White House nominate centrist Democrat Hubert Humphrey for President against the opposition of both these streams of insurgency. On the right, George Wallace had already declared his third-party candidacy, and the left—

thrown into bitter hostility by the Chicago convention debacle—sulked in its Manhattan-Cambridge-Berkeley tent.

In late September, with only 29 per cent poll support (to Nixon's 45 per cent and Wallace's 21 per cent), Humphrey had to make a choice—and he moved left, following the geopolitical trend of the sixties and wooing the McCarthyite wing of the party. These tactics succeeded, and by election day, Humphrey lost by only a hair (thanks to the Nixon-Wallace split on the right). His nearly successful coalition pivoted most of New England, New York, Pennsylvania, and Michigan. Far from doing poorly in the fashionable strongholds of the New Politics, HHH did well—thanks to his October shift. Chic knowledge-sector liberal areas such as Cambridge, Massachusetts; Scarsdale, New York; East Side Manhattan; Shaker Heights, Ohio; Ann Arbor, Michigan; Princeton, New Jersey; Berkeley, California; and Madison, Wisconsin; all gave Humphrey *stronger* support against Nixon than they had given John F. Kennedy against the same man eight years earlier. Humphrey held the affluent left easily enough; his problem lay on the right, with the many voters lost to Wallace and the other Wallaceites only brought back to the fold at the last minute because of AFL-CIO exertions and GOP inability to stress realignment social issues.

As Map 8 shows, Humphrey's top states were mostly in the Northeast. The next ten were in the Midwest and Pacific coast. Comparing Humphrey's 43 per cent in 1968 with the 38 per cent won by George McGovern four years later, there are not as many differences as New Deal coalition theorists typically argue. McGovern got probably one out of every five or six 1968 Wallace voters, mostly in the North, and thus the real measure of McGovern slippage among HHH voters is conceivably some six or seven percentage points. Across most of the old Confederacy, Humphrey and McGovern ran about the same, because there just wasn't much left to lose after 1968. McGovern scored about the same (and in a few cases, a bit better) than Humphrey in Wisconsin, Iowa, the Dakotas, and Oregon. The big Democratic 1968–72 losses—eight to fifteen percentage points—came in conservative Catholic and border areas: in the Catholic industrial cities of New England (especially Rhode Island), New York, Pennsylvania, and Michigan; in the coal-and-smokestack country of Appalachian Pennsylvania, West Virginia, Ohio, and Kentucky; in the border country of Missouri; in the Democratic rural strongholds of Oklahoma and Texas; in national-security-conscious Hawaii; and in the aerospace centers and trans-planted-Okie counties of Washington and California (e.g., Bakers-field—sometimes known as "Nashville West").

Except for these sloughed-off moderate Democrats, McGovern had much the same constituency as Humphrey had had. Both men ran best in the same regions: New England, the Middle Atlantic States, the upper Midwest, and the Pacific coast. McGovern held the East Side of Manhattan, Beacon Hill Boston, and a number of the Yankee towns that had never voted Democratic until they broke ranks in 1964. For the *fourth straight election,* New England was the most Democratic region in the United States, giving the South Dakota senator 46 per cent of the vote.

Which is to say that the basic "McGovern" pattern was actually laid down not by the "revolutionary" 1972 Miami Beach convention but by the post-industrial trend of the mid-sixties that drove the South and Wallaceites into revolt and shifted the soul of the Demo-cratic Party toward affluent interest-group liberalism. This transition can be moderated, its constituency broadened and made more ap-pealing to marginal groups that spurned McGovern, but it is unlikely to be reversed.

2. The Republican Evolution Since 1932, the Republicans, too, have had their convolutions. When Herbert Hoover left the White House, in 1933, the GOP's progressive faction, a thorn in the side of Coolidge, Hoover, et al., was based in the *West.* Progressive Republi-canism was a matter of farm, natural-resource, and economic policy, and, as such, it tended to center in the Midwest, the Rocky Mountains, and the Far West. The names of the leading GOP Pro-gressives are well known: Robert La Follette of Wisconsin, George Norris of Nebraska, William Borah of Idaho, Bronson Cutting of New Mexico, Hiram Johnson of California, and so forth. Anyone who suggested that, before long, party progressives would come from the Northeast, would have been laughed at: Northeastern Republicans were the economic-conservative henchmen of big busi-ness and corporate power. They cursed Roosevelt from the ma-hoganied, Persian-carpeted recesses of the Somerset, Links, and Union League clubs, and he mocked their Congressional spokesmen as "Martin, Barton and Fish"—two New York reactionaries and one from Massachusetts.

But if the eastern Republican establishment was conservative in

1933, things were changing by World War II. International-minded, drawn to FDR's pro-British foreign policy, and even increasingly able to live with certain aspects of big government, the eastern establishment was a force for moderate internationalist politics at the 1940 party convention. Meanwhile, the isolationist forces of the farm belt, Rocky Mountains, and Pacific coast let their opposition to Roosevelt's foreign policies also drag them toward economic conservatism. Wendell Willkie's nomination laid down a cleavage that prevailed for twenty years: eastern-establishment moderate Republicanism versus midwestern conservatism.

On the presidential level, the eastern establishment won. New York Governor Thomas E. Dewey was twice picked to run—in 1944 and 1948—and the Dewey group was largely responsible for nominating Eisenhower in 1952. Most of Eisenhower's campaign advisers were New Yorkers, and he was obliged to meet with Ohio Senator Robert Taft to reassure that powerful leader of midwestern conservative forces. To those who did not appreciate the *reversal* of midwestern and eastern party ideology, the election patterns of 1952 and 1956 looked a lot like those of the nineteen twenties, and observers sometimes thought in those terms, querying restoration of the old GOP majority rather than a major realignment. As on the Democratic side, the election of 1960 brought clear signs of change. The Republican nominee, Vice-President Richard Nixon, was not the first choice of the eastern, liberal wing of the party, and, to placate it, Nixon had to agree to the so-called "Treaty of Fifth Avenue" with Nelson Rockefeller. Election Day saw Republican strength shift more to the South and West than previously. Nixon became the first *losing* Republican presidential candidate to carry three southern states and most of the Rocky Mountains, all Democratic-leaning states normally found only in GOP *winners'* columns.

While Nixon's candidacy did not please the eastern GOP establishment, revolt was also near on the right: Arizona Senator Barry Goldwater, leader of the Republican Party's growing southern-western conservative axis, had almost bid for the 1960 nomination. After Nixon's defeat, and with the prospect of a civil-rights revolt making Dixie victory possible, the Goldwaterites launched a grass-roots bid for the 1964 GOP nomination. After polarizing the party, the southern-western axis succeeded in taking away the Republican presidential nomination from the eastern establishment for the first time. Goldwater's campaign was premature: too extremist-flavored and too segregationist-tinged. He won just 38 per cent of the vote, spinning the Republican Party on its geographic heels. Goldwater carried his home state of Arizona, plus Louisiana, Mississippi, Alabama, Georgia, and South Carolina. Meanwhile, rock-ribbed Republican counties from Maine to Kansas swung Democratic for the first time. But there was also more *continuity* than is usually noted. The fact that Goldwater scored highest in the South, the Rockies, and the Great Plains while doing *worst* in New England put meat—albeit of a lean cut—on the bones of a pattern that had taken shape in 1960. Nixon had been the first GOP presidential candidate to do better in the South and West than in the Northeast, and the shift that bore that electoral fruit in 1960 shaped the Goldwater candidacy— and also its excesses—four years later.

Despite the howl set up by northeastern Republicans in the wake of Goldwater's crashing defeat, the GOP did not hark back to the ideological and geographic *status quo ante*. While the conservative Goldwater hierarchs imposed on the Republican National Committee were replaced by moderates in 1965, the 1966 off-year elections confirmed the conservative, southern, and western drift of the party. And, in 1968, Richard Nixon came back from the political grave to win the presidential nomination as the candidate endorsed by Barry Goldwater and most of the South and West. The 1974 accession of Gerald Ford is likely to moderate (or scramble) the shift but not reverse it. The evolution to date is much too deep-rooted for that.

Chart 11 shows the steady evolution of Republican presidential strength in the South. Because of George Wallace's third-party candidacy, the 1968 election returns did not show a clear-cut pattern of a Republican South and West against a more Democratic Northeast. With Wallace cutting a wide swathe through Dixie, Nixon's best states were in the Great Plains and Rocky Mountains. It remained for the election of 1972, a straight two-way contest minus George Wallace, to produce the crystal-clear southern-and-western victory coalition. Map 5 shows the best GOP states in the election of 1972; the southern-western tilt is clear. The Republican Party left Washington in 1933 as the party of a conservative eastern establishment, and, as of the nineteen seventies, ruled again principally based on a southern-and-western coalition suspicious, by its own rhetoric, of the new liberal (and increasingly Democratic) eastern establishment.

1944	1948*	1952	1956	1960	1964	1968*	1972	Southern States Giving a Major Party Landslide Support (60% or over)
None	None	None	None	None	Miss. Ala.	(Other States diverted by Wallace) None	Ala. Ark. Fla. Ga. La. Miss. N.C. S.C. Tenn. Tex. Va.	Over 60% GOP
None	8 States	8 States	10 States	10 States	8 States	11 States	None	Neither Party over 60%
Ala. Ark. Fla. Ga. La. Miss. N.C. S.C. Tenn. Tex. Va.	Ark. Ga. Tex. (Other states diverted by Dixiecrats)	Ala Ga. Miss.	Ga.	Ga.	Tex.	None		Over 60% Democrat

*Most of the 1948 Thurmond vote would have stayed Democratic in a two-way race; 1968 polls showed that most of the Wallace vote would have gone to Nixon in a two-way race.

CHART 11
The Dixie Presidential Shift, 1944–72

The transition has been clear enough on the presidential level, but much more confused on the local level.

If the evolution of both parties is a confusing process, no such metamorphosis has taken place before. And it may not succeed. But, whatever happens to the existing parties, it is tempting to surmise that the divisions of the industrial era are slowly yielding to those based on the economics, culture, and morality of the post-industrial era. If these cleavages seem to follow some familiar lines, perhaps that is because culture, regionalism, religion, and ethnicity are not shed so easily as abstract theorists often suggest.

D. POPULISM, CULTURE AND ECONOMICS

Through the years, U.S. presidential patterns have shown an extraordinary tendency, particularly in realignment years, to cleave along certain persistent economic and cultural fault lines in American society. Despite the racial overtones of the Civil War period, these persisting fault lines can be perceived in the alignment of 1860, as well as in those of 1800, 1828, 1896, 1932, and 1968–72. Such repetition suggests that certain U.S. cultural, regional, and economic divisions are denominators of national politics. Inasmuch as political realignment is once again pivoting on historic tensions and divisions, upheaval must run deep. Race is a factor, but just one, in a much broader socioeconomic cockpit.

From the beginning of the republic, power and privilege have tended to concentrate along the northeastern seaboard in a way that has galled the citizenry—even the rich men—of the South and the interior. Whatever has gained fashion and success has focused on the Northeast, taken up residence there, imbibed establishment characteristics, and, in the process, influenced local outlook. Paranoia about "establishments" notwithstanding, the process seems to be a well-established sociological and political fact.

The first politics of privilege to be toppled was that of the Federalists in 1800. Map 9 shows that the Federalists were based along the New England-to-Delaware seaboard and that the Jeffersonian Democratic coalition bringing them down drew its strength from the South and the trans-Appalachian West. But, by the mid-eighteen twenties, the "Era of Good Feeling" had transformed the Jeffersonians into a one-party monopoly, and John Quincy Adams, son of the last Federalist President but himself a Democratic-Republican of sorts, rode this one-party, no-party system into the White House. In 1828, Adams, a Massachusetts man, lost to Andrew Jackson, who represented the raw insurgent forces of the South and West. The map shows the split through the rest of the country. While Jackson had strength all over the nation, he was by far and away strongest in the Deep South and easily weakest along the New England seaboard.

Arthur Schlesinger, Jr., and others have spent many volumes trying to sum up the "Age of Jackson"; this essay can hardly do so. Still, it is possible to sum up some obvious attributes of the Jackson constituency as against the constituencies of the wealthy seaboard: frontier vigor, egalitarianism (or, as one would call it today, *antielitism*), crude manners, economic individualism, and hostility toward the vested interests, a fighting, martial nature, a lack of communal morality, a relative disinterest in education, and so forth. A

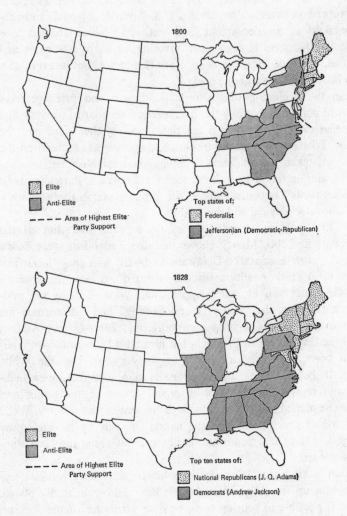

1800

Elite

Anti-Elite

- - - - Area of Highest Elite
Party Support

Top states of;

Federalist

Jeffersonian (Democratic-Republican)

1828

Elite

Anti-Elite

- - - - Area of Highest Elite
Party Support

Top ten states of:

National Republicans (J. Q. Adams)

Democrats (Andrew Jackson)

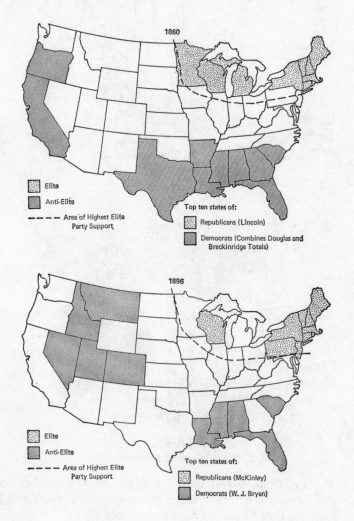

1860

Elite

Anti-Elite

- - - Area of Highest Elite
Party Support

Top ten states of:

Republicans (Lincoln)

Democrats (Combines Douglas and
Breckinridge Totals)

1896

Elite

Anti-Elite

- - - Area of Highest Elite
Party Support

Top ten states of:

Republicans (McKinley)

Democrats (W. J. Bryan)

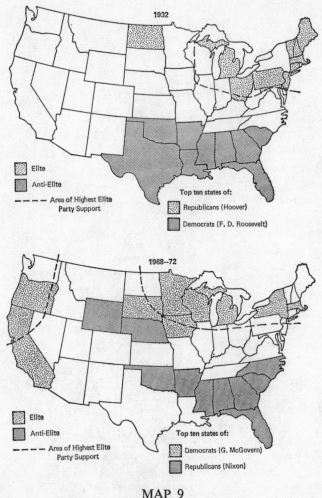

MAP 9
Critical Election Patterns

visitor to, say, Ohio, would have found the poor white farmers Jacksonian Democrats and the Yankee merchants, active in supporting free schools and libraries, of the contrary persuasion.

While pre-Civil War politics upset part of the Jacksonian cleavage, the new Republican/Democratic alignment of 1860 continued several vital divisions. To be sure, most southern Whigs turned Democratic (giving the Democrats an aristocratic infusion), and a fair percentage of northern Democrats turned Republican. Still, the Civil War party system *continued* the basic Jacksonian division between a Democratic Party based in the South and West while encompassing poorer whites (and Catholics) in the Northeast, and a Republican Party reiterating the predominantly northern commercial (and anti-Catholic) base of the Whigs. The Civil War obviously intensified the sectional ingredient of the party split, but there was also a considerable element of continuity.

Such books as *The Mind of the South,* by W. J. Cash, and *Cavalier and Yankee,* by William R. Taylor, describe some of the considerable cultural differences between Southerners and Yankees that colored the division between Jacksonians and Whigs, and to a greater extent between post-Civil War Democrats and Republicans. Some of these can be found even in the new coalitions taking shape.

With its more simplistic and individualistic agricultural roots, the South did not like a Yankee culture that blended industry, community morality, and intellectual condescension. Yankee penchants for education grated on Southerners who liked their good ole hunting dog, rifle, and a well-set table. Southerners predominated in the army; Yankees preferred factories, banks, and universities. Yankee industry demanded tariffs that hurt southern agriculture. Yankee bourgeois religion—quintessentially Congregationalist or the Unitarianism of Ralph Waldo Emerson—annoyed Southerners who were used to high-church aristocrats and fundamentalist "Yes, We'll Gather at the River" masses. And Yankee puritanism, obnoxious to Southerners since New England witch trials and Oliver Cromwell's time, was never more obnoxious to those below the Mason-Dixon line than when it pushed for abolition of slavery, a move that Southerners cynically saw as the linchpin of national Yankee industrial and political supremacy. To Yankees, Southerners were low-living scoundrels who talked states' rights as a cover for economic interests and immoral slaveholding. In such states as Ohio, Indiana, and Illinois, Yankee artisans and merchants sneered at the improvident farmers who stained their clothes with butternut dye.

All this is not "mere history." These mainstreams of American culture are alive today. One lives on in the hawkishness, economic individualism, dislike of government social programming, apathy-*cum*-hostility toward minorities, anti-elitism, and Massachusetts-baiting of the 1970s Nixon-Wallace element; and the second sprang to life in the social-reform fetishism, education orientation, concern for Negroes, disinclination to military service and blood sports, John Brown's Body moralizing, and rampant anti-southernism (plus muted anti-ethnicism) of the McGovernish New Politics set. There is much more to North-South sectionalism than race.

But back to history's recurrent divisions. In 1896, the Democrats nominated William Jennings Bryan for President, and once again, a realignment election pitted the South and West against the northeast establishment. Populist Bryan fell well short of victory. He rallied the silver miners of Colorado, the wheat farmers of Kansas, and the poor whites of the South, but his crusade against the northeast money power scared too many middle-of-the-road Americans. Not until the 1929 depression did the northeastern economic establishment fall on its face; then the old Populist coalition of the South and West formed the fulcrum of Roosevelt's victory. As earlier, the South and the West were the economic "have not" sections of the United States, and the New Deal promptly moved to aid agriculture; curb big industry, banks, and power companies; and build roads and other public works from Maine to California. Roosevelt catered to economic populism by telling the people that the vested interests hated him and that "I welcome their hatred." Big-business Republicans started talking about "social planners" and criticizing Social Security as "Bolshevism," but New Deal liberal measures were almost entirely economic: government harnessed on behalf of the *majority*.

Here is an important cultural distinction: The early New Deal had little of the social programming on behalf of *minorities* that was to come—and work drastic political change—in the nineteen sixties. Not only Lyndon Johnson but George Wallace and Strom Thurmond were strong New Dealers in the early nineteen forties. Throughout the New Deal (and throughout Harry Truman's Fair Deal as well), racial segregation was still permitted by the U. S. Supreme Court.

Truman annoyed the South by favoring civil rights, but John F. Kennedy's was the first Democratic administration to shift toward the northeastern establishment that had always been the other party's albatross. Poet Robert Frost had advised Massachusettsman Kennedy "to be more Irish than Harvard," but Harvard held its own—at least in professors coming down to Washington. First lady Jacqueline Kennedy brought French art and cuisine to the White House. Kennedy himself, a former journalist, became almost a cult among members of the booming communications industry. Education programs, civil-rights proposals, and Ivy League professors all flowed freely through the Kennedy administration. To make this point, it seems hardly necessary to reiterate the analyses of the evolutionary change that overtook the Democratic Party in the early and mid-sixties: Besides being the first Democratic President elected with New England as his strongest region, Kennedy's programmatic biases leaned in that direction. In the liberal landslide of 1964, the Democrats moved closer to the Northeast and its mushrooming knowledge sector. While the nature of this change doesn't lend itself to precise definition, there is enough justification for saying that sometime during the mid-nineteen sixties, the Democratic Party shifted its thrust from representation of an old economic liberal *antielite* to a new liberal *elite* principally based in the Northeast.

Using these conceptual approaches, the 1968 upheaval experienced by the national Democratic Party can be described as a dual insurgency of both elitist and anti-elitist forces. Poet-politician Eugene McCarthy, candidate of the elite, came to the Chicago convention with most of the delegates from primary victories in New Hampshire, Wisconsin, Massachusetts, Pennsylvania, Oregon, and New York. Alabama's George C. Wallace, hero of the old anti-elitist southern and working-class elements, opted to run as a third-party candidate. Organization Democrats, torn between their party's past constituency and the articulate, influential new class, leaned toward the new forces. George Wallace won 10 million votes, peaking in the anti-elitist strongholds of the South and Rocky Mountains, while Hubert Humphrey chalked up his best support in the affluent states where New Politics Democrats are strongest. Reluctant as Humphrey may have been, he wound up doing quite well in Cambridge, Scarsdale, and Sausalito.

By 1972, New Politics elements based in the states that Map 9 shows have always been on the elite, fashionable side of the alignment, took over the Democratic Party and nominated George McGovern. Although McGovern purported to represent a "populist" politics, his support in Bryan and Jackson country was negligible, and his elitism was manifest during the campaign. The *Christian Science Monitor* noted that about half of his advisers came from New England private colleges.[1]

Confronted with this type of national Democratic Party, the Wallace constituency went solidly Republican in 1972, and so did a large chunk of the anti-elitist Catholic, Appalachian, and border-state Democrats who had remained with Humphrey in 1968. In geographic terms, then, the 1972 *Republican* coalition represented the historic and anti-establishment grouping while the Democrats picked up the affluent, elite pattern. Granted that this analysis is superficial and needs some qualification, there is also a good bit of truth to it. The cultural difference between the Nixon and the McGovern coalitions fits at least part of the historic mold.

Achieved by the rise of the knowledge industry and the social upheaval of the sixties, the metamorphosis of constituencies is unprecedented. When the Republicans left Washington after the 1932 Roosevelt landslide, the GOP represented the rich, educated, fashionable sections of the country, notably the Northeast and Great Lakes —the principal regions of U.S. industrial wealth. Typically, the more educated and affluent a neighborhood or county was, the more Republican. Herbert Hoover, when he was defeated in 1932, won his best vote in prosperous, culture-rich New England. All the straw votes at the fashionable prep schools went his way.[2] Harvard and Yale graduates were routinely Republican. Not coincidentally, Hoover's best states were those with the most symphony orchestras, the highest number of library books per capita, the highest civic-awareness levels, the highest literacy rates, the most doctors and scientists, and the highest ratio of persons locally educated later named in Who's Who. Map 10 shows the top-rated states of 1930, and Map 11 shows those of 1970. By and large, they are the same.

This recurring elitist-versus-anti-elitist division in U.S. politics can be analyzed on three levels: 1) forms of economic organization, 2) cultural and ideological tradition, and 3) types of religion.

From the standpoint of economics, the United States is unique in that its internal settlement has occurred simultaneously with its evolution from agriculturalism to industrialism and then post-industrialism. Largely for this reason, the United States, more than most nations, has developed economically on an uneven regional basis, with certain areas being quasi-colonial in status. The South and the West have traditionally been the less developed areas, and their politics have tended to mirror this hostility toward eastern-seaboard domination. The political geography of elitism, mapped for 1828, 1860, 1896, 1932, and 1972, can also be squeezed into economic categories. For example, the critical election of 1828 pitted the generality of agrarianism, artisanry, and the frontier against established commerce.

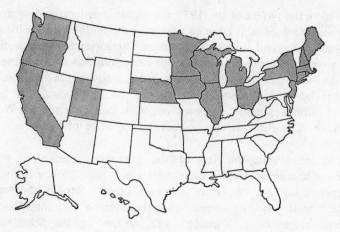

MAP 10

Top 18 States in Combined Wealth, Culture, Health-and-Security, and Civic-Affairs Criteria (1930)

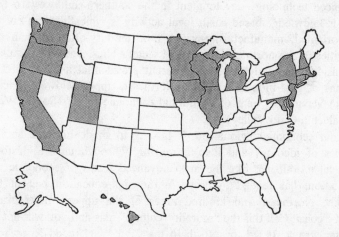

MAP 11

Top 18 States in Combined Wealth, Culture, Health-and-Security, and Civic-Affairs Criteria (1970)

Eighteen sixty saw the agriculture of the Greater South oppose the emerging industrial/commercial framework of the Yankee North. Then in 1896, agrarianism squared off against industrialism and lost. By 1932, after unfettered industrial Republicanism had been impugned by the advent of the 1929 depression, southern and western agrarianism joined with labor to overcome the northern-based industrial-financial sector. Granted that these categories are less precise than any neat classification implies, the basic point has merit: namely, that the Northeast (plus the Great Lakes and now the Pacific coast) tends to be the locale and chief exponent of the nation's most advanced form of economic organization, while the South and the West are more dependent on and politically supportive of less-advanced forms.*

Using this scheme, the Northeast has gone from representing preindustrial commerce (under John Adams and John Quincy Adams) to representing industry (from Abraham Lincoln through the post-World War II period) to representing the principal concentration of the knowledge sector. Through 1932, meanwhile, the South and West represented agricultural and extractive industry (mining, logging). Since World War II, however, the South and West have been the regions of most-rapid corporate and industrial growth. Although advanced technology development in the southern-southwestern Sun Belt is knowledge-based, such local activity is typically more corporate-oriented, manufacturing-oriented or military-oriented than the activities of the northeast knowledge sector. Thus, one can postulate a considerable economic base to recent presidential alignment: The regions of post-industrial thrust (Northeast, upper Midwest, Pacific coast) versus the areas of traditional economic forms (South, West, Appalachia-Ohio Valley).

From economic regionalism, it is easy to shade into the similar politics of ideology and ideo-moralizing. Throughout U.S. history, political moralizing, like the most advanced forms of economic organization, has tended to occur in the high-education belt of the Yankee Northeast and kindred areas of the upper Midwest and Pacific coast. Call this the "morality/culture" axis and you will not be too far wrong. It led the North in the Civil War. It led Roosevelt-era opposition to New Deal policies. Now there is a new social gospel —no longer that of abolitionist William Lloyd Garrison or anti-New Deal Republicans, but a new one of social progress and elements of a

* Reference to southern and western support of agriculture and manufacturing against the new class/knowledge sector applies only to presidential races. In state races, local politicians often do very well with populist-type opposition to business interests.

"Greening of America." George McGovern was its inept 1972 political prophet, and there is no better symbol of his constituency than the one state he carried: academic, anti-war Massachusetts, historic citadel of ability to blend economic interest and morality.

Because of this shift in the presidential base of the two parties, 1972 saw the Democrats *strongest* in states with the highest income, culture, education, health and welfare, and civic awareness. Forty per cent of the McGovern delegates at Miami's July Democratic Convention had advanced university degrees (M.A.s or better). Half of McGovern's staff came from New England colleges. And an October straw poll found that McGovern was favored 6–1 by students at the Harvard Law School, training ground of the nation's top professional elite. Yale and Princeton were not far behind. Chart 12 shows the sharp 1948–72 realignment of seven fashionable academic/knowledge-sector communities.

		Deviation from National % Democratic[*]							% Dem. 1968	% Dem. 1972
Community	Deviation	1948	1952	1956	1960	1964	1968	1972		
Mansfield, Conn.	National	−21.5	−11.0	− 8.2	− 4.4	+11.7	+13.8	+21.4	56.5	58.9
Orono, Me.	National			−17.0	− 5.2	+ 8.0	+13.5	+11.5	56.2	49.0
Amherst, Mass.	National	−20.6	−18.9	−16.7	−10.4	+ 9.0	+14.7	+30.6	57.6	68.1
Hanover, N.H.	National	−29.9	−19.0	−13.3	−11.6	+15.7	+11.4	+22.2	54.1	59.7
Princeton, N.J.	National	−15.9	− 4.4	− 6.2	− 3.0	+10.7	+15.2	+18.0	57.9	55.5
Oberlin, Ohio	National	−27.8	−13.4	−12.4	−11.4	+ 6.9	+12.2	+18.6	54.9	56.1
Swarthmore, Pa.	National	−40.7	−27.5	−25.2	−26.6	−10.5	− 5.4	+ 8.6	37.3	46.1

[*] Percentage Democratic of the total vote, 1948 and 1968; of the two-party vote, 1952–64.

CHART 12
Academic-Community Realignment

State-by-state rankings for everything from infant-mortality rates and new-car purchases to teachers' salaries offer a fascinating and revealing political correlation. New England's high cultural and educational levels are well known. Less well known are the kindred characteristics of the upper Midwest and the Pacific Northwest, states in large measure settled from the Northeast.

Take the upper Midwest, a strong Democratic region in 1968 and 1972. Wisconsin, Minnesota, and Iowa rank high in these ways: few poor people, few non-whites, high literacy, high per-pupil spending, frequent education of people later in Who's Who, relatively numerous symphony orchestras, low infant mortality, low violent crime, top-flight state legislatures, and high civic awareness. If there is a Scandinavia in the United States, this is it. The Pacific Northwest— Washington, Oregon, and northern California—shares many of the same characteristics. Even such peripheral states as Montana and the Dakotas share part of this pattern with respect to high literacy, civic awareness, and library books per capita. South Dakota, seventh in the nation in *per-capita* library books, leads every other state outside the Northeast.

New England, the upper Midwest, and the Pacific Northwest have relatively few poor people, few black or Chicano minorities, and relatively little violent crime. Put this together with Yankee and Scandinavian morality, comparative affluence, and a tradition of civic awareness, and you get the parts of the country most supportive —McGovern's vote proved it—of current-day liberal politics. As Map 8 shows, New England, the upper Midwest, and the Pacific coast were the Democratic nominee's three top regions. Voter amenability declined, and McGovern lost many traditional Democrats in southern California, Illinois, greater Detroit, Ohio, Pennsylvania, New York, and New Jersey. The reasons? Less tradition of political moralizing, more poor people, higher minority ratios, more big cities, more crime. From Pittsburgh to Bakersfield, local Appalachian and Okie Democrats, to say nothing of big-city ethnic whites, balked at their party's new "Greening of America" presidential philosophy. These same areas—from greater New York City to southern California—had been politically suspicious of Civil War-era Yankeedom.

In contrast to McGovern, Richard Nixon's campaign aimed at America's *traditional* anti-elitist constituency, especially the states that were Populist William Jennings Bryan's best in 1896: the South, the Great Plains, and the Rockies. Moralizing northeastern elites have never fared too well in these areas, and the same held true in November 1972. Catholic voters also turned away from McGovern in droves. Statistical data sketch an interesting character portrait of the top Nixon states of the South and West: low incomes, many poor, relatively low literacy, low per-pupil expenditures, relatively few symphony orchestras, few library books per capita, low health and welfare, high infant-mortality rates, high motor-vehicle fatality rates, high rates of violent crime. Map 12 shows the geography in question.

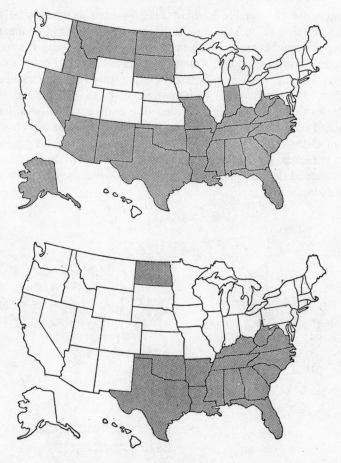

MAP 12

Two Dozen Lowest-ranking States Based on 1970 Census Data for Wealth and Education, and Miscellaneous Data for Culture, Health, and Civic Affairs as Tabulated in Lifestyle *magazine, November, 1972*

The Bottom Fifteen States in Per-capita Literacy, Media Consumption, Education, Symphony Orchestras, Libraries, and Scientists

Extraordinary as it may sound, these political, economic, and cultural divisions can also be related to *religion*. Years ago, R. H. Tawney linked Protestant reform and the rise of capitalism; and current scholars—notably Richard Jensen—have analyzed vital religious correlations in U.S. politics.[3] Since the early days of the republic, persons having the highest education and pursuing the most advanced form of economic organization have tended to concentrate strongly among certain religions: Congregationalism, Quakerism, Judaism, Presbyterianism, Unitarianism, and to a lesser extent, Methodism. Persons having less education and connected with less-advanced economic organizations have been disproportionately members of Catholic, Lutheran, Baptist, or other, simpler, more authoritarian churches. Emphasizing the nineteenth-century Midwest, Jensen has examined these alignments in great depth—and they are relevant again today.

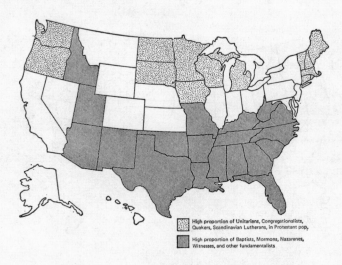

High proportion of Unitarians, Congregationalists, Quakers, Scandinavian Lutherans, in Protestant pop,

High proportion of Baptists, Mormons, Nazarenes, Witnesses, and other fundamentalists

MAP 13
Geography of Protestant Church Membership

To Jensen, the central division is between "pietistic" denominations and "liturgical" denominations. Pietists are reform-minded: opposed to elaborate ceremonies, rituals, or traditions; in favor of revivalism, individual information, *personal* attainment of grace, abolition of sinful institutions. In this group, Jensen includes Congregationalists, Disciples of Christ, Quakers, Methodists, Unitarians, Presbyterians, Scandinavian Lutherans. As he notes, "the Pietists fostered interdenominational voluntary societies to distribute bibles,

conduct missionary work, abolish slavery and promote total absti-
nence . . . specifically the Midwestern pietists demanded that the
government halt the spread of slavery (or even abolish it), overthrow
the saloon and the sale of liquor, and (among many pietists) restrict the pernicious and corrupting flood of Catholic immigration."[4]

Revivalism and religious conflict were important elements of nineteenth-century upheaval, and the pietist-versus-liturgical combat was
omnipresent, coloring debate on the major issues of the period. On
the liturgical side were these churches: Roman Catholic, Baptist
(Primitive), Missouri Synod (German) Lutheran, Episcopalian.
The liturgicals emphasized institutionalized formalities and rituals
and historical doctrines. Salvation required faithful adherence to
the creed, liturgy, sacraments, and hierarchy of the church. "For the
liturgicals," observes Jensen, "moralistic social action groups that
were not an integral part of the church structure were illegal, un-
scriptural and unnecessary, since the church could attend to all matters of morality without outside help. . . . Heresy, pride and in-
novation, rather than impure behavior, were the cardinal sins for
the liturgicals . . . liturgicals, as a rule, opposed prohibition, denounced abolitionists (even if they disliked slavery), and avoided
the nativist agitation. The intrusion of government into affairs of
morality was, in their eyes, a threat to the primacy of the church . . .
the liturgicals feared that 'fanatical' (their favorite epithet) pietists
would use the government to further their moralistic crusades."[5]

Given the centrality of the slavery, immigration, and prohibition
issues to nineteenth-century politics, the pietist-versus-liturgical division reflected itself in party alignments, as Jensen's data prove quite
conclusively. Chart 13 shows the correlation between religious denomination and Republican Party identification in late-nineteenth-
century Indiana and Illinois.

Regional and political correlation between Republicanism and
pietist church membership was overwhelming from the late 1850s to
the late 1950s. Such denominations as Unitarians, Quakers, Congregationalists, and Disciples of Christ were solidly Republican,
and their chief states—from New England to the upper Midwest—
were the strongholds of the party. In contrast, Roman Catholics and
Southern Baptists were heavily Democratic, with only a few major
exceptions (for example, in such machine-controlled cities as
Philadelphia, where Catholic GOP voting persisted well into the New
Deal). These basic divisions remained valid until the Post-Industrial

Ethnic/Denomination	Per Cent Republican
Old Stock Congregationalist	97%
Swedish Lutheran/Methodist	96%
Old Stock Unitarian	96%
Old Stock Methodist	91%
Old Stock Baptist (Free Will)	91%
Old Stock Presbyterian	75%
German Lutheran	67%
German Catholic	25%
Irish Catholic	0%

Party, by Denomination, Hendricks County, Indiana (1875)

Denomination	Per Cent Republican
Friends (Quaker)	96%
Christian (Disciples)	74%
Methodist	73%
Presbyterian	64%
Free Will Baptist	57%
Regular Baptist	17%
Roman Catholic	4%
(No denomination)	47%

CHART 13
Party, by Ethnic Religious Groups, Geneseo City/Township, Illinois
(1877)

Revolution began exerting its greatest socioeconomic pull upon the same elements that had been in the vanguard of the Industrial Revolution: the high-education, reform-minded, affluent strata of the North. As a result, groups with emphatic GOP traditions were among those drawn most strongly toward liberal (and often Democratic) politics. Herman Kahn places these groups—Quakers, Unitarians, Reform Jews, Yankee abolitionist descendants—in the forefront of the move toward the New Left. Voting data support him. Meanwhile, related forces have been eroding the traditional Democratic loyalties of ethnic Catholics and Southern Baptists.

On all three counts—culture, religion, and regional economics— one can see a reversal in the traditional party support bases. This reversal pattern has been increasingly clear on the presidential level; below that, it remains blurred. And even on the presidential plane, there is considerable confusion. Massachusetts and Mississippi have polarized in the new mode, but *within* many states, many old alignments still hold sway. The fact is: *No such reversal has ever occurred before within a continuing two-party framework.* In many states, and among many groups, Republican and Democratic loyalties are still shaped by the cultural and economic loyalties of a bygone era. Young voters, much more inclined to make their decisions based on current circumstances, have better reflected the new divisions.

During the 1972 election, considerable attention was focused on Democratic appeal to college youth, while the GOP fared better with non-college and blue-collar young people. This pattern among 18–24-year-olds represented a *reversal* of that prevailing, say, among persons aged 45–60 whose attitudes reflected New Deal-to-Eisenhower economic and cultural denominators. Two thirds of 58-year-old college graduates are probably business-oriented Republicans; two thirds of 58-year-old blue-collar workers are labor-oriented Democrats. But, among their children, upper-middle- and lower-middle-class backgrounds have been forging a different sociopolitics. Surveys by the Opinion Research Corporation of Princeton, New Jersey, found the reversal beginning in the 1968 election. In a 1971 article, ORC statistical director Michael Rappeport observed that the historic relationship between education and party affiliation was *turning around:* The Democrats are now the party choice of the educated young while the Republicans are the party choice of young blue-collar white unionists. According to Rappeport, only 19 per cent of blue-collar union whites aged 21–24 voted for Humphrey in 1968, 48 per cent chose Nixon, and 33 per cent picked Wallace; but among 21–24-year-old white-collar workers, 45 per cent backed Humphrey, 43 per cent Nixon, and 12 per cent Wallace.[6] A study of the 1971 municipal elections in Cambridge, Massachusetts, yielded a similar result:

Young people from working-class families tended to vote for conservative incumbents, while young voters from upper-middle-class families favored liberal-radical candidates. These results were especially noticeable in the School Committee race. Advocates of discipline, patriotism and basic skills did well in poorer areas of the city, while those favoring open classes, experimental programs and student rights did well in wealthier areas.[7]

The 1972 election, if anything, made the reversing pattern even more obvious. George McGovern won by 3–1 and 4–1 majorities in straw polls in leading Ivy League colleges and law schools; among 18–19-year-old mechanics and farmboys in Oklahoma, he lost by more than those ratios. Youthful allegiances probably indicate the ideological cleavage of the future, and they seem to confirm the nature of post-industrial realignment.

More troublesome is the question of whether or not the existing two-party system can handle such a reversal-*cum*-realignment. While the usual regions and cultural groups are keynoting an anti-establishmentarian surge, they are not—as in 1828, 1896, or 1932—working within the traditional framework for such upheaval. On the presidential level, at least, the Democratic Party has been reshaped by the new class. But it is doubtful whether the GOP can accommodate itself to the Populist reversal. In short, there are reasons to wonder if the Post-Industrial Revolution may not force a reconstitution rather than a mere realignment of the parties.

E. THE RISE OF TICKET SPLITTING

Debunkers of the idea of a "new majority" in U.S. politics raise a telling point: Based on historical precedents, no new presidential majority could be taking shape without bringing a Congressional majority in its wake. Thus the post-1968 and post-1972 assumption of stalemate: Republicans searching for a Congressional breakthrough, and Democrats assuming that, as long as they controlled Congress, no new and adverse presidential majority could be forming.

There is no doubt about the past pattern. Each party taking over the White House in a new cyclical wave has also won or held Congress—in 1800, 1828, 1860, 1896, and 1932. However, there are a number of interrelated reasons why the link is now dubious: 1) the institutionalization of members of Congress, 2) the unique circumstances of metamorphosing southern Democratic loyalties, 3) the influence of the media, and 4) the rise of the ticket-splitting phenomenon. *Once again, the impact of the Post-Industrial Revolution is central.*

From George Washington's days until the nineteen forties, Congressional-election returns often swung wildly, both in off years and mirroring presidential tides. For example, the Democrats lost fifty-nine House seats in 1920, seventy-one in 1938, and fifty-five in 1946, while the GOP lost seventy-five in 1922, a hundred and one in 1932, and seventy-five in 1948. From 1948 to 1972, incumbents survived better. Party House losses never exceeded fifty, and in the three elections of 1968, 1970, and 1972, the shifts were in the dozen-seat range. Much of this shrinking turnover can be credited to blurry party lines and issues, to the impact of the Communications Revolution, to the growth of federal defense and domestic programs (and to the congressman's consequent pork-barrel and ombudsman role), and to the incredible, supportive growth of Congressional staffs.

In 1940 or thereabouts, the average congressman had only two or three employees. Committee staffs were also small. As of 1974, each congressman was entitled to sixteen employees, and Democratic members usually enjoyed committee staff patronage as well. Most use this support—together with the franking privilege and TV-radio spots—to build up their local support base on personal rather than purely party grounds. The extent to which staff and communications assistance has burgeoned since the mid-sixties probably goes a long way to explain diminishing turnover. Able to carve out personal identities, congressmen and senators have tended to go easy on ideology when their party's position has seemed dangerous. (According to a September 1972 *National Observer* survey, only 49 per cent of the Democrats running for Congress that year were openly backing presidential nominee George McGovern by name. This sort of fluidity explains why party identification doesn't mean too much in Congress, why realignment tides have had only limited impact, and why House Democrats were able to survive the McGovern debacle with a loss of just twelve seats.[1])

Year & Party of Winning Presidential Candidate	Number of Districts	Number of Districts With Split Results	Percent Split Election Results
1920R	334	11	3.2%
1924R	356	42	11.8
1928R	359	68	18.9
1932D	355	50	14.1
1936D	361	51	14.1
1940D	362	53	14.6
1944D	367	41	11.2
1948D	422	90	21.3
1952R	435	84	19.3
1956R	435	130	29.9
1960D	437	114	26.1
1964D	435	145	33.3
1968R	435	139	31.6
1972R	435	190	43.7

CHART 14

Ticket Splitting—Congressional Districts with Split Election Results: Districts Carried by a Presidential Nominee and U. S. House Nominee of Different Parties, 1920–72

No small part of the political anomaly of the nineteen seventies rests on Dixie schizophrenia—on the fact that the South has been increasingly Republican on the national level and still substantially (conservative) Democratic in Congressional, state, and local offices. As Chart 14 shows, the real growth of ticket splitting in U.S. politics began in 1948, when the South began to break away from the presidential Democratic Party while still electing Democrats to Congress and almost every other post.[2] After picking up steam during the nineteen fifties, ticket splitting really came into its own during the nineteen sixties as the civil-rights revolution took hold below the Mason-Dixon line. The GOP response to this—choosing Barry Goldwater as the 1964 nominee—created a massive wave of ticket splitting, with Goldwater losing a hundred or so northern districts carried by GOP congressmen, and LBJ being defeated in several dozen in the South that sent Democrats to the House. Party lines were becoming unprecedentedly irrelevant.

Again, in 1968 and 1972, the South spurned the presidential Democrats. Texas alone backed Humphrey in 1968, and McGovern lost all eleven ex-Confederate states in 1972. Meanwhile, Congressional and local Democratic strength suffered only gradual erosion. Because of the growth of ticket splitting, conservative southern Democrats were able to sidestep the presidential party and run on their own; many almost overtly supported Nixon. A century of local tradition was important, but institutional prerogatives also counted heavily: vital seniority on the Democratic side of the Congressional aisle, with pivotal committee chairmanships and other leverage to deliver the South's more-than-fair share of domestic and defense projects. With Southerners chairing such key House and Senate committees as Agriculture, Appropriations, and Armed Services, all vital to the regional economy, the reasons for voting Republican presidentially did not apply to Congressional contests. An unprecedented two-tier utility was apparent.

No new political cycle has faced a similar challenge: overcoming the *central* loyalty of the previous era. Back in the thirties, the New Deal coalition nibbled at the weak fringes of the old GOP supremacy—at farm-belt and western progressives and the inert ethnic electorates of factory and anthracite country. Luckily for FDR, his success did not depend on converting the rural Yankee core of the Civil War GOP coalition. And, seventy-five years earlier, the new Republican electorate forged by Abraham Lincoln and his allies broke off an important northern Free-Soil segment of the Jacksonian coalition, but they did not have to break into the northern urban working-class and southern core of Democratic loyalty. Which is to say that the current GOP need to win over the Deep South—an obvious part of any Congressional conservative ideological grouping—is *an unprecedented chore*. Instead of picking at the fringe of the Democratic coalition, the Republicans have been attempting to budge the element with the deepest, albeit obsolescent, traditional loyalties. On the presidential level, the South seems to have shifted; on the Congressional level, change is dubious.

Nevertheless, a definite pattern has been apparent in southern Republican Congressional gains. The areas of first Republican penetration were the states of the outer South—those not voting for George Wallace in 1968. Here the Republicans have been winning presidential victories since the nineteen fifties (save for 1964), and by the nineteen sixties, GOP success was trickling down to the local level. The first Dixie Republican was elected to the Senate from Texas in 1961; then Tennessee and South Carolina followed in 1966; then Florida in 1968; then Tennessee elected a second in 1970; then Virginia and North Carolina in 1972. By the beginning of the Ninety-third Congress, the outer South had seven GOP U. S. Senators, four Democrats, and one independent.

The citadel of ticket splitting is the 1968 Wallace bloc: Georgia, Alabama, Mississippi, Louisiana, and Arkansas. These states are the most conservative in the South, but they are also the "Heart of Dixie"—as Alabama auto license plates proclaim—and the repository of Civil War Democratic tradition. As the Ninety-third Congress opened, the contrast between the outer South and the Deep South could not have been more striking: While the outer South elected a predominantly Republican Senate delegation, Wallace states were represented by ten Democrats (mostly conservatives) and not a single Republican.

The pressure on these states is considerable. As their huge 1972 Nixon majorities illustrated, they are ideologically out of kilter with the national Democratic Party. Secondly, the nineteen-seventies Democratic Congressional trend toward rule by party is eroding the importance of conservative seniority and independent committee power. Lastly, the Deep South's Congressional power is exercised by a handful of aging men, such as Committee Chairmen Eastland and Stennis of Mississippi (aged 72 and 75 respectively in 1974), Sparkman of Alabama (74), McClellan of Arkansas (78), plus a few younger men such as Long of Louisiana and Talmadge of Georgia (aged 56 and 61 respectively in 1974). When these men die or retire, they will leave a regional power vacuum on the Democratic side. No one will be in position to pick up their dropped baton.

For all these reasons, Deep South Congressional realignment is likely before the end of the decade. Should this happen, it would swing most of the Wallace states, plus similar lagging "deep southern" areas of the Carolinas, northern Florida, and western Tennessee. Whether the Republican Party framework can handle the shift is conjectural. But if our politics are realigning onto an ideological base, there seems no way that the Republicans or a new conservative party can achieve a Congressional majority without the adherence of the South.

While the principal national impact of ticket splitting occurs in the South, the phenomenon has spread into every region. Whether ticket splitting *preceded* blurry party lines or vice versa is one of those chicken-and-egg situations; certainly the two are closely related. A 1971 study of ticket splitting by political analysts Lance Tarrance and Walter De Vries saw a new multilevel structure of U.S. politics based on rising voter interest and issue politics rather than traditional non-ideological party loyalty. Education and communications were seen laying much of the groundwork, both by increasing issue orientation and spreading realization that each major "party" stands for different things in different localities and at different levels of government.

Fifty years ago, straight-ticket voting was the rule. Post-industrialism has undercut such behavior. According to Tarrance and De Vries, "Enormous changes in the social matrix of the Nineteen Sixties —changes in social structuring, educational attainment and media influence—have given us a more selective electorate."[3]

As for the characteristics of ticket splitters, Tarrance and De Vries dispute the oft-spoken academic view that independents are the cross-pressured dregs of the electorate: "Split-ticket voters appear twice as likely to come from Democratic family backgrounds. They are print-media oriented. They are disproportionately Catholic in religious background. They also seem to be anchored into suburban white-collar values, and they exhibit a higher-than-average interest in the electoral system. In many ways, but not all, they are close to Republican party types."

The importance of the Tarrance-De Vries theory is the way it explains contradictions that cannot be resolved by the criteria of the survey research centers—Gallup, the University of Michigan, and others—whose methodology goes no deeper than superficial party self-identification. Tarrance argues that "The Gallup Model of 'Do you consider yourself a Republican, Democrat, Independent or what?' is unfortunate. The constant repetition of 'party stability' does not square with the electoral dynamism of the last few elections. Party identification is indeed important, but it does not completely control the vote as we have seen. The increase in ticket-splitting Republicans and Democrats appears to be producing electoral instability for the future that will have far reaching effects on the two-party system."[4]

This theme has some further implications. Because of ticket splitting, party identification is losing importance as a yardstick of presidential coalition building. Political scientists such as the late V. O.

Key began referring to southern Democrats who were "presidential Republicans" as early as the nineteen forties. Now the phenomenon is spreading, and thus the party identification data put out by the Michigan Survey Research Center may bear little relation to the new lines forming in U.S. presidential politics. For the first time, a coalition may be emerging on the national (presidential) level without meanwhile emerging as a Congressional majority. The spate of political "majority" books published in 1969–72 hardly dealt with the possibility of such a multitiered system.

One such tome was *The Real Majority,* published in 1970 by law-and-order Democrats Richard Scammon and Ben Wattenberg. Ticket splitters were not discussed, and independents were shrugged off as "impotents" who chose not to register by party. The authors described as "myth" the idea that the American electorate consists of alert, vigilant citizens who are motivated by the issues. Instead, Scammon and Wattenberg quoted approvingly from *The American Voter,* the standard academic text of many years: "Far from being more attentive, interested and informed, Independents tend as a group to be somewhat less involved in politics. They have a somewhat poorer knowledge of the issues. . . ."[5]

On the liberal side, *A Populist Manifesto: The Making of a New Majority,* published in 1972 by New Left Democrats Jack Newfield and Jeff Greenfield, simply shunned any analysis of the independent and ticket-splitting voters.[6] More awareness of these groups appeared in *Changing Sources of Power: American Politics in the Nineteen Seventies,* published in 1971 by former Kennedy aide Frederick G. Dutton.[7] He saw the United States heading into an era of party inadequacy, stalemate, and instability, such as we had during the eighteen forties and eighteen fifties.

By and large, analysts agreed that the large Democratic leads in voter registration and self-identification did not mean much in terms of presidential voting. But little attention was paid to the impact of the media and the possibility of multitiered politics. As for *The Emerging Republican Majority,* the first version, written in 1968 and published in 1969, likewise ignored ticket splitting. The preface to the paperback edition, published in 1970, merely stated that the theory of a rational ebb and flow of presidential politics does not extend to non-presidential races: "State and Congressional races do not necessarily (although they may) follow the presidential pattern."

The earliest major analysis of *separate* presidential and Congressional behavior tiers came from one of the most penetrating U.S. political observers, Professor Walter Dean Burnham of M.I.T. In his 1970 book *Critical Elections and the Mainsprings of American Politics,* Burnham suggested that decomposing parties made classical realignment impossible; in 1972 he argued that the presidency was both centralizing power and creating its own new orbit of coalitions quite apart from those prevailing in Congressional races.[8] To Burnham, the key to the dominant presidential coalition was cohesion of the white middle class, and the Presidents elected by that coalition, he prophesied, would necessarily come into conflict with Congress. In 1973, Samuel Lubell produced a quite similar interpretation of the alignment and implication of the 1972 election.[9] Only by 1972–73, it is fair to say, were the implications of ticket splitting becoming clear.

In the meantime, the gap between party presidential coalitions and party representation in Congress had become larger than ever. By 1972, as the presidential Democratic Party nominated George McGovern, there remained sufficient well-ensconced conservative southern (and other) Democrats in Congress to suggest several probabilities: 1) that the GOP probably could not capture both houses even in a Nixon landslide; 2) that an unprecedented number of Congressional Democrats would refuse to endorse McGovern; and 3) that the Nixon administration, being exclusively preoccupied with presidential politics, would make scores of Congressional deals to safeguard pro-Nixon Congressional Democrats in return for other considerations. After the election, Capitol Hill Republicans were livid to learn that the White House had made over one hundred such pacts with Democratic congressmen, ignoring party lines and making no real attempt to transfer presidential-level realignment patterns to Congressional Republicans. As a result of this attitude, plus the lack of a White House GOP domestic policy appeal, Richard Nixon abrogated the usual coattail patterns. (It is not true, as sometimes argued, that Nixon's coattails were no weaker than those of Dwight Eisenhower. In 1956, the GOP elected 194 congressmen outside the South, and presidential coattails were obvious in such states as Connecticut, New York, and New Jersey. No such pattern existed in 1972, when only 158 GOP congressmen were elected outside the South.)

Although ticket splitting has been growing steadily since the late nineteen forties, White House 1972 actions constituted the first explicit strategic divorce of presidential and Congressional-level party fortunes. Moreover, it is unlikely that ticket splitting can be overcome by returning party discipline, what with the weakened party system of the mid-seventies and the steadily growing role of the media.

F. THIRD PARTIES AND
IDEOLOGICAL TRENDS

Since the beginning of modern U.S. party politics, in the eighteen thirties, emerging splinter-party tides have usually signaled the next major national regimes. The pattern—and it's surprisingly clear—seems to rest on the peculiar nature of U.S. coalitions. Unhappy electoral streams shake progressively looser from the majority coalition, and as the predominant stream of discontent becomes clear, this movement foreshadows the realignment that will shape the *next* coalition.

At least, this has been the technique to date: alignment, partial disintegration, emergence of a new theme, realignment. If these precedents hold, then the right-wing splinter parties emerging in presidential politics since 1956—attaining critical thrust by 1968—suggest the ideological shape of the near future.

In the past, political scientists have given minimal attention to third-party tides. And although most analysts devoted considerable attention to the 1968 George Wallace electorate, they ignored the million votes won in 1972 by American Party candidate John Schmitz, a John Birch Society member. Yet Schmitz's support deserves notice as yet another barometer—besides the successes of George Wallace and Richard Nixon—of the rightward drift of U.S. politics in the late sixties and early seventies. By winning 1.1 million votes, Schmitz did quite well; the only third-party candidates to do better were George Wallace (1968), Robert La Follette (1924), and Theodore Roosevelt (1912). Schmitz tallied about the same raw vote as that cast in 1948 for Dixiecrat Strom Thurmond (1,169,000) or Progressive Henry Wallace (1,157,000). What makes the Schmitz total even more significant is its occurrence in what could be called a credibility and media vacuum: In sharp contrast to previous third-party candidates able to pull over a million votes, Schmitz was dismissed and given little or no publicity. His bigger-than-expected turnout must be chalked up to a deep-seated splinter-type alienation on the right wing of U.S. politics.

The importance of this spur should not be underestimated. Chart 15 shows just how dominant presidential splinter-party regimes have prophesied cyclical shifts in the major parties. (Before 1840 the technique does not work, because major party cleavages—and names—had not yet jelled.)

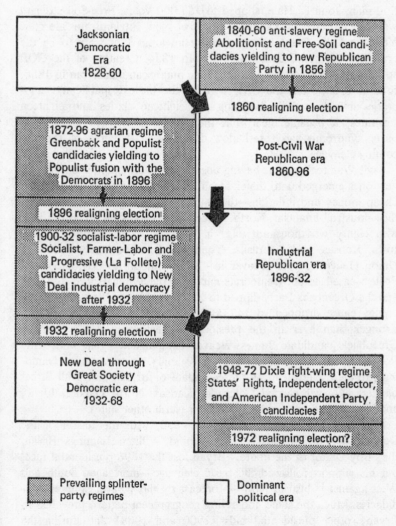

Jacksonian
Democratic
Era
1828-60

1840-60 anti-slavery regime
Abolitionist and Free-Soil candi-
dacies yielding to new Republican
Party in 1856

1860 realigning election

1872-96 agrarian regime
Greenback and Populist
candidacies yielding to
Populist fusion with the
Democrats in 1896

Post-Civil War
Republican era
1860-96

1896 realigning election

1900-32 socialist-labor regime
Socialist, Farmer-Labor and
Progressive (La Follete)
candidacies yielding to New
Deal industrial democracy
after 1932

Industrial
Republican era
1896-32

1932 realigning election

New Deal through
Great Society
Democratic era
1932-68

1948-72 Dixie right-wing regime
States' Rights, independent-elector,
and American Independent Party
candidacies

1972 realigning election?

Prevailing splinter-
party regimes

Dominant
political era

CHART 15
Prevailing Presidential Splinter-Party Regimes in U. S. History

Minor-party emergence began in 1840, with the candidacy of Abolitionist James G. Birney. From seven thousand votes that year, the Abolitionist Party climbed to sixty-two thousand in 1844. Then, in 1848, anti-slavery forces ran under the Free-Soil label, and former President Martin Van Buren captured 291,000 votes—just over 10 per cent of the U.S. total. In 1852, a less well-known Free-Soil man, John B. Hale, slipped to 157,000 votes. Free-Soil strength was concentrated in Yankee districts of New England, upstate New York, and the Great Lakes, exactly the areas that were to be the cradle of the new Republican Party in 1854. Creation of the GOP split the existing party structure. Three major candidates ran in 1856, four in 1860. After the Civil War, as the basic Republican/Democratic division stabilized during the eighteen sixties and eighteen seventies, it became clear that the Abolitionist/Free-Soil splinter-party syndrome had foreshadowed the basic dynamic of the upcoming cleavage.

Civil War realignment having absorbed the old splinter parties, no new ones emerged until the eighteen seventies. The new dynamic was cheap money and inflation—the war cry of the debtor West against the industrial-financial North. Greenback candidate Peter Cooper won eighty-two thousand votes in 1876, scoring best in Indiana, Iowa, Kansas, and Nebraska. Then the Greenbackers ran former Union General James Weaver in 1880, climbing to 309,000 votes. Protest eased as the Democrats captured the White House in 1884, and the Greenback Party dipped to 175,000 (and in 1888, the cheap-money cause dropped to 147,000). But discontent bounced back stronger than ever in the presidential election of 1892: Former Greenback candidate James Weaver campaigned again under the Populist label and gathered 1,041,000 angry agrarian votes. Damning President Cleveland as the candidate of British and Wall Street bankers, Weaver carried Colorado, Kansas, North Dakota, Idaho, and Nevada and ran a close second in several other states.

Agrarian protest consummated in 1896, with the fusion of the Democratic and Populist parties behind William Jennings Bryan, the "Boy Orator of the Platte." Bryan lost the 1896 presidential race, but his support followed the basic cleavage—mortgaged South and West against industrial North—forecast by the Weaver splinter candidacies. Much the same underlying geographical pattern prevailed in Bryan's other presidential bids (1900 and 1908) and during the Woodrow Wilson years (1912–20). Populist regionalism substantially guided the Democrats until the Al Smith upheaval of the twenties. Moreover, even though the Populist movement was not victorious in the partisan political sense, historians agree that most of their ideological goals—from railroad regulation to easier money —were ultimately realized.

No sooner had the Bryan revolt worked its fundamental 1896 upheaval in the shape of U.S. politics but a new insurgency caught fire in the socialist anger of urban working classes and middle-class reformers. In 1900, Eugene Debs made his first of five Socialist campaigns for the White House, winning ninety-five thousand votes while the Socialist Labor Party candidate won thirty-three thousand. Four years later, Debs's vote grew to 403,000 and the Socialists were clearly established as the major U.S. political splinter movement. By 1912, Debs's Socialist vote doubled, to 902,000. Most of it was labor support—from the timberlands and canneries of Washington State to the German districts of Milwaukee and Cleveland to the sweatshops of New York City's Lower East Side. Debs was jailed during World War I and, without him, the Socialists slipped to 585,000. Then, in 1920, the Socialists and the Farmer-Labor Party co-ordinated in several states: the Socialists got 920,000 and the Farmer-Laborites 265,000.

Whereas Theodore Roosevelt's 1912 Bull Moose charge was really a factional division within the Republican Party, Robert La Follette's 1924 third-party Progressive candidacy was substantially in the radical splinter mold. Because of La Follette's reform reputation, the Socialists stood aside for him, and indeed in some states the Wisconsin senator ran on the Socialist ticket. Granted that his 4.8 million votes (17 per cent) greatly surpassed Socialist strength, they pinpointed cleavages that would create a new politics in the nineteen thirties. The Democratic nomination of New York Governor Al Smith in 1928 moved the party further in the progressive direction. The Socialists mounted only a token race against Al Smith, and party candidate Norman Thomas gathered just 267,000 votes. Even before the great crash, the Democratic Party was moving to absorb the farmer-labor impetus represented by Robert La Follette and Eugene Debs.

In 1932, as most of America was voting for Franklin D. Roosevelt, Socialist Thomas won 884,781 votes, down just a bit from Eugene Debs's peak. But the great bulk of nineteen-twenties dissidence—from Al Smith's city sidewalks to La Follette's mining camps and Dakota grain-elevator towns—swelled the vote for FDR. Thus, despite the pangs of depression, 1932 proved a sunset year for the Socialists, because the labor politics and industrial democracy of Roosevelt's New Deal stole their anti-business thunder. Only 187,-000 persons cast ballots for Norman Thomas in 1936, plummeting the Socialist vote to its lowest point since 1900! In 1940, Thomas' vote dipped to one hundred thousand; in 1944, to eighty thousand; and in 1948, Thomas netted 139,000, in his last race. Thereafter, Socialist presidential campaigns became a quadrennial joke, with Socialist Labor and Socialist Workers candidates finishing in the 20–50,000 vote range.

With Socialists and Progressives for the most part entering the new Democratic coalition, the splinter baton passed to extremism. Nineteen thirty-six Union Party candidate William Lemke, who won eight hundred thousand votes with a mixture of socialism and sympathy for European fascism, was the only major third-party candidate of the Roosevelt era. At the left end of the spectrum, the Communists pulled 103,000 votes in 1932, eighty thousand in 1936, and forty-six thousand in 1940 (their last race until 1972). The far left's last hurrah came in 1948 with the Communist-backed Progressive Party candidacy of former Vice-President Henry Wallace. Hopeful left-liberals saw a "Gideon's army" of 10 million votes, and when Wallace flopped with 1.1 million, the left threw in the splinter-party sponge. The Progressives drew only 140,000 votes in 1952, and did not bother to run in 1956.

Movement since then has been on the side of the rightward splinter-party shift that traces back to the Dixiecrat revolt of South Carolina's Strom Thurmond. In 1948, Thurmond won 1.1 million votes, capturing the electoral votes of South Carolina, Alabama, Mississippi, and Louisiana. Four years later, many of these voters backed independent electors pledged to Republican Dwight Eisenhower. Then, in 1956, the leading splinter-party candidate was States' Rights nominee T. Coleman Andrews of Virginia. His 111,000 votes came largely from the South. Meanwhile, Alabama, Mississippi, Louisiana, and South Carolina cast a total of 196,000 votes for un-pledged, independent-elector slates.

Southern states were the major focus of splinter-party politics during the fifties, and this regionalism continued in 1960. Louisiana and Mississippi cast 286,000 votes for unpledged-elector slates, and States' Rights candidate Orval Faubus of Arkansas won forty-five thousand votes. This lure of splintering Dixie loyalties was a key factor in the 1964 nomination of Republican "southern strategy" candidate Barry Goldwater. Just as Al Smith's 1928 realignment candidacy dried up Socialist opposition, Goldwater's headed off both further States' Rights splintering *and* the threatened independent candidacy of Alabama's Governor George C. Wallace. But, like Smith, Goldwater represented too much too soon, and he lost badly.

Consummation of the Dixie breakaway came in 1968, with the biggest third-party movement in U.S. history. Running as the candidate of the new, right-wing American Independent Party, George Wallace pulled 10 million votes. Although his support was lopsidedly southern, Wallace also did well in the Rocky Mountains and the blue-collar North, two other emerging areas of insurgency against the new *bête noire* of U.S. politics: the social-issue liberalism of the eastern establishment. His drainage of right-wing votes almost cost the GOP an expected easy victory.

The new Republican administration of Richard Nixon moved erratically to sew up the 1948–68 right-wing splinter vote while the Democrats solidified their hold on the New Politics side. Nixon won re-election in a landslide, and the 1972 results showed the right far stronger than the left on the minor-party level. Here is the scorecard for leftist minor parties: People's (Benjamin Spock), seventy-nine thousand; Socialist Workers, sixty-five thousand; Socialist Labor, fifty-four thousand; Communist, twenty-five thousand. American Party candidate John Schmitz far overshadowed these totals with his 1,080,541 votes. These included 233,000 in California (3 per cent of the state total), eighty thousand in Ohio (2 per cent of the state total), 7 per cent of the vote in Alaska, 9 per cent in Idaho, 5 per cent in Louisiana, 4 per cent in Montana, 5 per cent in Oregon, 6 per cent in Utah, 5 per cent in Washington State, and so forth.

Map 14 shows the way in which the 1968 and 1972 right-wing patterns, like other dominant splinter regimes before them, may signal the direction of the new presidential coalition built on their absorption. As previously indicated, the new Republican coalition of 1860 followed the contours of the abolitionist third parties. Then the post-1896 Democratic Party followed much of the geography of the 1892–96 agrarian insurgency. Next, the new Roosevelt Democratic coalition largely reflected the addition of La Follette, Socialist, and Al Smith electorates to traditional party backing. Likewise, the

Top 10 American Independent Party states (Wallace) 1968—**W**
Top 10 American Party states (Schmitz) 1972—**S**
Second 10 Wallace states (1968)—w

MAP 14
Right-Wing Splinterism—1968–72

vital 1972 build-up of the presidential GOP seems to have come in the southern, Rocky Mountain, and urban blue-collar areas stirred by the Wallace insurgency (and, in the case of the South, by two previous decades of third-party and independent-elector efforts).

Since 1860, each cyclical upheaval in U.S. presidential politics has coincided with a peaking of splinter-party activity, as well as the issue focused by that activity. In 1860, the slavery issue; then, in 1896, the agrarian issue; then, in 1932, the economic issue (with its corollary "labor" and "city" issues). The late-sixties fulcrum was the social issue: racial concern, plus hostility to the liberal sociology, morality, and lifestyle promulgated by the new affluent intelligentsia. Each of these issues triggered growing third-party concern, ultimately shuffling coalitions.

On the basis of these trends and numbers, it seems fair to say that the dominant political shift of the sixties and seventies is the splintering of the right wing of the old Democratic coalition: the South, much of the Rocky Mountains, part of Appalachia, and a large chunk of the Catholic, ethnic, and blue-collar North. Some of this disintegration is also apparent in state and local races. For example, the two independents elected to the U. S. Senate in 1970 largely represent the two major voter streams leaving the Democratic Party: Harry Byrd of Virginia exemplifies southern conservatism, and James L. Buckley of New York stands for the Irish and Italian ex-Democrats who now back the Conservative Party in New York.

Many analysts downplay the possible meaning of the right-wing movements of the late sixties and early seventies by arguing that cyclical upheaval can come only from the left. This, in essence, is the thesis of Professor Harry Jaffa, who delineates four watersheds in U.S. political history: 1800, 1828, 1860, and 1932 (Jaffa does not include 1896). Inasmuch as each of these upheavals was in the direction of greater equality, Jaffa defines them as movements to the left. Anyone embracing his approach must doubt the watershed nature of 1968–72 politics. However, the *real* denominator of U.S. cyclical politics has been *popular* upheaval, not leftward movement per se. Until the rise of post-industrial society and the knowledge sector, popular political revolutions necessarily focused on a *conservative* economic elite. But now that the typical voter has climbed to middle-class status, while public resentment targets a liberal elite, it may be possible for cyclical upheaval to come from what has been described as the right.

Moreover, in light of third-party-movement persistence, the growth of populist conservatism (in lieu of the traditional variety), and the weakness of the Republican Party, the post-Watergate era gave rise to speculation that a new party might be emerging, somewhat in the way the Republican Party did in the eighteen fifties. Any such new party would come from the insurgent South and West (and conceivably blue-collar neighborhoods) and be heavily anti-Establishment in nature.

From 1956 through 1972, the ascendant third-party impetus in U.S. politics, with all its implications, has come from the right. The fact that this thrust has not yet been digested to cause a transformation of one of the existing parties also supports the notion that a new party system could be in the works.

G. A NEW POLITICAL CYCLE?

Given the historical pattern of regional shifts and 32–36-year cycles, the evidence is overwhelming that defeat of the Democrats in the 1968 election wrote an end to an era. Coming thirty-six years after the undisputed beginning of the New Deal, the victory of a Republican president, resting on a *new* version of South and West against Northeast, presumably signaled a new cycle, and nineteen sixty-eight has to be counted a critical election. But the post-1968 "cycle" bears little resemblance to preceding ones.

First and foremost, Congress did not change hands. The partisan upheaval of 1968–72 occurred on the presidential level alone. As indicated earlier in this chapter, thanks to the Communications Revolution and its concomitant of ticket splitting, national-level shifts may now occur without upsetting local patterns. Voters can create short-term or medium-term *presidential* coalitions without necessarily going through a parallel *local* rebuilding process. If one accepts the further implications of this change, 1968 may mark the beginning of a post-industrial transition to short, superficial cycles heavily influenced by the media. Here are the alternatives:

1. *Eight-to-twelve-year presidential cycles with no corresponding movement at the local level:* Under this circumstance, the GOP cycle that began in 1968 could peter out in 1976 or 1980. Local politics would mirror some of this national-level shift, but there would be no clear parallel. In support of such a notion, one can point out that, since 1952, the United States has had eight years of one party, then eight years of the other. The phenomenon of incumbency is also involved: Presidents win re-election (none have lost), and then the opposition takes over, beginning a new eight-year regime. Prior to 1952, there are no such examples of eight-year alterations, and party regimes were longer lasting. Election of a Democrat as President in 1976 would suggest a recurring eight-year pattern.

Hitherto, new cycles have invariably meant a lengthy initial period of unbroken rule for the party taking over. From accession in 1828, the Jacksonian Democrats governed twelve years until the brief Whig interregnum in 1840. Abraham Lincoln's GOP did not yield power from 1860 to 1884—twenty-four years. When McKinley beat Bryan in 1896, that signaled a straight GOP reign lasting until Woodrow Wilson won in 1912. And from 1932, when FDR won, the Democrats held the White House for twenty consecutive years. The impetus that brings a regime to national power has invariably kept it there for the first twelve years of the new cycle, and usually more. A Republican loss in 1976 would indicate that post-industrialism has made 32–36-year cycles a thing of the past.

2. A medium-length cycle slowly taking hold on local levels: This is a theoretical cop-out, suggesting that cycles may simply be getting shorter and less related to Congressional and local patterns, without any precise definition of that new relationship. A Republican presidential victory in 1976, coupled with continued Democratic control of Congress (and thus incomplete southern realignment), might support such analysis.

3. A full 32–36-year presidential cycle: Should the Republicans hold the White House in 1976, one could argue that the 32–36-year pattern may still be in operation, especially if southern Democratic realignment seems to be occurring. While this would not indicate a conventional cycle of the 1828, 1860, 1896, and 1932 varieties, neither would it be too different.

4. The end of the present party system: Lots of people seem to agree with David Broder's book title *The Party's Over*.[1] Maybe. But maybe not. Each period of cyclical change has also been a time of shifting, blurring party loyalties—enough to make observers wonder if the two-party system mightn't be cracking up. Yet, during the industrial era at least, it never has. Without fail, the two-party system has sorted itself out, and parties have come back stronger than before.

The election of 1828 is generally counted as the beginning of the modern party system. Andrew Jackson's victory over incumbent John Quincy Adams broke up the one-party system which had developed out of James Monroe's "Era of Good Feeling." As might be expected, party labels were in a wild state of flux. In 1828, Jackson's people called themselves "Democrats"; Adams forces used the label "National Republican." After Jackson's election, it took a while for anti-Jackson forces to consolidate. In 1832, they ran—and lost—as Democratic-Republicans. By 1836, after a decade-long shuffling, the basic Jacksonian-era rivalry emerged: Democrats versus Whigs.

As regionalism and slavery made Whig/Democratic rivalry untenable by the early eighteen fifties, the two-party system seemed about to dissolve. After the formation of the Republican Party, in 1854, three major parties ran in 1856: the Democrats (who captured 45 per cent of the popular vote); the new Republicans (33 per cent), and the Whig, or "American," Party (22 per cent). In 1860, there were *four* parties: Republican (38 per cent), northern Democratic (30 per cent), southern Democratic (19 per cent), and Constitutional Union (13 per cent). During the Civil War, the future of the party system was cloudy. Abraham Lincoln ran for re-election in 1864 on a "Union" ticket. But, by 1868, a new two-party system was established along a war-related, Republican/Democratic cleavage.

The next two cyclical upheavals—in 1896 and 1932—also caused substantial dislocations of previous party loyalty. Gold, silver, and inflation were among the big issues of 1868, and economic ideology threatened to dissolve party lines. Hard-money "gold Democrats" deserted William Jennings Bryan, either backing third-party candidate John Palmer or supporting Republican McKinley. Meanwhile, "silver Republicans" and Populists of nominal GOP identification swung to Bryan. Populist economics had been loosening old ties since the eighties, and, by the nineties, there were plenty of politicians who thought that third parties and third-party issues would break up the existing parties. Instead, Populism versus Industrialism triggered a pro-Republican shift within the basic partisan framework of the period.

Likewise, Franklin D. Roosevelt's 1932 success by no means convinced the experts that a new, Democratic era was beginning. Once again, party lines blurred. Many progressive Republicans left the party and/or endorsed Roosevelt in 1936. At the same time, the 1924 and 1928 Democratic presidential nominees—John W. Davis and Al Smith—endorsed 1936 Republican candidate Alf Landon. Huey Long's assassination, in 1935, removed what had been shaping up as a major third-party candidacy in 1936, and the year's one substantial splinter bid, William Lemke's Union Party (backed by right-wing radio priest Father Coughlin) fell short of expectations. Not until the late nineteen thirties was it apparent that the two-party system was once again surviving.

Considered in these historical contexts, the 1968–72 breakdown in party loyalties—with some conservative Democrats and liberal Republicans changing parties, and a surge of independent voters—may be part of another lengthy realignment within the existing framework. More likely, though, the old framework is crumbling. Accept the idea that the revolution in education and communications has created a syndrome of ticket splitting and separate presidential and Congressional-level coalitions, and you have a situation that might very easily sustain a growing body of floating or independent voters while reducing parties to a new, minimal role. Unfortunately, because we have no way of measuring the rise and ebb of voter identification as "independent" in previous upheaval periods, no comparison can be made with the late sixties and seventies. However, the current poll data shown in Chart 20 (p. 204) put independent self-identification at such unprecedented levels as to support the notion of a new, less-anchored electorate (which, in turn, probably suggests shorter presidential cycles).

In many ways, the current political and partisan disarray is reminiscent of the 1830–65 period, when the United States and Britain shed the "agricultural era" politics of Whig-Tory and Federalist-Jeffersonian cleavages for the new conflicts of the Industrial Revolution: Liberal versus Conservative, Democratic versus Republican. During the period that politics and party lines required to "straighten out," independent affiliation was widespread in Congress and Parliament. It was a time of great uncertainty. Nobody quite knew where party politics was heading, because of the tremendous adjustment necessary in shifting society from an agricultural base to an industrial base. As much confusion may now occur in the transition of U.S. society and politics from an industrial base to a post-industrial, increasingly communications-oriented base. The old framework and the old 32–36-year cyclical pattern may no longer apply.

4

THE DISRAELI ANALOGY

WHATEVER VIEW history may take of the Disraeli cult pervading
the 1971–73 White House, there *are* parallels between the political
circumstances of the nineteen seventies and the eighteen seventies.
In this respect, the Disraeli analogy has some merit. Setting aside any
personal comparison between leaders, there is a larger analogy between the difficulties of the partisan and ideological transformation occurring with the Industrial Revolution and those now taking
place as a result of the Post-Industrial Revolution. The U.S.
parties of the seventies face many of the same problems—new issues,
roles, and constituencies—that reshaped political life during the
Victorian era.

Chapter 2 has already indicated the importance of the Industrial
Revolution in shaping an entirely new nineteenth-century political
context, then postulating the likelihood that the communication/
knowledge explosion is shaping an upheaval of similar importance.
To assess the general impact on U.S. politics, the logical comparison
would seem to be with industrial-era America rather than with
British politics of the same period: What did the Industrial Revolution do to the politics of the *United States* rather than of Britain?

In one, basic respect, however, the British analogy is more appropriate. To be sure, the Industrial Revolution worked a major change
in U.S. politics, helping to bring about the Civil War and a new
Republican/Democratic partisan context (more on this in due
course). But, for the best evidence of the initial impact of the

Industrial Revolution on politics, one must look to Britain, for the simple reason that the United Kingdom was the first country to experience the upheaval: it began there, with absolutely no precedents in other nations, a genuine economic and political revolution. America's Industrial Revolution came somewhat later than Britain's, and lacked the early intensity. For example, as of 1850, despite roughly comparable populations, the value of Britain's manufactures was about five times the value of U.S. manufactures. In historical terms, Britain, and not the United States, was on the cutting edge of the Industrial Revolution. American political reaction to it was piecemeal, slower, and less original. Similarly, the United States, rather than Britain, is experiencing the first decisive national impact of the Post-Industrial Revolution.

To measure the political cutting edge of post-industrialism in the United States, it is useful to examine the nineteenth-century political consequences of the Industrial Revolution on *both* sides of the Atlantic: not just the obsolescent, vulnerable dependence of current U.S. party patterns on the industrial era, but the shattering nature of an upheaval like Britain's on the first nation in the world to experience its force. Many precedents for what computers and television cameras are doing to circa-1975 politics can be found in the confusion that steam and railroads caused in the England where they were first found.

And yet the parallel of the Industrial Revolution has one major flaw: The new economics and politics of the early-nineteenth century replaced a land-based aristocratic structure that had little popular depth, elaborate organization, or magnitude. New parties could be created with little by way of old parties to supplant. Legislation was a hobby, and parliamentary and Congressional membership turned over with great frequency. In contrast, any new *post-industrial* system must supplant or transform the parties and institutions of the past century and a half: deeply sunk in middle-class democracy, elaborate in industrial-era organization, and vast in social and economic magnitude. While there are many similarities between this era and Disraeli's, there are also some essential differences.

A. PARTIES IN FLUX

Indisputably, the Industrial Revolution created the basis of modern politics—in public electoral participation, in ideology, and in party divisions—which the Post-Industrial Revolution is now displacing, and Great Britain served as the original crucible. Prior to the steam engine and the spinning jenny, British partisanship was based on aristocratic cliques and factions. Neither "party" had social or organizational depth. Adherents of the Duke of Devonshire fought allies of Lord Bolingbroke. Moisei Ostrogorski, whose early-twentieth-century works pioneered in the field of Anglo-American party-organization studies, effectively capsuled the superficiality of pre-industrial British party divisions:

> Subdivisions as they were of the same society, separated by rivalries and grudges and to a slight extent by principles, Whigs and Tories in parliament were animated by the same spirit and the same passions. It was a struggle of Capulets and Montagues. Social discipline made each party into a living chain that nothing could break: a flux of ideas, pressure of public opinion, revolts on the part of individuals, were not strong enough for the purpose. The questions in dispute were few in number and not of recent date; in those days, people were slow in raising problems and a long time in solving them. . . . The pressure of public opinion, apart from exceptional cases, was still felt by the politician. There hardly existed any opinion outside parliamentary circles and the drawingrooms connected with them. . . . The general public paid little heed to politics. It was the pet hobby of a select group, the sport of an aristocracy.[1]

As the Industrial Revolution increased middle-class influence and affluence, new pressures threatened these patterns and divisions. By the 1820s, reform followed reform, culminating in the great Act of 1832, which enfranchised the middle classes, giving British politics a mass base (albeit still only 10 per cent or so of adult males). Confronted with the new electorate and its issues, the old parties made progressively less sense. After all, they were rooted in another era: the royalist struggles of the seventeenth century. The name "Whig" came from "Whiggamore," the name given to a group of rebel peasants in the Jacobin West of Scotland, so the name signified rebels, enemies of the king. In turn, the king's partisans of 1688 were given the nickname of "Tories," after that given to certain footpads or bandits in Ireland, to imply that they were no better than Irish Catholic rebels. Beginning as jibes, these nicknames became badges of honor and official party names by the middle of

	1815	1820	1825	1830	1835	1840	1845	1850	1855	1860	1865	1870
Population of England and Wales (millions)		12		14		16		18		20		23
Miles of railroad	150			200		2,000		5,000		9,000		13,560
Power looms	2,000[1]		15,000		116,000			300,000				
Coal production (millions of tons)	16	17	21	25	30	38	44	50	65	70		110
Iron production (thousands of tons)	250			678	1,000	1,500		2,000	3,200	3,900		6,000
Exports (millions of pounds)[2]		36		43		59		71		136		200

1. For 1818
2. Multi-year averages.

CHART 16

England: The Chronology of the Industrial Revolution

Britain's period of political upheaval closely paralleled the take-off years of the Industrial Revolution: "The years between 1815 and 1847 have been described, probably with truth, as the period of swiftest development of domestic resources in the whole of Great Britain's economic history." W. H. B. Court, *A Concise Economic History of Britain from 1750 to Recent Times* (Cambridge, England, 1958), p. 177.

the eighteenth century. But as steam and soot marked the spread of British industry in the years after Waterloo, the terminology of Whig versus Tory became a babble of confusion.

It was just about this time that Benjamin Disraeli began his career. He ran for parliament in June 1832, offering himself to the thirty-two voters of Wycomb as an independent. He lost, and ran again in the October 1832 general election, by which time the Reform Act had expanded the voting rolls to almost three hundred. Disraeli harangued on the fading adequacy of partisanship: "I care not for party. I stand here without party. . . . Englishmen, rid your-selves of all that political jargon and ficticious slang of Whig and Tory—two names with one meaning, used only to delude you—and unite in forming a great national party which can alone save the country from impending destruction."[2]

Perceptive words, these. British historians tend to single out the period from 1828 to 1846 as the years when the old order of things was overcome by the surge of industrialism and the arrival of the middle class. Chart 16 shows how this was the era during which industrialization reached its peak momentum. It was also a period of reforms—in the electorate, in the local government, in the Church of England, and in the economy. One scholar has analyzed these events as a "composite attack on the legal privileges of the landed interest which the shift of wealth, power and population to the towns had already rendered out of date and anomalous."[3]

Effective consummation of this shift came in 1846, when Tory Prime Minister Sir Robert Peel acquiesced in the repeal of the famous and controversial corn laws, which functioned to protect British agriculture. Peel's action infuriated the squirarchy that was the bul-wark of the Tory Party; repeal was regarded as the ultimate be-trayal of the Tory interest in the face of onrushing industrialism, and it split the party in twain, causing Peel's government to fall.

Party upheaval triggered by the corn-laws controversy ushered in what the Oxford History of England describes as a "long period of confusion and instability." Professor E. L. Woodward, writing in the Oxford volume on *The Age of Reform (1815–1870)*, de-scribed the instability:

From the beginning of the year 1846 until the passing of the Reform Bill of 1867, there were nine administrations; between 1846 and 1852, from 1856 to 1859, and from 1866 to 1868, no

ministry had a stable majority in parliament. . . . Party discipline was still very loose; it was impossible, after a general
election, to know the exact state of the parties until the first
division had been taken in the new parliament. . . . The very
names of the parties were unstable for a time. The terms "conservative liberal" and "liberal conservative" came into use,
though [Lord] Russell thought whiggism a simpler term than
"conservative progress" and the protectionists were inclined to
give up the name "conservative party" owing to the odious as-
sociations with Peel. . . . Leaders of parties were as unde-
cided in their allegiance as their followers. . . . These facts
merely reflect the hesitancy and quick changes of opinion inevitable at a time when issues were so much confused and in
many cases so new that the old party distinctions did not apply
to them.[4]

In *Democracy and the Organization of Political Parties,* Ostrogorski offered a kindred analysis:

Soon the traditional party ties slackened all along the parliamentary line; discipline ceased to exist, and no one could depend on his followers. . . . Every day, in fact, the difference
between the two great historical parties grew less marked. You
could not tell a moderate Tory from a Whig. Personal considerations invariably become factors of importance in parliamentary combinations. A policy was combated one day and
adopted the next by the victorious coalition; ministers left
office by one door and crept in at another. Members of parliament transferred their allegiance to another leader without
being false to their political convictions, because they had none
to speak of; others withheld their support because they enter-
tained opinions which they were not disposed to sacrifice to
the calculations of parliamentary strategy. From one motive
to another, the individual asserted his independence within the
halls of parliament as well as elsewhere. . . . Political veterans
deplored the perversity of the new generation, and were at a
loss for words to denounce the inconsistency and insincerity
displayed by members of all parties. These censors, like all
laudatores temporai acti, little dreamed, in clinging to their
traditional ideas, that they were applying old principles to a

new society, or at all events, to a society in course of transformation.[5]

The upheaval in British politics was more profound than its
transatlantic cousin. Whereas Tory and Whig rivalry had deep
historic roots, American party loyalties were newer and looser.
Federalism had collapsed during James Monroe's one-party Era
of Good Feeling, from 1816 to 1824, and new party lines did not
take shape until the 1830s. Even then, they were shaky and loose,
in large measure because both the Whigs and the Democrats tried
to sidestep the confrontation of the southern agricultural slaveoc-
racy and the rapidly industrializing economy of the North. Liberal
Democratic activist Frederic Dutton, who has found current-day
parallels in pre-Civil War chaos, sketched this portrait of U.S.
political fragmentation during the period of comparable British confusion:

> During the 1840's and 1850's, first two, and then three major
> candidates contested for the presidency in the same election.
> Finally, in 1860, there were four. No man was able to hold
> onto that office for more than a single term between 1840 and
> 1860. Indeed, not a single chief executive during those twenty
> years of change and upheaval was even renominated by his
> own party! One took himself out of consideration before the
> end of his term—Polk, of the Mexican War; the other four
> incumbents (two of them Vice-Presidents who had succeeded
> through tragedy to the White House) simply were sacked at
> the end of their term. The victors in the 1856 and 1860 pres-
> idential elections were elected by considerably less than a
> majority of the votes cast. Lincoln gained the White House
> by the smallest percentage in the nation's history: 39.8%,
> almost 4% less than Nixon in 1968.[6]

Independents were numerous in Congress. Party names counted
for little. But one must hesitate at drawing too many analogies
between U.S. and British parties in the mid-nineteenth century,
because of 1) the sectionalism dominating events in the United
States and 2) the *later* chronology of the Industrial Revoultion in
the United States. To be sure, there is a superficial parallel in the
fact that U.S. party loyalties firmed up at about the same time—

after the Civil War—as did those in Britain, where the first ministries of Disraeli (1868) and Gladstone (1868) are generally taken as signaling the new party system. Even so, the U.S. alignment was an early industrial cleavage; the United States did not experience the velocity of 1830–60 British industrialization until the last years of the nineteenth century. Likewise, the U.S. reaction—the Progressive movement—came later.

In both Britain and the United States, the process of solidifying a new party system out of the upheaval of the Industrial Revolution took place over a considerable, albeit different, period of time. With ten times as many voters in 1860 as there had been in 1800, the new parties had much more social and organizational depth. Transformations of political ideology also played a vital role, because the new lines in British politics could not harden until new middle-class ideological differences had clarified in place of the old disputes between Whig and Tory. Britain's evolution of ideology during the mid-nineteenth century suggests several patterns that seem to be recurring with the impact of the Post-Industrial Revolution, namely: 1) the assertion of the ideology/technology of progress under the liberals, 2) the ideological turmoil of a conservatism defending the interests of an obsolescent socioeconomic system and no longer able to field a useful doctrine, and 3) the regrouping of the (Conservative) opposition around new ideas, programs, and constituencies, which in turn gives a new logic to partisanship.

During the third, fourth, and fifth decades of the nineteenth century, the United Kingdom was caught up, as Alfred Tennyson poeticized, in the concept that a more perfect world was being built by new developments in industry and transportation. The idea of progress, while promoted by previous generations, enjoyed a heyday. Scholarly assessments normally trace its origins to the rise of science, philosophy, and commerce in the seventeenth century. French philosophers of the Enlightenment had expounded the theme at great length, but it was left for Britain, the first nation to experience the Industrial Revolution, to take the theme of a handful of intellectuals and make it a currency of middle-class politics and ideology. Herbert Spencer, in his book *Social Statics* (1850), saw industrial *laissez faire* leading to a new world in which "The ultimate development of the ideal man is logically certain. . . . The things we call our immorality [must] disappear . . . man must become perfect."[7]

As indicated, the repeal of the corn laws, taken as signaling the end of squirarchical Britain, was traumatic for the Tory Party. So was the onrush of industrialization at home and revolution abroad. By the 1860s, although party ideologies were badly blurred, Tories were the more despondent of the two groups. Between 1830 and 1866, Liberal ministries ruled Britain for all but seven out of thirty-six years. This was the zenith of Industrial Revolution and reform, and conservatism was demoralized:

> The ruling classes, who were sunk in stagnation, had no resistance to offer; they were without ideas, without strong convictions, and consequently without strength. The rising tide of new ideas convinced the Conservatives that all hope was lost, that a relentless fatality was dragging England towards the abyss of radicalism and democracy. The Tories of the old school had lost faith in the strength of their cause, and the new men had never possessed it.[8]

To some extent, the repeal of the corn laws had also gotten rid of a philosophic millstone. Sir Robert Peel had acted to repeal the protection duties in order to keep the Tory Party from being ruined. Old-line Tories were losing the confidence of the country by clinging to obsolescence. Some historians see Peel's action as marking a watershed:

> "After Peel's ministry, both parties accepted the broad principles of the Liberal creed and differed mainly over the speed and methods of their application. It thus became possible to have a real system of party government with parties alternating in power without each repealing the measures recently passed by its rivals. . . . Socially it rested on the domination of both parties by the middle classes."[9]

The two ideas are hardly contradictory: Conservative demoralization and basic acceptance of Liberal ideas went hand in hand. One could argue that Peel's ministry served something of the function that Samuel Lubell has assigned to the Eisenhower administration of 1953–61: essentially ratifying the permanence of the political changes already in motion. In each instance, Conservatives were demoralized because they really had no choice but to ratify developments they disapproved, and they were frustrated because no new role for them had yet emerged.

The fortunes of British Conservatives began to change during the late 1860s and 1870s. If the period from 1866 to 1874 can be counted as a transition era during which Liberal-versus-Conservative competition firmed up, the era from 1874 to 1905 was one of Conservative hegemony, their ministries being in power twenty-three out of thirty-one years. At some risk of oversimplification, here are the ingredients of Conservative party and philosophic comeback.

> *First, the completion of the original middle-class Liberal*
> *impetus to break the hold of the agricultural gentry*
> *and open up the country to industrialism.*

By the late 1860s, this process was all but finished, and middle-class Liberalism was beginning to shift gears toward representation of working-class objectives. Such measures as the (electoral) Reform Act of 1867, the Education Act of 1870, and the Irish land and church reforms went well beyond the Liberal ideas of aristocratic Whig leaders and Manchester industrialists.

> *Second, the changing constituency of the Liberal Party.*

After the Reform Act of 1867, which doubled the electorate, the center of party gravity shifted to the working-class urban districts. Liberalism lost ground in the boroughs and counties where middle-class and rural voters grew more suspicious of their party's increasingly radical thrust. By the mid-1870s, much of the affluent strata of the Liberal Party—merchants, shopkeepers, industrialists, et al.—was in motion toward the Conservatives. The (financial) City of London, Liberal through 1870, was Conservative by the 1880s. The same was true of the prominent old-line Whig aristocratic families that had maintained their loyalties through the Palmerston period.

> *Third, the changing tenor of post-1870 Liberalism.*

Lord Palmerston, who as Foreign Secretary or Prime Minister dominated the Liberal ascendancy from 1830 to 1865, was the man who put the word "jingo" into the English language as a synonym for aggressive nationalism. Palmerston represented expansionism: industrial and financial at home; diplomatic gunboat-style elsewhere. Cambridge Professor David Thomson describes Palmerston's policy as "conservative at home and jingoistic liberalism abroad," saying that he "almost personally embodied the character and outlook of the commercial and industrial middle classes."[10] Palmerston himself knew that his death would release the more radical forces in the Liberal Party: The year he died, 1865, he said, "Gladstone will soon have it all his own way, and whenever he gets my place, we shall have strange doings."[11] His words were prophetic, because Gladstone sharply reversed the tone of Palmerston's day. Liberalism lost interest in nationalism and industrialism, adopting instead the causes of education, religion, and oppressed minorities. In many ways, Gladstone was to Palmerston as George McGovern was to John Kennedy and Lyndon Johnson. He stranded the Liberal Party on the shoals of isolationism, military defeatism, insufficient protection for British industries, and Home Rule for Ireland. The importance of these interacting issues cannot be overstated. By the 1890s, the Marquess of Salisbury, Conservative Prime Minister, could go so far as to say, "Politics are Ireland," and the combined issues of Ireland, imperialism, and protection were responsible for a major realignment of conservative Liberals (Unionists), who joined the Conservatives in protest against Liberal policies.

The Industrial Revolution ended one era in British politics but did not create a definite new cleavage until the excesses of Liberalism enabled Conservatism to rally around a set of issues entirely unlike those that went by the wayside in the earlier upheaval. For all the talk about "Tory Democracy" and the party's need to forget Pall Mall clubdom and appeal to the people, expanded Conservative appeal was basically shaped around issues—Irish Home Rule, anti-imperialism, free trade—in which Liberalism had gone too far for the nationalism and self-interest of the British people. To be sure, Conservatism was obliged to accept—and even innovate— social and economic legislation of a liberal variety. But only after Liberalism changed color could the Conservatives put together a winning majority that drew substantially on working-class support. In 1874, as in 1972, liberal moralism—at home and abroad— had much less appeal than economic liberalism, and working-class voters were amenable to issues of imperialism, economic nationalism, and ethnic rivalry.

While any attempt to relate these patterns to the circumstance of contemporary U.S. politics can be picked apart on this or that specific, there *is* an over-all parallel: 1) The Post-Industrial Revolution in the United States had displaced the Republican industrial elite in somewhat the same way as the Industrial Revolution displaced Britain's agricultural gentry; 2) the emergence of the knowledge economy has destroyed the relevance of traditional Republican party lines and ideology just as the old Tory-Whig system and outlook was rendered obsolete by industrialization; 3) post-industrialism has gotten carried away with the idea of progress, going too far and alienating traditionalists, just as industrial Liberalism did; 4) "conservative" forces, who have hitherto lacked ideological bonds, can now regroup around a new coalition including disillusioned liberals, just as the Conservatives of the 1870s and 1880s fashioned a coalition including many of their former Whig opponents. The Industrial Revolution ideologized British politics, replacing the non-ideological divisions of Tory versus Whig; and the Post-Industrial Revolution is ideologizing U.S. politics by wiping out the regional and hereditary traditions of the Civil War orbit.

The disintegration of U.S. party loyalties during the nineteen fifties and nineteen sixties hardly needs restatement. Lack of party loyalty, lack of party ideological lines, emphasis on support for individual politicians, and the practice of ticket splitting all go hand in hand. In this respect, current U.S. politics bear a great resemblance to circa-1855 Britain (or, indeed, circa-1855 America). Just as the dissolution of Tory-versus-Whig loyalties coincides with the 1820–50 surge of British industrialism, the decline of U.S. party cohesion in the fifties and especially the sixties seems to correlate with the rise of post-industrialism. The question is whether a new party system/cycle will emerge as the two parties slip into a logical orbit of post-industrial-society debate and conflict. And this problem is doubtless linked to the problem of rekindling voter interest. During the nineteen sixties, as the logic of the existing national parties collapsed, so did voter turnout, reaching an extraordinarily low 56 per cent level in 1972. In most northern states, voter participation was lower in that year than in any other since the Civil War (Chart 17 shows the pattern in Massachusetts and Indiana). For kindred reasons of obsolescing party lines, the 1970–72 turnout was also extremely low in Canada and Britain.

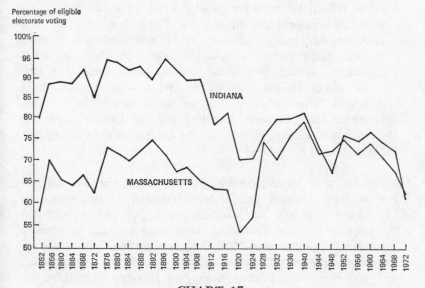

CHART 17

Voter Turnout in Presidential Races, 1852–1972, Indiana and Massachusetts

As chapter 2 shows, the U.S. reaction against nineteen-sixties liberalism can be described as something of a traditionalist reassertion. Liberal politics narrowed its constituency by moving beyond the economic into the cultural, and this raises another parallel with industrial-era British Liberalism. The last Liberal Prime Minister of the golden era, Viscount Palmerston, stood for economic expansionism, international belligerence, and a relative dearth of social moralizing at home. In the 1860s and 1870s, Gladstone shifted gears by emphasizing morality, education, religion, and oppressed minorities (everywhere from Ireland to Bulgaria to the Sudan), and de-emphasizing military prowess and British imperial glory. This shift from an economic liberalism to a cultural/moral credo bears considerable relation to the Kennedy-to-McGovern metamorphosis of U.S. liberalism.

Under the circumstances, the basic 1960s direction of party realignment should continue. Walter Dean Burnham oversimplifies, but is basically correct, in describing the cleavage this way:

> The potential fracture lines around which a sixth party system would be organized are, unlike those of the New Deal realignment but very much like those of all preceding ones, overwhelmingly horizontal: black against white, peripheral regions against the center, "parochials" against "cosmopolitans," blue collar whites against both blacks and affluent liberals, the American "Great Middle," with its strong attachment to the values of the traditional American political formula, against urban cosmopolitans, intellectuals and students who have largely left that credo behind.[12]

Granted that his demographic framework leaves out the important GOP business and technical/managerial component, the "traditionalist" middle-class coalition does appear to lack skills that the demands of post-industrialism have made essential to effective government. Britain's circa-1874 Conservatives faced the new challenge of government with most of the country's industrial, commercial, and professional men in their ranks. And although Disraeli, as one observer put it, "discerned the Conservative workingman [in the inarticulate mass of the English populace] as the sculptor perceives the angel prisoned in a block of marble," he ran the nation with the talents of the British elite—talents that were very much available to his party.[13] Circa-1974 U.S. "conservatism" lacks that talent; its business and middle-class constituencies do not readily provide the sort of skilled professionals necessary to cope with the problems of post-industrialism.

Unfortunately for the U.S. political system, effecting a transition from industrialism to post-industrialism may be more difficult than the nineteenth century's shift from agriculture to industrialism. The management problem of post-industrial society is infinitely more challenging: the comparison of government size, budget, and complexity of decision making, being in the range of 1:20, is no comparison at all. Those who have studied post-industrialism generally agree with Daniel Bell's analysis that "a post-industrial society is one in which there will necessarily be more conscious decision-making. . . . [The key] is bargaining between groups. But in order to bargain, one has to know social benefits and social costs."[14] Thus the political arena becomes pivotal as the place where a broader and broader range of decisions are made; however, effective use of that arena requires complex skills. To quote Bell again: "The relationship of technical and political decisions in the next decades will become, in consequence, one of the most crucial problems of public policy. The politician, and the political public, will have to become increasingly versed in the technical character of policy, aware of the ramified impact of decisions as systems become extended."[15]

Herein lies the weakness of the "traditionalist" sector: lack of governmental and related expertise. Some Republicans have reiterated Disraeli's famous saying, "You cannot form a party of resistance pure and simple, because change is inevitable in a progressive country; the question is whether Reform shall be carried out in the spirit of the national customs or traditions, or whether you will follow abstract principles and general doctrines."[16] Richard Nixon said much the same thing in a well-publicized 1972 pre-election interview: "I would say that my views, my approach, is probably that of a Disraeli conservative—a strong foreign policy, strong adherence to basic virtues that the nation believes in and the people believe in, and to conserving these values, and not being destructive of them, but combined with reform, reform that will work, and not reform that destroys."[17] But the domestic policy record of 1968 to 1972 obliged even sympathetic observers to doubt that the Nixon administration possessed 1) a sufficient social and cultural grounding to understand those values and 2) the programmatic and analytic capability to retool government policies accordingly. Even the usually sympathetic *Wall Street Journal* lamented in mid-1972:

> To maintain some claim to political power in such times, a dominant party or elite needs to have articulated some vision of the common good—something a party can stand for beyond its won continuation in office. That this requires intellectual skills is a major reason no such vision is apparent after four years of Republican rule.[18]

The dearth of GOP intellectuals is an incontrovertible fact. Attenuating the historical division between the party of wealth and the party of intellect, the GOP has a substantial but diminishing share of the wealth—industrial-era or corporate-*nouveau-riche* variety—but very little of the intellect, which is heavily Democratic. Media analyst Edith Efron painted an accurate picture:

> President Nixon gets in the White House and in four years there never has been a Republican brain trust. The last four years there could have been a tremendous collection of brains walking in and out of those White House doors, and there would have been a whole group of prominent intellectuals of a contrasting persuasion if Mr. Nixon had simply shed his light upon them, but he didn't do it. . . . Books are not something that they deal with. When they think of a powerful man, they think of a big industrialist who could manipulate the materials of the earth in a long range and potent way, and that is power—that's one kind. But they will not look at a broke little intellectual and understand that he contains the ammunition they need for a very different kind of battle.[19]

No small part of the nation's 1968–72 difficulty can be traced to the inability of the Administration to understand and conceptualize the national mood and counterrevolution that was implicit in their constituency; and this same weakness limited the extent to which that constituency could be deepened and broadened in 1972. Looking back on the election, Seymour Lipset and Everett C. Ladd, Jr., found that while academicians cast 43 per cent of their votes for Nixon, a GOP record, the Republicans missed a larger opportunity than anti-McGovernism. Lipset and Ladd argued that faculty members, reacting against the societal turbulence of the sixties, were undergoing "a change in conceptual orientation that touches strains historically associated with conservatism."[20] However, they suggested that, in another sense, 1972 was a story of opportunities missed by the Republican Party. In view of the antipathy of faculty for Republicans, a concerted effort by the minority party was required to win academic support. Instead, the prevailing Republican tone was one of suspicion, if not outright anti-intellectualism. By and large, the GOP remained locked in the psychologies of industrial-era politics, failing to substitute an articulate indictment of knowledge-sector miscalculation for country-club know-nothingism.

The definite lack of philosophic mooring which characterized the first Nixon administration has a peculiar historical logic. Indeed, as we have already noted in several places, the 1820–40 era of the early Industrial Revolution was similarly bankrupt or confused. Note Ostrogorski's comment (pp. 156–57) on the parallel dearth of principles and lack of differences between the parties in mid-nineteenth-century Britain. And as for the United States, one can usefully recall the advice that agents for 1840 Whig presidential candidate William Henry Harrison got from his campaign manager, Nicholas Biddle: "Let him say not a word about his principles of creed— let him say nothing, promise nothing. Let the use of pen and ink be wholly forbidden."[21] Richard Nixon's domestic chief, John Ehrlichman, from time to time expressed kindred anti-philosophic sentiments.

There are other Nixon-Whig parallels. During the upheaval of the mid-nineteenth century, ideological cleavages tended to blur, and the least-ideological concern was often in the minds of members of the party primarily concerned with trying to preserve old economic privileges amid rapidly changing circumstances. Paul Murray, writing about Whig politics in nineteenth-century Georgia, described the overriding concern: "The compelling aim of the party was to get control of the existing machinery of government the better to serve the dominant interest of the group."[22] Under White House major-domos H. R. Haldeman and John Ehrlichman, the Nixon administration practiced an extraordinarily similar neo-Whiggish managerialism, although it was clique-oriented rather than party-oriented. Heavy emphasis was put on organization and management rather than ideas.

But if the Disraeli analogy is to hold up, then a consolidationist/ traditionalist body of political thought ought to be emerging in the wake of liberal excess and failure. Here there are reasons to wonder whether post-industrialism may not raise a much deeper dilemma. Perhaps the Nixon-administration pattern was an aberration and the traditionalist coalition will yet interact with the more chastened segment of the knowledge sector—per Herman Kahn's synthesis hope and the Lipset-Ladd theories of opportunities at hand in 1972. If so, this might create a constructive new coalition able to pursue the usual unifying function of U.S. politics.

On the other hand, the 1968–74 pattern may bespeak a fundamental breakdown: excessively institutionalized branches of government; lack of concern for party; lack of talent able to forge positive policies and bonds; and reliance on managerialism, propaganda, and other negative, manipulative techniques of the sort apparent in the Watergate syndrome. Communications-age Whiggery rests on a far more powerful base than the dollar-a-vote variety of the eighteen forties. In November 1972, Walter Dean Burnham observed: "If Nixon were another Theodore Roosevelt, he could have fashioned a landslide against this [eastern] 'Establishment' out of positive support for himself and his persona. Since he is not, the landslide became almost wholly negative-based."[23] Samuel Lubell raised similar post-1972 fears: that instead of moving into an era of creative conservatism, we may be moving into an era of negative Manager-Presidents. Clearly, the Watergate syndrome has affected the evolution of Lubell's Manager-President, but our system may lack the institutional fluidity and party efficacy needed for the sort of realignment that took place in Disraeli's day. Post-industrial parties will play a very different role from those of the industrial era.

B. THE ROLE OF PARTY

Looking back over the past century and a half of U.S. politics, the importance of party organization peaked—and, more recently, diminished—with the tide and ebb of the industrial-era party structure.

This is logical enough. The parties of the era of the smokestack make less sense in the era of television; their structure has atrophied with their *raison d'être* and industrial-era cohesion. Part of their function has been taken over by the Department of Health, Education and Welfare, part by CBS News. Over all, the Communications Revolution has been the central factor in undercutting the get-out-the-vote function of party organizations, straight-ticket voting, and traditional adherence. The importance of changing national economic patterns can hardly be overstated. Because of the striking extent to which the past evolution of U.S. parties has been linked to the Industrial Revolution and its socioeconomic ramifications, the Post-Industrial Revolution—here as in virtually every other context—may signal a major shift. What is more, a major change in the *role* as well as the *alignment* of parties seems inevitable.

Eighteenth-century thinking was hostile to the idea of parties, and, in the first years of the republic, there were none, albeit Federalist and Jeffersonian factions evolved quickly enough in Congress. Thomas Jefferson's two administrations (1801–9) saw the party caucus rise to considerable power (as an instrument of the White House), and Jefferson's Democratic-Republicans were successful enough in party terms to more or less extinguish the Federalists. But the crumbling of the opposition during the administration of James Madison (1809–17) took away the pressure for party organization and effectiveness. Professor Edgar Robinson's summary is a fair one:

> With the accession of Madison, party guidance became uncertain and was presently lost. Party history for twenty years thereafter becomes an account of struggle of factions and cliques, only occasionally revealing distinct party action in government affairs.[1]

As noted earlier, much the same factional bickering described the Montague-Capulet nature of the Tory-Whig struggle in British politics between Waterloo and the passage of the Reform Act of 1832. In England and the United States, the old party systems were obsolete, and the emerging industrial era, with its middle-class economic interests and spreading male enfranchisement, had not yet created new ones. In the early-nineteenth century, then, party —and party organization—did not count for much.

In the 1830s, "party" began to take on a new meaning. Hitherto, as used by Federalist and Democratic-Republican leaders alike, "party" referred to clique-based loyalties, and was built upon both a restricted electorate and general public disinterest save in times of crisis. But the democratization processes of the 1820s and 1830s changed these circumstances. After 1817, the new states coming into the Union ignored taxpaying or property qualifications on suffrage, and many older states changed their constitutions. In Britain, the Reform Act of 1832 did away with most "rotten boroughs" and increased the number of eligible voters tenfold. On both sides of the Atlantic, this explosion of the electorate had two principal effects: first, it forced nomination processes farther out of the grasp of the few and nearer to the hands of the many; secondly, it obliged the nation's "interests" to set up organizations that could handle the technical side of appealing to five or ten times as many people—people without familiar aristocratic decision-making criteria.

Hardly any textbooks disagree: the great early-nineteenth-century expansion of the electorate laid the basis for modern party organization. In the United States, the process began in such states as New York and Pennsylvania. Old family leadership was displaced by the emergence of politicians who could organize and deliver votes. By the 1830s, the convention system of nominating candidates, a product of New York, was extended to the national level to create electorally disciplined national parties in lieu of the cliquish chaos of the 1820s. The decade following the inauguration of Andrew Jackson in 1829 witnessed a tremendous surge of party organization (although the party phenomenon was still new enough in 1834 to be missed by Alexis de Tocqueville in his otherwise insightful study of democracy in America).

So, too, in England. Before the Reform Act of 1832, the number of electors in any constituency was typically too small to require a register of voters, to say nothing of organizational efforts. Many seats were controlled by individuals or families, and estimates as late as 1815 found 487 members of Parliament owing their seats to the government or powerful families, while just 171 were democratically elected.[2] Although the great families of England remained powerful after 1832, electoral attention shifted to the newly formalized lists of voters. Even before passage of the Reform Bill, in 1831, the Conservatives formed the first party central organization: London's Carlton Club. The Liberals quickly followed suit, and both parties created a network of local party registration societies and canvassing operations. The leading statesman of the era, Sir Robert Peel, said that the watchword should be "Register, Register, Register."[3] He might have said, "Organize, Organize, Organize."

By 1840, the party ambiguity in U.S. politics had been replaced by clear partisan divisions pitting the Democrats against the Whigs. But they soon proved themselves to be rival political machines rather than philosophic rivals. Organization and tactics were everything, principles nothing. On several occasions, the Whigs even avoided announcing a party presidential platform. This outlook had a peculiar logic, because the great party-organization upsurge of the thirties had barely taken hold before the issue of slavery— which cut across pro-Jackson and anti-Jackson party lines—raised its head. Such ideological assertion would destroy the all-important party organizations. Thus, to avoid the slavery issue, the parties tried to avoid issues in general. In 1840, 1848, and 1852, for example, the Whigs nominated presidential candidates who were army generals—Mexican War heroes—and ran as men above politics (and thus, presumably, above the issues).

On one hand, the circumstances of the 1840s and early 1850s showed that U.S. political parties had come of organizational age, attaining unprecedented structural significance. Yet, on the other hand, it was also becoming apparent that the two parties dared not stand for much of anything and had few real issues between them. Each had only one compelling interest: holding office. As the slavery issue became more and more dominant, the two parties were unable to smother it with calls to organizational loyalty, and, slowly but surely, that loyalty and organizational strength eroded. Mass-based parties could not sidestep powerful issues the way factions sometimes could. Ultimately, as the elections of 1856 and 1860 proved, national party organizations could not sustain themselves on parties unable to straddle emerging ideological and geographic divisions.

The fault lay in lack of solid party alignments. But after party alignments sorted themselves out during the 1860s, political organizations rooted on that new solid ground became stronger than ever. In the post-Civil War North, Republican Party machines grew hand in hand with industrial corporations. A number of excellent studies have described the workings of the late-nineteenth-century political machines. Suffice it to say that machines commanded a unique importance in the United States because of the federal system. Decentralized political power made city halls and state legislatures important as they could never be in Britain—and local parties had a lot more favors to dispense and many more offices to hold or capture. Then, too, the federal government was obliged to cater to local machines—for votes in Congress and support in presidential elections—in a way that British ministries were not. This wide-open situation played into the hands of American industry, little regulated in the era of *laissez faire,* and most of the party organizations on the Republican side were dominated by corporate interests and used by those interests as a go-between for controlling government and legislation. Ostrogorski's pioneering study on party organization painted a picture of post-Civil War U.S. party organizations as the creatures of big business:

. . . With interests extending over the economic surface of the country, and with an unquenchable thirst for gain, they

needed . . . the compliance of Congress and of the State Legislatures. But to buy their members singly . . . was not such an
easy matter. . . . The party Organizations very often provided
a way of getting around them more cheaply and more effectively: the representative elected with the all-powerful aid of
the Organizations . . . had contracted obligations towards them
which had no need to be expressly stated; they flowed from
the nature of human relations. Entering into an alliance with
the Organizations, by means of heavy contributions to their
funds, or even by paying them the whole bill of the election
campaign, the corporations obtained a hold over the representatives. . . .

Under one aspect or another the party Organizations appeared as the base of operations for all the great private interests in their efforts to bend the power of the State to their
own selfish ends, efforts which have filled the greater part of
the history of the United States since the Civil War.[4]

Historian Richard Jensen takes a broader but not contradictory
view. Party organizations might have been convenient, easy prey
for big corporations, but they also reflected the intense tribalism
of the electorate—ethnic, cultural, and religious. With all these
divisions underscored by important cultural issues from Civil War
memories to Prohibition, politics had a real fervor quite apart
from the bribes and objectives of banks or railroads. To Jensen,
the political organizational style of the period lends itself to charac-
terization as "militarist" in the sense of armies drawn up for combat
with well-staffed organizations, partisan newspapers, and a pro-
clivity for huge rallies and parades.[5] He estimates that 750,000
people from all over the country visited McKinley's home during
the "front porch" campaign of 1896, a figure that amounts to 5
per cent of the total vote and 13 per cent of the Republican vote
in November! Activity of this magnitude clearly bespeaks an intensity of commitment beyond the scope of Standard Oil or the
New York Central. Blending Jensen and Ostrogorski, one can say
that the importance of U.S. party organization in the late-nineteenth century was a function of 1) democratization of the franchise,
spurred by the Industrial Revolution; 2) the needs of the corporate
interests created by the Industrial Revolution; and 3) the cultural,
regional, and religious animosities sharpened by the conflicts that

came in industrialism's wake. This definition is not intended to be complete, but rather to emphasize the centrality of the Industrial Revolution.

Under the circumstances, it is not necessary to dwell on the British pattern. However, the limited transatlantic parallel continued. The Reform Act of 1867 came more or less at the time when the Liberal-versus-Conservative cleavage was achieving the basic shape it would maintain through the Victorian era, and this further expansion of the electorate led to a further increase in party organizational activity. Liberal Party leaders formed the Birmingham Federation as an instrument of local party organization and control. Disraeli attacked it as a "caucus," with implications of American-style maneuvering, wire-pulling, and graft—and the name stuck. But the Conservatives moved in the same direction. Expansion of the electorate via the reform bills of 1867 and 1884 underscored the need for organization, and the fires of party activism were fanned by public intensity over such issues as Ireland and religion.

In many ways, the period of Gladstone and Disraeli or McKinley and Bryan symbolized the heyday of party combat and party organization. From the pre-Civil War realignment era to the end of the century, party organization was probably at its peak as a determining factor in U.S. politics. In the late 1850s, as the new parties took shape around the great issues dividing America, voter turnout ratios began to climb. Extended Civil War and partisan loyalties kept turnout high through McKinley's day, and well-oiled political machines controlled nominations, reaped political spoils, and mobilized their adherents to go to the polls. These were the years of Tammany Hall and Boss Tweed, of the Whisky Ring, of powerful congressmen and senators who doubled as state political bosses tied to industrial interests, of huge political picnics, torchlight parades, and other examples of the cultural role of political organizations, especially in the big cities teeming with immigrants newly arrived from Europe. Not that political organization fattened more on immigrants than native Americans. Anglo-Saxon Indiana, for example, was closely divided by the politics of Civil War memory—Yankees versus Copperheads and Peace Democrats— and powerful party machines grew up to manage the fight. From 1868 to 1896, Indiana presidential turnout was huge, typically 90–95 per cent, and the margin of either party's victory was usually very thin. Circumstances like these were the stuff on which political organizations fattened and became indispensable.

Although Britain's political organizational forms were maturing rapidly, they tended to relate more to the need of parliamentary electioneering, playing less of a role—much less—in everyday life. For several reasons, the United States was unique in the cultural pervasiveness of its political parties. First of all, from 1865 to 1896, the United States had a far higher ratio of voter turnout than any other foreign nation, and party organization played a unique role in managing this electoral participation. Secondly, as indicated, U.S. industrialists used party organizations to advance their own interests in a way that would have been lessened in other countries (and was in Britain) by the influence of the landed aristocracy. Thirdly, the United States had a) unparalleled numbers of uneducated immigrants and b) rural and small-town native Americans still easily mobilized against one another by recent Civil War partisanships. As a result, no other nation had party organizations along the lines and significance of those in the United States.

Before describing the ebb of this organizational power, it is useful to profile it at the zenith.

On a geographic basis, the areas of strongest party organization were the Great Lakes, Middle Atlantic, and New England states —in short, the industrial North. After Reconstruction ended, in 1876, the rural South became solidly Democratic, and the peculiar socioeconomics of the Great Plains and Rocky Mountain states admitted to the Union between 1860 and 1896 did not lend themselves to the strong party organizations one found in New York, Pennsylvania, and Indiana. Frequently in the grip of Populist or other agrarian insurgency, the western states were more rambunctious. Powerful party organization was mostly a northern phenomenon.

After McKinley's defeat of Bryan broke up the national political stalemate of 1876–96, the case can be made that party organizations began losing their impetus. Presidential elections no longer pivoted on the outcome of voting in marginal Connecticut, New York, New Jersey, and Indiana (as was the case from 1876 to 1892). Tenure in Congress began to institutionalize. The tight post-Civil War balance fell apart in 1896, and, until 1932, these and other industrial states were *almost always* Republican in presidential contests and *usually* Republican on the state level. In states that became less marginal after 1896—and this includes most northern states—turnout began to fall off, with the assistance of registration laws, literacy tests, and other devices to curb the fraudulent practices especially prevalent in the big cities. Only in a few such border states as Missouri and Delaware, which became more marginal (i.e., somewhat more Republican), did turnout increase. In most northern states, turnout peaked during the 1876–96 stalemate era.

Once the stalemate of rival political armies had been broken, reformers and businessmen alike took steps to reduce the importance of the political machines. In addition to registration laws and literacy tests, the late 1890s and the early-twentieth century saw widespread introduction of the Australian ballot, authorization of voter initiatives, institution of party primaries, direct election of senators, non-partisan elections, and the like. All of this tended to weaken the militant organizational structure of late-nineteenth-century parties. To the considerable extent that big business ran the United States, political-party organizations were less important; that hurdle was cleared with the decisive 1896 defeat of Bryan.

While analysts disagree as to exact chronology, there can be no doubt that the importance of party organization has been steadily diminishing throughout the twentieth century. Full-fledged institution of the seniority system in Congress undercut party power there in 1910: The introduction of primaries eroded the control of party organizations, as did the push for non-partisan elections. The cutoff of immigration during the 1920s greatly reduced the sustenance of the big-city machines. As for partisan factors, the depression of 1929 ruined the Republican machines in many northern states, and it was no longer so easy—or necessary—to build new ones.

The considerable impact of Franklin D. Roosevelt's fireside chats suggested another vista of decreased political organizational importance. And, in the wake of the Second World War, the enormous revolution in communications, plus the trend to suburbia, brought about further erosion in the efficacy and importance of party organizations. One by one, state and city machines lost their hold. Increasing voter education and affluence reduced the appeal of political jobs and small favors, hitherto the lifeblood of organizational strength. Perhaps even more important in this same vein was the impact of federal, state, and local welfare and assistance programs: What had been the tool of local political machines was now the role of government. Ticket splitting grew (as described in chapter 3). On the national level, the parties lost ideological cohesion and saw more and more of their influence drained by the institutionalization of Congress and the presidency. Party organizational impact gave way to the leverage of incumbency and to massive candidate spending on management and communications packages.

All told, the sum effect of the Post-Industrial Revolution has been *to very nearly dispense with the party organizations that came together in the early, alignment period of the Industrial Revolution.* Post-industrialism has 1) confused old party lines, 2) increased the education and independence of the electorate, 3) substituted welfare-state machinery for Tammany turkeys, and 4) substituted the media for party organizations as the principle means of communicating with the electorate. Campaign-management firms have multiplied to take up the slack. Richard Nixon's 1968 and 1972 presidential campaigns were managed by media-oriented personal organizations and not by the Republican Party. George McGovern's 1972 campaign was also run this way. With many congressmen and senators relying on incumbency, media coverage, and personal networks or organizations, powerful party organizations are becoming fewer and fewer.

Chart 17 shows how twentieth-century voter participation has dropped in several of their states, with the biggest dip usually coming in the past decade. Every available poll and index of opinion suggests that the key is public disenchantment with a politics that is confused, corrupt, and devoid of clear party or philosophic lines. Much the same malaise must have been present in the revolutionary Europe of the 1830s and 1840s, and in the festering pre-Civil War United States when existing parties and politicians tried to sidestep unavoidable issues.

But if the Post-Industrial Revolution has created societal turmoil and substantially eliminated the old organizational role of political parties, the *new* role of party remains unclear. Hitherto, after each realignment period, the two-party system has snapped back with a new logic. How or whether it will do so under post-industrialism remains to be seen. A shift to media-and-communications-based politics may represent as much of a transition in the nature and importance of the party system as the changeover from eighteenth-century aristocratic factionalism to the middle-class party politics of the Industrial Revolution.

Bear in mind that the prevailing pattern of the agricultural era saw political arbitration and patronage in the hands of great landowners—from Whig and Tory aristocrats in England to families such as the Schuylers, Van Rensselaers, and Livingstons in New York's Hudson Valley. As the Industrial Revolution and the party system took hold together, arbitration and patronage tended to flow to business: by the 1890s, entire states were dominated by steel, railroad, and lumber interests, and parties were their creatures. Now, at least in the United States, the Communications Revolution seems to be shifting the essential patronage and arbitration-of-issues role to the media. Not only do the media determine the issues and careers that advance, but many defeated or hopeful politicians (people who once might have courted Schuylers or U. S. Steel) are beginning to seek commentators' positions as the best way to remain in the public eye. Thus, further evolution of the media as the pivotal intermediaries in U.S. politics may mean the end of parties as we have known them, and governmental institutions will also be greatly changed.

C. EXECUTIVE AND LEGISLATIVE INSTITUTIONALIZATION

Since the 1960s, scores of books have been written about the institutionalization of excessive presidential power, but few have dwelt on its effect on party politics. Only a handful of books have been written about the institutionalization of Congress, and, by and large, these have dealt only cursorily with the impact of that shift on the national role of parties. More examination is warranted, because the separate and increasingly hostile institutionalization of Congress and the presidency were major factors in the ineffectiveness of our party system during the 1960s and early 1970s.

Here is the point: For modern party systems to be effective, they must be free to reflect and arbitrate public needs and demands. The American party system has not been able to do this, especially in the past decade, because of the tendency at *both ends* of Pennsylvania Avenue—in Capitol and White House alike —for elected officials to institutionalize their power and maintain their hold on office by technical, managerial, and communications techniques rather than on the basis of party or philosophical appeal. Congressmen, senators, and Presidents alike have clutched eagerly at mushrooming numbers of staff aides and communications tools. And with party differences and labels generally weaker, these predictions at once add to this problem and take advantage of it: Huge staffs and expert communications techniques tend to be especially effective in such a climate.

While Democrats and Whigs might have done the same thing in the pre-Civil War era, they lacked the technical wherewithal and the evolutionary base of the past century. As a result, the realignment years of the 1850s had a political and institutional fluidity able to respond to changing public opinion—even to the point of choosing a President whose election sundered the Union. The Thirty-fifth and Thirty-sixth Congresses were not full of senior and un-beatable committee chairmen or members whose sixteen-man staffs, personal service machinery, and communications advantages enabled them to buck the ebb and flow of weakened party tides. Likewise, such chief executives as Millard Fillmore, Franklin Pierce, and James Buchanan were a pale shadow of current-day Presidents able to almost automatically use incumbency to gain a second term. Indeed, the extent to which politicians in the legislative and executive branches have institutionalized the power (and thus the non-responsiveness) of their offices raises a question of the extent to which the party system is capable of reconstituting itself in a traditional realignment process. The 1972 elections showed that each of the presidential and Congressional "wings" of both parties operated without much real concern for the other wing's interests and tapped substantially different electorates.

Analysis ought to begin with the self-aggrandizement of the executive branch, which, reaching its zenith in the hands of Richard Nixon and the clique of H. R. Haldeman and John Ehrlichman, subordinated the Republican Party of the early 1970s. Most scholars, in characterizing the Nixon administration, take the growth of executive abuse of power back to Lyndon Johnson or John Kennedy. But the dislocating effect of executive growth on the *party system* is a slow but steady progression of changes and circumstances reaching back to the early-nineteenth century.

During the 1840s and 1850s, when the old party system was

dying and the Civil War cleavage gathering embryonic ideological shape, Presidents were ineffectual political animals. Of the seven taking office between 1840 and 1860, not one served more than a single term—and not one was even renominated by his party. As a measure of impotence, this is hard to beat. The period was one of legislative dominance, and, not coincidentally, also one of *laissez faire*. Legislatures dominated when there was little governing to be done, and the shining stars of political Washington were the great Senate orators. The great bulk of the Cabinet came from Congress, the logical source of talent. (Congress was not institutionalized then either; more on that later.)

Like most other conflicts, the Civil War fueled the power of the chief executive. In 1864, Abraham Lincoln became the first President since Andrew Jackson to be renominated and re-elected. Ulysses S. Grant also served two terms (1869–77). Grover Cleveland served two non-consecutive terms (1885–89 and 1893–97) and ran as the Democratic presidential nominee in three straight elections (1884, 1888, and 1892). With the exceptions of men who succeeded to office through death (Andrew Johnson, Chester A. Arthur), presidents during the 1860–96 political cycle were generally renominated. Still, 40 per cent of the Cabinet officers chosen came from Congress.

The next cycle (1896–1932) saw further political power accrue to the President. Without exception, sitting Presidents were renominated for a second term if they wanted it. All won re-election save for William Howard Taft—whose party split in 1912—and Herbert Hoover in 1932. Moreover, such was the emerging leverage of the presidency that even Vice-Presidents succeeding to office through death commanded the wherewithal to win nomination and election to a full term (Theodore Roosevelt, Calvin Coolidge). Fewer Cabinet members were selected from Congress—under one quarter.

1828–1860

After Andrew Jackson's two terms, the presidency was generally weak:

No President was renominated by his party (or re-elected).

Half of the Cabinet came from Congress.

Vice-Presidents were not renominated.

1860–1896

Presidents were often renominated.
Lincoln, Grant and Cleveland were elected to second terms.
40% of the Cabinet came from Congress.
Vice-Presidents succeeding to the presidency were not renominated.

1896–1932

Presidents were invariably renominated if they desired.
Presidents were re-elected except William Howard Taft (a party split) and Herbert Hoover (Great Depression).
20% of Cabinet came from Congress.
Vice-Presidents succeeding to the presidency were renominated and re-elected in their own right.

1932–1972

Presidents were invariably renominated if they desired.
All Presidents seeking re-election won.
15% of Cabinet came from Congress.
Vice-Presidents succeeding to the presidency were renominated and re-elected in their own right.
Vice-Presidents became heirs apparent for their party presidential nominations (Nixon, Humphrey, Agnew, Ford).

CHART 18
The Evolutionary Political Institutionalization of the Presidency

Chart 18 is an attempt to graph the increasing political power of the presidency. The 1932–68 cycle witnessed a major surge. Franklin D. Roosevelt became the first President elected for four terms. All Presidents won renomination; all were re-elected. Not only did Vice-Presidents succeeding to office win another term in their own right, but the vice-presidency became the best jumping-off point for the White House. This represents an extraordinary turnabout. Nobody paid any attention to pre-World War I Vice-Presidents: Thomas Marshall, Garret Hobart, and company. But since Eisenhower's day, Vice-Presidents have invariably become Presidents or presidential candidates: Richard Nixon, Lyndon Johnson, Hubert Humphrey, Spiro Agnew, and Gerald Ford.

These years saw an enormous build-up of executive-branch authority and manpower. Civilian federal employment mushroomed from 1933 to 1968, and the federal budget increased twentyfold. Four new federal departments were created: Defense; Health, Education and Welfare; Housing and Urban Development; and Transportation. The executive branch picked up enormous regulatory powers over business and industry. And, more than that, the post-1933 years saw the growth of a sizable, independent White House staff: up from several dozen when Roosevelt took office to hundreds under Lyndon Johnson (and hundreds of others assigned to the White House by various agencies and departments).

Executive leverage of this magnitude tended to subordinate Congress. During the New Deal, only 2 per cent of the major laws passed were the result of Congressional initiative. A generation earlier, the figure had been nearly 50 per cent. In the first eight years of the New Deal, only 20 per cent of the Roosevelt Cabinet had Congressional experience; between 1941 and 1963, the figure declined to 15 per cent. One expert notes that of *all* the political federal appointments made between 1933 and 1963, only 4 per cent of the appointees had had Congressional experience: "While Congress assiduously insulated itself from executive encroachments, presidents came to rely on a pool of business, academic and military talent that had little experience with legislatures and even less patience, once they were appointed, for dealing with them."[1]

Through the political realignment of 1932, the growth of presidential power, while clearly apparent, was not such as to distort the party system. The White House staff was very small. Presidents worked through their party organizations, albeit with less reliance than in the late-nineteenth century. Interaction with Congress was still important, and former members of the House or Senate were frequently found in the Cabinet. In short, despite the onset of institutionalization, political fluidity prevailed. Presidents tended to be re-elected, but incumbency had not yet lent itself to the theory of the sure thing; and national tides of opinion registered huge turnovers in the membership of Congress, usually guaranteeing that Presidents taking office with new programs did not face hostility on Capitol Hill. Besides which, Democratic or Republican Presidents drew their votes from the same cultural and geographic sources as the congressmen and senators of their party. There was no institutionalization-*cum*-ticket splitting to create the anomaly of the Deep South being Republican for President and Democratic for Congress. At the risk of repetition, there was political fluidity—just as there had been in 1800, 1828, 1860, and 1896.

By the mid-1960s, as countless studies have elaborated, the institutionalization and self-aggrandizement of presidential political power had become notorious. Lyndon Johnson multiplied the White House staff, ignored Congressional wishes, starved the Democratic National Committee, and engineered the nomination of Hubert Humphrey in 1968 despite the fact that the Vice-President had been obliged (largely by time factors not his fault) to sit out the party primaries. Although Johnson had been, at least in part, forced to eschew re-election by public opinion, even the sunset hours of his presidency were strong enough to control and warp party actions.

The election in 1968 of Richard Nixon, committed to reversing the flow of power to Washington and the build-up of bureaucratic power, served to consummate this trend. Thus the political era beginning in 1968 sought not only to ignore the (by now institutionalized) Democratic Congress but to draw power away from the rest of the executive branch (bureaucracy) and into the White House. Richard Nixon's preferences were already in this direction—an inexperienced media-oriented personal clique had run his 1968 campaign—and he gave them free rein. The White House staff was so greatly enlarged, as one disgruntled Republican noted, that the once-prestigious title of Special Assistant to the President had been awarded to advertising account executives and advance men who had earned their spurs handling campaign baggage at the Phoenix airport. Congress was ignored, and even Capitol Hill Republicans were treated with occasional hostility. The Republican National Committee was milked and subordinated. As the years passed by, Nixon's Cabinet was increasingly 1) made up of nonentities and 2) kept under the thumb of the White House staff.

By 1971–72, the stage was set for the impact of this new "fourth branch" of government on the party system. The President's advisers created a Committee to Re-Elect the President separate and apart from the Republican National Committee. The committee (CRP) established its own advertising agency and arranged local deals and pacts with Democratic officeholders as readily as with Republicans. Nixon's 1972 get-out-the-vote mechanism was principally aimed at identifying and bringing to the polls *Democrats* for Nixon although their balloting in other races would presumably hurt the Republican Party. The financial mechanisms of the committee (Finance-CRP) deliberately sopped up money that might otherwise have helped other party candidates, and as late as two weeks before the election, the White House reiterated approval of a policy designed to maximize the Nixon vote at the expense of any other party candidates who might be in the way.

With the Watergate syndrome as an obvious corollary of this behavior pattern, critics have often overlooked some of the unfortunate—but yet understandable—political roots of the runaway presidential clique. First, the influence of the Communications Revolution upon campaigning—beginning in the primaries and later in the general election—has obliged presidential candidates to develop their own personal media and managerial teams outside the party framework. Strong candidates take on an almost feudal coloration: Signing on with a candidate likely to be successful is like choosing which duke or earl for whom to fight in the thirteenth-century wars of plunder (and occasionally a cause or two). The roots of Nixon cliquism go back to John Kennedy and beyond.

What helped make Nixon cliquism so extreme was the multiple influence of 1) a conspiracy-minded reaction to the rifts and the social upheaval of the late sixties and 2) a siege-psychology attitude toward the Washington liberal power structure, which blocked GOP attempts to reform or cut back the programs of the sixties. While the Nixon administration's awareness of these issues was, at best, erratic during the 1969–72 period, there also can be no doubt that the White House faced an unprecedentedly institutionalized Congress and bureaucracy not interested in making such changes. Circa-1972 and -1973 observers liked to argue that the Nixon administration really had no program mandate, because the Democratic Congress had a mandate, too, and the two substantially negated one another. But this was not true. Richard Nixon was elected President by a large majority of Republicans and southern Democrats. Republicans and pro-Nixon conservative Southerners together received about 55–60 per cent of the vote for both House and Senate, and senators and representatives openly or covertly supporting Nixon were a majority in both houses. This point, made less often than it should be, is central to any analysis

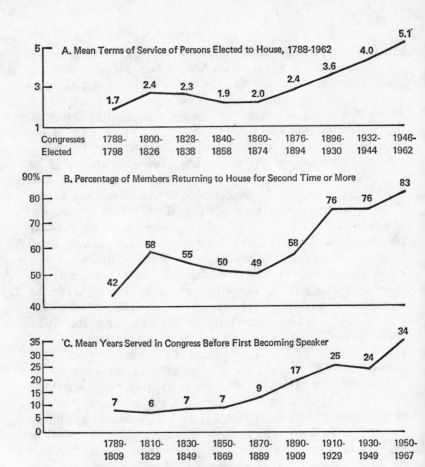

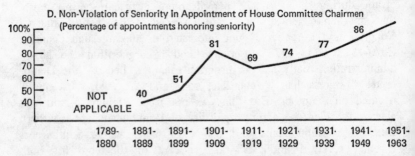

Note: Charts A, B, and D are adapted from data in "The Institutionalization of the House of Representatives," by Nelson Polsby, in *The American Political Science Review* (March 1968). Chart C appears on p. 149.

CHART 19

The Institutionalization of the House of Representatives

of the way in which *Congressional* institutionalization played its own role in the development of governmental non-responsiveness and White House cliquism.

In an era of more fluid politics, the southern Democratic/Republican anomaly would probably have given way before a more logical realignment. National party preferences and Congressional preferences would have shifted in parallel fashion, and Nixon would have had partisan majorities in Congress. Much of his programmatic and political-siege psychology would have been dissipated by interaction with a more sympathetic Capitol Hill leadership. It is possible that southern realignment would have lessened *pre*-Nixon cliquishness as well: Liberal Democratic presidents also regarded Congress as troublesome, with their nominal party majorities often worthless because of the southern Democratic factor.

Essays on GOP/southern Democratic similarities typically gloss over a number of important differences in cultural and political style. Even so, much of the continuing anomaly flows from Congressional institutionalization: 1) lingering questions of seniority and committee rank that have kept key southern conservatives in the Democratic Party and thereby left undisturbed the Democratic majority status that supports a liberal leadership structure and an increasing number of liberal committee chairman, and 2) large staffs and important communications benefits that enable congressmen and senators to avoid the decimation that used to accompany major swings of public opinion. If the realignment of the sixties and seventies had occurred in the fluid institutional context of the 1840s or 1850s, Congress might well have shifted with the presidency. In those days, there was no seniority, no institutionalized committee structures, and no elaborate personal staff or communications mechanisms. So, too, in the realignment period of 1896. By 1932, the seniority system was established, and the beginnings of institutionalization were obvious, but not to the point where political realignment was affected.

The institutionalization of Congress to a point where most of its members can avoid political tides merits brief elaboration.* In the days of Thomas Jefferson, Congress was almost a parliament. Orders came from the White House, and Representative Giles of Virginia, Jefferson's leader in the House, was sometimes referred

* A good discussion, from which some of the following statistics are drawn, is Nelson Polsby's article "The Institutionalization of the House of Representatives," in the June 1972 *American Political Science Review*.

to as the "Prime Minister."[2] Committee chairmen were appointed on the word of the President. But, as party organization weakened under James Madison, Congress seized its own reins and took over effective control of its own appointments and committee structure. Even so, there was no seniority; in the House, committees were appointed by the Speaker; there was little more staff than one would expect in a debating society (as Congress was in this largely *laissez-faire* era); and the job of House Speaker did not go to long-term, experienced, professional legislators but to prominent politicians or public figures who moved in and out of Congress more or less at will. In turn, as shown earlier, former members of the House or the Senate accounted for 40 per cent of the men appointed to the Cabinet between 1860 and 1900. Needless to say, under these conditions the House and Senate were subject to decimation by election swings.

The Civil War brought about little additional institutionalization. Power to make committee assignments still rested with the Speaker, not a seniority system. Staffs were negligible. Speakers continued to come from non-legislative backgrounds and move on to other jobs. Typical members of Congress stayed in office for only one or two terms. As late as 1882, the House of Representatives experienced over 50 per cent membership turnover in one election! Part of the turnover rate reflected the ebb and flow of political tides: off-year Democratic or Republican losses in the House often ran in the 60–100 range during the thirty years after Appomattox.

After the party alignment firmed up, in 1896, things began to change. Representatives began to stay in office longer. The tenure-of-service mean climbed from 2.25 terms in 1895 to 3.11 terms in 1900 and 3.62 terms in 1910. Turnover decreased. The election of 1908 was the first of the century in which less than 20 per cent of the Representatives elected were first-termers. Staff and clerical assistance began its first, hesitant stage of growth. The old House Office Building was built in 1909. Beginning with Representative Joe Cannon of Illinois, in 1903, Speakers tended to be professional legislators with a record of long service in the House. Most important of all, the seniority system began in 1910, with membership and rank on House committees being determined by seniority rather than the whim of the Speaker. As a result of this development, committee jurisdictions also firmed up, and institutionalization got under way.

Not that the process was very far advanced by 1932. Personal and committee staffs remained very small, and the entire Congressional housekeeping appropriation was only $8 million, up from $2.6 million in 1890 and $5 million in 1914. Although biennial turnover in the House of Representatives was in the 13–27 per cent range through the 1920s, it climbed to 37 per cent in the 1932 elections, enough to indicate that real fluidity prevailed in that realignment period. Thereafter, especially during and after World War II, the institutionalization of Congress began in earnest.

Between 1945 and 1974, the budget of the House of Representatives rose from $12 million a year to $145 million a year. The number of clerks and staff assistants allocated to each congressman rose to sixteen—an incredible number compared with the negligible personal staff of a British or Canadian M.P. Part of the explanation is surprisingly simple: As the executive branch gathered more and more control over budget making, defense, foreign affairs, and the like, Congress expended its own staff structure to watch—and counter—the executive. Meanwhile, Congress also kept increasing the staff and communications resources of committees, individual representatives, and senators. Consequently, committees became more and more unresponsive—the creatures of a senior chairman, key professional staffers, or interest groups exerting their leverage from outside. Incumbent senators and congressmen became increasingly difficult to defeat. By 1965, the mean length of service in the House of Representatives was 5.65 terms, more than twice as long as the mean in 1895.

During the nineteen fifties, ticket splitting grew apace, and the election of 1956 marked the first time that less than 10 per cent of the Representatives chosen were first-termers. In 1968 and 1970, the number of first-termers elected stayed in the 10–12 per cent range. Such were the new advantages of staff assistance and communications that legislators were becoming steadily more difficult to beat. Chart 14 shows the growth of ticket splitting in federal elections, a pattern becoming especially strong in the Deep South. Across the Cotton Belt, state after state, district after district, endorsed Republican (or third-party) presidential nominees but elected conservative Democratic senators and congressmen. Many of these men had first gone to Washington during the 1930s, 1940s, or early 1950s—in days when the national Democratic Party was still relatively acceptable below the Mason-Dixon line—and had since accumulated considerable seniority. As of 1968, virtually every deep-southern Democratic senator chaired an important committee. Kindred circumstances prevailed in the House. Because this power would have been lost if these states and districts had elected Republicans, they split their tickets—ignoring Democratic presidential nominees and re-electing their local legislators.

After failing to make any major Congressional gains in 1968, Richard Nixon made one more try—in 1970—and missed again, although the GOP showing was much better than the usual off-year election pattern. But the central weakness of the Nixon administration was its cliquish nature, its disposition to narrow tactics, its relative disinterest in domestic policy on any other grounds except as necessary to maintain itself in office, and—especially —its inability to collude with Congress, Republican Party organizations, and other partially or substantially amenable segments of the community at large.

Such is not the stuff of an administration able to overcome institutionalized forces and bring presidential and Congressional voting patterns into parallelism. On the contrary, the Nixon administration aggravated institutionalized separatism. Nixon's White House chief of staff, H. R. Haldeman, told writer Allen Drury: "I don't think Congress is supposed to work with the White House—it is a different organization, and under the Constitution I don't think we should expect agreement."[3] So motivated, the White House saw no kinship with Republicans in Congress, did little to support them in the 1972 elections, all but endorsed a number of senior southern Democrats, and made over a hundred deals with Democratic congressmen, who, in general, got free rides in a year when an administration of greater depth might have achieved a major realignment. In turn, many Democratic congressmen did their part by totally turning their backs on their presidential nominee. Non-parallelism of party interest and electoral support between Congress and the executive branch reached unprecedented importance.

After the 1972 election, institutional tension between Congress and the White House grew stronger, spurred by the Watergate syndrome (which, in turn, had been nourished by the White House's institutional siege pyschology). But, as of the mid-seventies, there are signs that the institutionalization tide is ebbing—at *both* ends of Pennsylvania Avenue. The Watergate uproar has cut short the White House clique trend. The December 1972 attempt of Richard Nixon and his chief aides to pull all executive-branch power into the

White House may be seen by history as the high-water mark of the runaway presidency. De-institutionalization of Congress also seems to be in motion. Seniority is losing its sway; long-established committee jurisdictions are being reshuffled. Southern influence is fading. Large numbers of senior members decided to retire in 1972 and 1974, giving the turnover rate an upward push.

Institutionalization has been a pivotal factor in the political warp of the late nineteen sixties and early nineteen seventies, blocking party realignment, aggravation systemic non-responsiveness, and contributing to the general malaise of the electorate. De-institutionalization probably required some sort of confrontation—like that which occurred over Watergate—and the extent to which our institutions continue to regain fluidity will play an important role in determining the future of the party system.

5

THE FUTURE OF AMERICAN POLITICS

So FAR, the post-industrial future of American politics has been mapped out only as a series of probable perimeters: the probable imminence of a sixth party system; the possibility that the parties will shed their traditional roles and take a new form in a post-industrial communications society; the need for Congress and the White House to shed their institutionalized hostility and draw closer politically; the obsolescence of "conservative" and "liberal" classifications in a post-industrial society; the probable economic divisions of post-industrial confrontation (traditional sectors versus the non-profit institutions, communications media, and knowledge sector); the regional geography (South and West versus the northeastern and Pacific areas of most-advanced post-industrialism); the political geography of black-white cleavages; the thrust of population trends (youth versus age, South versus North, urban versus suburban); and the difficulty of containing the Post-Industrial Revolution in a traditional, democratic framework.

Within this broad arena, predictions have been general: implications left by the development and statistical presentation of trends that have prevailed up through the mid-1970s. In this final chapter, an attempt will be made to project those trends and statistics forward in time.

A. THE PARTY SYSTEM

By the mid-1970s, speculation on the obsolescence of the existing party system, far from being confined to the United States, was on the upswing from Canada and Australia to Scandinavia. While the pattern varies from country to country, a general pattern does emerge: voters are becoming less and less content with a party system rooted in either a) industrial-era cleavages between conservative and labor/social-democratic parties or b) traditional (often pre-industrial) regional, ethnic, and religious divisions.

Persons interested in full documentation of these international shifts will have to find it elsewhere, but here is a quick portrait. To begin with Britain, by the nineteen seventies, public fatigue with the Conservatives and trade-union-dominated Labourites had stimulated a revival of the Liberal Party, based on two major new sources of strength: a) Celtic-fringe rural areas (Scotland, Cornwall, Devon, and others) historically suspicious of both capital *and* labor, and b) middle-class areas substantially populated by young professionals and white-collar workers disenchanted with both major parties and receptive toward the Liberal Party's vague progressivism and emphasis upon decentralization and industrial profit sharing. Observers reported voters describing both parties as overidentified with yesteryear's class conflicts and economic divisions. For a while in 1973, British polls showed the Liberal Party actually drawing abreast of Labour and the Conservatives.

Across the Atlantic, more and more Canadians have been jumping out of *their* nineteenth-century-based system—Tories versus Liberals, both parties essentially middle class and middle-of-the-road in outlook—in order to support the New Democrats, a reform party somewhat akin to the McGovern Democrats and similarly weighted with academicians, minority groups, students, and young professionals. By 1974, the New Democrats controlled three provincial governments.

In Germany and Scandinavia, social-democratic parties have followed their doctrines steadily leftward, stirring middle-class apprehension at the prospect of more socialism and the reality of more taxes. But early-nineteen-seventies election results suggested that such parties, rooted in the conflicts of the industrial era, are reaching a point of diminishing returns as more voters move into middle-class status and lose empathy with class-conflict and socialist doctrine. Meanwhile, traditional conservative parties have not been the principal beneficiaries of public unrest (for example, Germany's Christian Democratic Union was slipping during the post-Adenauer decade, Sweden's Conservatives felt obliged to change their name, and Denmark's Conservatives lost as heavily in the 1973 elections as the Socialists). Instead, inroads have been made by new parties approximating the ideological appeal of Britain's Liberals, although sometimes—as in the Danish general election of 1973—voicing a stiffer position against oppressive income-tax levels.

In a kindred vein, the Netherlands' old party system is also eroding. But, in this instance, it is a case of religious parties based on traditional Catholic-Protestant rivalry. Young people and white-collar professionals are leading the shift to non-religious parties. Outside of northern and western Europe and the English-speaking nations, the recurrent pattern is less obvious.

Minimally relevant as these circumstances may seem to the changing pattern of U.S. politics, there *is* a common link: Britain, Canada, northern Europe, the Netherlands, and Australia, along with the United States, make up Herman Kahn's Zone 1. By Kahn's criteria, this is the old industrial-era stronghold of Protestant-ethic economic motivation and middle-class morality, now the center of exploding communications and technology—in short, of the *Post-Industrial Revolution*. Not surprisingly, this shift is reflected in the weakening of parties based on yesterday's socioeconomics. At their 1973 Conference, the liberal parties of seven western European countries saw a "liberal renaissance in Europe" at the expense of conservatives and socialists. Representatives of the various liberal parties emphasized their shared broad concern for individual rights—expressed in such policies as profit sharing and worker participation in industry, and decentralization of government. Vague as these principles may be, they tap the alienation of the new class from both industrialist-*cum*-landed-gentry conservatism or socialist labor-union militance and preoccupation with nationalization of industries. Some European politicians have made direct reference to the industrial-era-based obsolescence of existing party systems: to wit, this November 1973 statement in the House of Lords by Lord Alport, a former Conservative government minister:

. . . The foundations of the Industrial Society of the 19th and 20th Centuries upon which the prosperity and livelihood of the people of this country was based—abundant and easily accessible raw materials, and unchallenged superiority of technical skill and industrial know-how, cheap food, protected imperial markets and worldwide prestige—have all largely disappeared. Yet the political posture of the great parties and the organization and the attitude of management and workers to each other and to the community have, in general terms, changed hardly at all.[1]

Some of the same points can be argued with respect to the U.S. party system, and the follow-up question poses itself rather starkly in two parts: 1) Can we expect a post-industrial party system (or sixth party system, to adopt Walter Dean Burnham's terminology) to use the existing Republican and Democratic party frameworks; and 2) once new party alignments are clear, can we expect post-industrial-society party organizations to function in the traditional nineteenth–twentieth-century style?

As chapter 3 should have made clear, the *presidential*-level Republican and Democratic parties have tentatively realigned themselves along ideological, regional, and demographic lines fundamentally compatible with post-industrial cleavages. Evolutionary rather than revolutionary, the shift took place in the presidential elections of 1960, 1964, 1968, and 1972. Map 15 shows how the 1972 presidential-party alignment closely parallels the relative conservatism or liberalism of state Congressional delegations. This being the case, our politics would have a post-industrial coherence except for one compelling difficulty: mixed-up parties. The relative liberalism or conservatism of state Congressional delegations may correspond very closely to party voting for President, but, *within* the House and Senate, there is only partial correlation between ideology and party. Although one can safely describe most Democratic legislators as liberals, the most conservative states—Alabama, Mississippi, Louisiana, et al.—continue to elect conservative Democrats to Congress. Meanwhile, some of the most liberal states—for example, Massachusetts—elect GOP "progressives," whose voting records are out of kilter with most of their GOP colleagues.

Most-liberal states: 1973 Americans for democratic action ratings: states where House delegation and/or Senate delegation was rated over 65 per cent correct in voting.

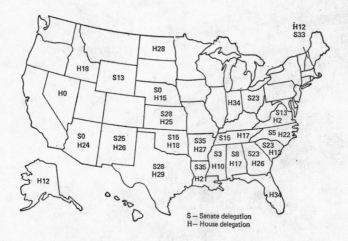

Most-conservative states: 1973 Americans for democratic action ratings: states where House delegation and/or Senate delegation was rated under 35 per cent correct in voting.

MAP 15
The Ideological Division of National Politics

A) THE DEMOCRATS

States over 40% for Eugene McCarthy in 1968 presidential primaries

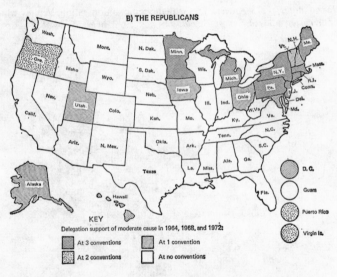

B) THE REPUBLICANS

KEY
Delegation support of moderate cause in 1964, 1968, and 1972:

At 3 conventions   At 1 convention
At 2 conventions   At no conventions

MAP 16
The Common Geography of Intraparty Ideology

In recent years, the ideological anomaly has been easing: such liberal areas as the upper Midwest and New England are electing more and more liberal Democrats to Congress, and such conservative regions as Dixie are electing more and more conservative Republicans. Even so, there is still a major lag, and on the courthouse and municipal level, the lag is greater. For many reasons, ranging from local organizational strength and institutionalized government to ticket splitting and pure convenience, the local party system in the United States still reflects industrial-era divisions: business on the Republican side, organized labor as a mainstay of the Democrats; rural Yankee courthouses in GOP hands, southern counties run by the Democrats. This factor keeps over-all party lines blurred and unclear, and hinders the parties from developing new vitality based on clearly post-industrial ideological identities.

Neither of the broad-based traditional parties seems able to make the adjustment. On the presidential level, the internal alignment of the Republican Party reflects the divisions of post-industrialism. Map 16 was prepared by the liberal-Republican Ripon Society to show the states that backed the progressive GOP cause at the 1964–72 national conventions. By and large, the liberal votes came from the areas of most-advanced post-industrialism: New England, the Northeast, the upper Midwest, and the Pacific coast. Dominant-party conservatives tend to be concentrated in the South and West. But this regionalism only illustrates that the ideological lines apparent in presidential voting have little local logic.

On the Republican side, party organizations tend to be dominated by businessmen and lawyers—heavily Protestant, Anglo-Saxon, and middle to upper-middle class. This coloration has changed little from industrial-era days. Blue-collar, ethnic, and poor-rural elements, increasingly amenable to casting conservative ballots, are minimally represented in GOP leadership ranks. Thus, despite the shift in control of the national party from the northeastern establishment to the new forces of the South and West, one can only say that power has passed from the boardrooms of Manhattan and the clubrooms of Boston to the petroleum clubs of Texas and the defense-industry suburbs of California; as of 1974, it has not passed to blue-collar workers, northern urban ethnics, or southern Wallaceites.

Continuing middle-class WASP domination has been a major problem for the GOP. If the Yankee farmers and businessmen of New England, upstate New York, or Ohio were unappealing to the average Polish-American or southern poor white, so are the country clubbers of Phoenix, Anaheim, and Orlando. What is more, neither

WASP element—old-line Yankee moderates or Arizona country-club conservatives—has been anxious to welcome ethnic or Wallaceite recruits on a basis of social and decision-making equality. The conservatives fear their populist economics; the moderates worry about their cultural populism.

Because of this old-line WASP demographic base—underscored by the parade of short-haired Anglo-Saxons before the Watergate Committee—many observers doubt that the Republican Party can become the instrumentality of a new majority. Or at least there is good reason to doubt that it can do so in the traditional manner of politics: by a metamorphosis of leadership and growth of local strength. Instead, the technique of the presidential-level Republicanism epitomized by the 1972 Committee to Re-elect the President, has been to take advantage of the leftward tilt of the presidential Democratic Party, to ignore the grass-roots GOP, and to concentrate on media activity and campaign technology. While this communications-based approach has had superficial success on the national level, it has contributed to the atrophy of many state and local Republican parties, and to GOP weakness in Congress, state legislatures, and municipal government. Nor is any traditional-pattern renaissance likely. Little has been done to attune local GOP organizations to post-industrial alignments, and party organizations are losing adherents among young people and middle-class professionals.

This underscores the possibility that the Republican Party is nearing the end of its service as the traditional-type vehicle of American politics: On one hand, the GOP is losing chunks of its upper-income industrial-era constituency, from New England to the Pacific Northwest, and on the other hand, it has not been able to recruit and organize day-to-day support among the new blue-collar and Wallaceite "conservatives" of the post-industrial era. Party identification has been slipping (from 28 per cent in 1969 to 24 per cent in 1974, according to the Gallup Poll). Given such erosion, some observers speculate that the party may succumb to history and give way to another, better able to mobilize post-industrial constituencies.

In this case, the GOP might "go the way of the Whigs." Back in the eighteen fifties, although the Jacksonian Democratic coalition had clearly outlived its philosophic logic, the Whigs were not the party to take advantage of the crumbling Democratic majority. Although their "Know-Nothing" political kinsmen scored heavily in the elections of 1854, the Whigs faded dramatically by 1856. Throughout most of the North, nearly all (85 per cent) of the Whig electorate went into the GOP, and so did a critical bloc of Jacksonian Democrats (mostly Free-Soil and anti-slavery Yankees) who had refused to join the Whigs. The result was a new alignment and a new majority. If the seventies are to witness a traditional party-system reconstruction, then the parallel may be a good one: The collapse of the Whigs signaled the collapse of an entire party system, including the old *Democratic* coalition. More likely, though, traditional party systems are finished—undercut by the Post-Industrial Revolution—and Republican/Democratic disintegration no longer implies the evolution of a new grass-roots, organizationally based party.

In contrast to the GOP, the Democrats are much stronger at state and local levels than they have been in presidential contests. Many of these local loyalties—meaningless in a national context—go back to obsolescent criteria of 1860, 1896, or 1932, and this grass-roots kaleidoscope of cultural and ideological groups enables Democratic strategists to make continual references to breadth of appeal and plausibility of coalitional revitalization. However, just as the presidential GOP hasn't broken through at the grass roots, Democrats have trouble at the national level. Since 1964, their conventions have exhibited how little the shared name "Democrat" means in the hot ideological cockpit of focused national issues. Many voters who find the name locally palatable have routinely voted for GOP Presidents since the 1950s. In both the 1968 and 1972 elections, about 30–40 per cent of those calling themselves Democrats—mostly moderates and conservatives—declined to vote for their party presidential nominees. Infidelity of this magnitude underscores the exhaustion of the New Deal coalition.

Nor are the divisions within the Democratic Party temporary ones likely to ease. As previously indicated, the University of Michigan Survey Research Center analyzed the Democratic "coalition" after the 1972 election and found its conservative and liberal wings more ideologically at odds with each other than the sum total of Democrats were with the sum total of Republicans. The Michigan researchers found that liberals were dominant by a 2–1 ratio, and this squares with the 1960–72 evolution of the presidential Democratic Party as a creature of northeastern, upper-midwestern and Pacific Coast liberalism. There is no reason to anticipate any basic reversal of this pattern even if national Democratic candidates do manage to move enough toward the center to substantially exceed their 1968 presidential vote (43 per cent) or their 1972 level (38 per cent). For the Democrats to undo the evolution of the sixties—and subordinate post-industrial left-liberalism—would be a turnabout without historical precedent.

Far more likely, the presidential Democratic Party will continue to pivot on a national base of post-industrial interest groups, middle-class liberals, and minority groups. Despite possible short-term renaissance, the blue-collar-based AFL-CIO, big city machines, and senior Southerners are likely to continue losing power in the *long term* because of their roots in another era. At the same time, there is little likelihood of the Democratic Party collapsing or seeking a new presidential-level name, however weak party loyalties and organizational ties may be. In contrast to the name "Republican," the label "Democrat" is a link to a *majority* past and tradition rather than a *minority* one; besides which, the name and image is no obstacle to picking up support from young voters and liberalizing professional classes (whereas the name "Republican" is a major cultural block to wooing many Southerners, ethnics, and labor-union members).

If the Whig analogy comes into play, the Democrats of the nineteen seventies, like the Democratics of the eighteen fifties, seem ready to split. Alienated conservatives are ripe for a new alliance. But communications-age circumstances may not lend themselves to—or even permit—the type of grass-roots realignment and new party organization that took shape just before the Civil War.

More likely than not, the sixth U.S. party system will not have the organizational depth of its predecessors. Broad-based nineteenth-century parties, like those still existing in the last (1932) realignment, appear doomed. The new presidential parties will focus on two things: 1) ideology and 2) communications technology. Both denominators flow from the increasing impact of post-industrialism.

Ideology: While previous U.S. party systems have emphasized issues along with regional, economic, and cultural tensions, ideology has never played the role that it is already playing under post-industrialism. After analyzing the 1972 presidential election, four scholars from the University of Michigan Center for Political Studies argued that "for the first time in twenty years, party identification was less important than issues as an explanation of the vote."[2] This issue politics has been building up for a number of years, the CPS analysts asserted, partly in response to communications upheaval: "The past 12 years have witnessed an increased articulation of the ideological differences between the parties, as well as profound social and cultural turbulence that has been immediately and widely transmitted by the mass media."

Speculation that the United States is shifting to European-style ideological and class politics misses the point. Such European cleavages occurred in the context of industrial-era conflict, but the issues focused in the communications cockpit of U.S. post-industrialism are substantially different: more *social* (lifestyle) and less *economic* (in the direct labor-capital sense). After all, social conflicts in post-industrial American politics are a far cry from the tensions of the Ruhr or Welsh coal-mining country. For one thing, the new U.S. politics of ideology are based in relative affluence rather than relative deprivation. In contrast to such European issues as nationalization, government housing, family allowance, and higher taxes on the rich, the CPS 1972 election study identified a basically cultural-lifestyle string of top U.S. issues: Vietnam, economic guarantees for minorities, campus unrest, treatment of criminals, legalization of marijuana, busing, and urban unrest. *This* is the sort of ideological controversy that flows from intensive media coverage of post-industrial-society tensions.

In the wake of the 1972 presidential election, a growing number of academicians believe that ideology is here to stay and that mobilization of the country along ideological lines probably dooms the traditional parties to decomposition and/or metamorphosis into a different breed of institution.

Communications Technology: Increasingly ideological U.S. politics—developing in the context of a decaying party system—are both a consequence of, and a further invitation to, emphasis on communications. As the old party lines lose meaning, politicians and strategists are turning to media, marketing, and image-shaping techniques. In *The Election Men,* David Lee Rosenbloom describes how the cost of elections has soared—"up to $1 billion may have been spent in pursuit of all the elective offices available in the U.S. in 1972"—as professional campaign managers, consultants, and media planners took over functions previously handled by the parties. The great surge, of course, came during the nineteen sixties.

Most analysts agree that the Republican Party has been in the vanguard of this trend, with GOP candidates and managers demonstrating the greatest penchant for high-cost, high-technology politics. This reflects the GOP's relative affluence, bias toward business (and marketing) approaches, and dearth of interest in ideas. But, in recent years, as the white-collar and professional New Politics element has come to the fore in the Democratic Party, the use of skilled political technology has become general. As a consequence, Walter Dean Burnham and others see U.S. parties evaporating as broad intermediaries between the people and their rulers, and assuming a mixed function of screening candidates, providing a name and limited vote base, and furnishing a basic communications and financial framework. If the Communications Revolution is transforming the national parties into vehicles of such limited function, the chance of any broad-based realignment is negligible. New parties could operate easily without year-to-year organizational magnitude. Increasingly ideological quadrennial selection of a president would take place on a plane all its own. Presidential-level changes need not occur locally; indeed, they cannot.

None of this means that history, culture, ethnicity, and regionalism won't be important: They will be—but as presidential coalition-assembling factors that can be appealed to with diminishing reference to national party names and loyalties. If the national parties become such limited-function vehicles, their own future is blurry. As of the mid-seventies, after post-industrial evolution, the national Republican Party has been the vehicle for casting a center-right (or moderate-to-conservative) vote in presidential elections, while the Democratic Party has been the vehicle for left-to-center presidential preference. Ideological division is likely to intensify if new parties or fusion arrangements bring about further changes in the existing system.

B. POST-INDUSTRIAL
IDEOLOGY

Despite the difficulties of applying conservative-versus-liberal terminology to the political circumstances of the seventies, the electorate has been little concerned with strict semantics. Since the early sixties, according to virtually every public-opinion survey, liberals have lost ground and more people have identified themselves as "conservative."

Louis Harris found reaction against Watergate pushing voters toward more-liberal over-all views. But most pollsters disagreed.

Pollster Albert Sindlinger, finding that conservatives outnumbered liberals by more than two to one in early 1974, asked both ideological groups how they came to their present status. Only a handful of upper-middle-class people identified themselves as liberals who had once been conservatives. In contrast, about 40 per cent of the moderates and conservatives identified themselves as onetime liberals (see Chart 20). Most pinpointed their change as coming after 1963. For many, it was a question of becoming economic "haves" instead of "have nots" and no longer seeing merit in social programs that help the poor or minority groups. Others blend these attitudes with ideological animosity toward busing, marijuana, pornography, drug pushers, and criminals.* Socioeconomic selfishness—a concern for status security—rather than commitment to tradition, underlay the new "conservatism." Many of the new conservatives were Democrats or ex-Democrats from southern, blue-collar, or ethnic electoral groups with Populist traditions. To call them conservatives may be superficially useful, but it is technically inaccurate.

While fewer people identify themselves as liberals, they also do so for a mixture of partly accurate and partly obsolescent reasons. Some think of themselves as part of pollster Louis Harris' coalition for social change, but a considerable number of "liberals" still call themselves that because of Roosevelt-era economic traditions, and they are uncomfortable with the liberalism of the post-industrial new class. If ideology is to serve as the basis for a new political system, a little more ironing out will be necessary first.

Both "sides" seem to be aware of this. "Old liberals" of the Henry Jackson-George Meany stripe have continued to describe themselves as liberals, while taking pains to differentiate themselves from the "new" liberals—whom they sometimes attempt to characterize as nonliberal elitists. Meanwhile the New Politics "liberals" describe the Jackson-Meany set as conservatives or reactionaries. Jumping over to the Republican side, the liberal Ripon Society has taken to calling such GOP moderates as Charles Percy the "Old Right" in contrast to a "New Right" which is not genuinely conservative but radical. Meanwhile, the New Right—from Southern California John Birch members to the New York Irish—likes to style itself as conservative, and dis-

---

* In a survey published in January 1974 by the New York *Times*, pollster Daniel Yankelovich found that New York City voters had moved to the right between 1970 and 1973 in response to these and other social issues.

Public Trend Away from Liberal Viewpoint

REPUBLICANS, DEMOCRATS, INDEPENDENTS: AN IDEOLOGICAL PROFILE

"Do you think of yourself as a conservative, moderate or liberal?"

	Democrats	Independents	Republicans	No Interest	Total Population
Conservative	22%	38%	55%	13%	34%
Moderate	47%	44%	30%	25%	41%
Liberal	29%	14%	12%	7%	18%
Other	2%	4%	3%	55%	7%

THE EROSION OF LIBERAL SYMPATHIES

If moderate or conservative, "did you ever consider yourself a liberal?"

	Democrats	Independents	Republicans
YES	35%	41%	10%
NO	64%	56%	89%
Don't Know/ Refused	1%	2%	1%

PRINCIPAL REASONS FOR CHANGE CITED BY FORMER LIBERALS

(Exceeds 100% because of repeated mention)

	Democrats	Independents	Republicans
1. Economic Conditions/ Need to Save Money	39%	36%	16%
2. Taking Care of Self/ Social Advancement	26%	34%	21%
3. Viewpoints Changed With Age/ With Marriage	24%	23%	22%
4. Radical Changes Not Always Good	10%	19%	10%
5. Do Not Agree With Current Liberal Viewpoints	14%	7%	14%
6. Political Leanings Follow Those of President	10%	21%	3%

CHART 20
Public Trend Away from Liberal Viewpoint

misses the moderate Republicans of the Northeast as "liberals." Here again, the confusing babble is reminiscent of politics in the 1850s.

As discussed in chapter 2, the terms "conservative" and "liberal" are creatures of nineteenth-century economic relationships, and they do not make much sense in the politics of the nineteen seventies. Even so, inasmuch as they are so prevalent and persistent in everyday political usage, it is necessary to try to sort out where the various semantic factions are headed. To this end, it is useful to refer to the maps of presidential and Congressional ideological patterns (Maps 15 and 16, pp. 195 and 196).

The old liberals and the New Right share a general electoral base in the South, the West, and in ethnic or middle-class northern neighborhoods. More people in these areas label themselves as "conservative" than do so in the nation as a whole, and those who continue to call themselves "liberal" tend to do so for fading industrial-era economic reasons. In 1972, these were the most *conservative* parts of the country in presidential and Congressional voting, but a similar set of maps for 1932 would show that these areas were then the most *liberal* sections of the nation, when industrial-era economics was front and center. Note that this "conservatism" is hardly the staid, traditional variety and that the predominant political heritage of these sections is *Democratic* rather than Republican. Few persons in "Conservative Movement" politics understand these changing dynamics or their implications, and conservative economic policy has shown little ability to make the necessary adjustment, although the 1974 elections stirred winds of realization and change.

At the same time, upper-middle-class elements formerly on the conservative Republican side—i.e., the Old Right—are clearly finding more and more in common with elite liberalism and less and less with a "conservatism" taking on the coloration of Lockheed Aircraft, George Wallace country, and the Italo-American suburbs of New York City. Congressional Republicans from fashionable northern urban and suburban areas clearly moved to the left during the 1964–74 decade, and the same can be said of William F. Buckley's social respectability-questing journal *National Review*. From St. Mark's and St. Paul's to Stanford University, the children of the Old Right are demonstrating growing affinity for the New Left (assuming one describes the New Left not in the *passé* terminology of Mario Savio but in the economic context of new-class liberal elitism).

Confusing as it may seem, the hubbub can be made to yield a logic. On one hand, the Old Left and the New Right seem to be in a convergence pattern with respect to many social issues, and economic-labor issues constitute the lingering divisions. Likewise, the Old Right and New Left—the elite knowledge-sector axis of both parties —seem bound to move closer. Again, though, economic/labor issues have a divisive effect. But as post-industrial economics take hold, the divisions between Old-Left blue-collar workers and the New Right will ease, and so will those between the old elite and the new. The meeting ground is a combination of social "conservatism" and economic activism.

In a 1974 book *The Jaws of Victory,* the liberal Republican Ripon Society began to focus on the split within "conservatism"—and the probability of a division whereby the northeastern-based Old-Right minority split away to ally with the liberals, leaving the New Right to edge toward the statist ideology of the populist-labor Old Left.[1] They argue that "the independent economic interest is fast disappearing, and like so many reform movements in the Republican past, the Old Right must rely now more upon intellectuals and non-economic concerns for its support."[2] Although technically perceptive, the Ripon analysis is a bit argumentative—categorizing the Old Right as committed to personal, political, intellectual, and economic freedom while criticizing the New Right for bias toward corporatism, nationalism, national security, and government paternalism.

Under such circumstances, the New Right, although borrowing the name "conservative" from industrial-era elitism, would be profoundly *unconservative.* Historically, conservatism has traditionally advocated a minimal or reduced government role and has opposed a build-up of executive-branch or White House power. These attitudes may be changing. To be sure, the New Right will continue to oppose welfare and social spending. But there is likely to be increased support for middle-class economic-security programs, control of the economy, assistance for troubled industries, and regulation of media power. Meanwhile, many liberals are picking up the old conservative theme of restraining government power. The embryonic turnabout is important: the old conservative ideology is a carryover from a period when conservatism was an economic elite fending off government activity, whereas the New Right recognizes different circumstances arising from a) the populist nature of its new constituencies and b) the historic pattern for anti-elitists to use government activity to restrain the power of an economic elite.

As of the mid-nineteen seventies, the new U.S. establishment is liberal: the media, universities, bureaucracies, and the rest of the emerging knowledge-sector elite. Forty years of government action and growth have made this aggregation of power a *fait accompli,* absent a major basic shift in the direction of government. Balanced budgets, marginally reduced government spending, and minor pruning of public payrolls—all the shibboleths of the Old Right—*can no longer undo the basic institutionalization of liberal power.* Many among the new class are showing a new interest in restraint of government lest its power be harnessed—as the Nixon administration attempted—to curb liberal freedoms, privileges, and interests.

Because of the increasing *reversal* of elite functions between liberals and conservatives, historic attitudes toward the activist role of government may also be shifting. The Ripon Society has expressed fear that the activist doctrines of the New Right "provide the logical philosophy to unify the New Majority coalition of Southerner, Northern working-class Catholic and Republican businessman, thereby bringing into the 'Republican' Party the two largest elements of Franklin Roosevelt's Democratic coalition."[3] They argue that "we have seen how the doctrine of economic security might unify business and labor; it is also easy to demonstrate how the doctrine of status security can unify the Southern Anglo-Saxon conservative Protestant and the Northern ethnic conservative Catholic." Daniel Bell's sociological theses of post-industrial political decision making also support an analysis that "conservative" groups must take a course of governmental activism to assert their interests and restrict their elite foes in the fashion of the Jefferson, Jackson, Bryan, and Roosevelt coalitions.

Media power may turn out to be among the most important focal points of this activism. More and more conservatives are perceiving its centrality. In March 1974, White House aide Patrick Buchanan argued that the national liberal media stand as a bigger obstacle than the Democratic Party to a successful conservative counterrevolution. And Dartmouth Professor Jeffrey Hart made the same point to the American Political Science Association's 1974 convention:

> The capacity of the media to determine the terms of the public debate gives it, at least for extended periods, a political

leverage that may well be superior to that of a variegated and often ill-informed Congress. . . . The key struggle, on the frequent occasions when a centrist or a conservative occupies the White House, will be between the President and the media, and it will be a contest over public opinion.[4]

If this theme intensifies, debate over the status of the media—pubic versus private control—may become as important an item of the agenda of post-industrial politics as control of capital has been for the industrial era. What is more, the theoretical parallel may be very real, with the populist-conservative position representing a kind of McLuhan-era Marxism.

With traditional conservative and liberal ideology more and more obsolete under the conditions and economic alignments of post-industrialism, new categories are likely to evolve in order to better represent the ideas and constituencies in conflict. Because the existing terms "conservative" and "liberal" camouflage or blur emerging divisions within their obsolescent nomenclature, they should diminish in currency. The terms "right" and "left," also having had their genesis in the French Revolution, are also obsolescent.

Thus, as of the mid-seventies, terminological-*cum*-ideological realignment seems necessary and probable to recast political debate and division around the issues of the post-industrial society. That these divisions will continue to support broad-based parties is unlikely; more plausibly, national politics will ideologize on a *communications* rather than a *party* base (which in turn will intensify the post-industrial nature of ideological conflict).

C. THE DEMOGRAPHY OF POWER

In contrast to most modern nations, where basic settlement patterns have been fixed for centuries, U.S. population shifts have played a major role in national life—and in national politics. The rise of the trans-Appalachian "New West" played a major role in establishing the Jacksonian coalition. Then, in the 1850s, as the demographic balance began to tilt in favor of the westward-expanding North against the South, changing population patterns helped bring on the Civil War. By the nineteen twenties, the coming of age of the immigrant cities—high birth rates going hand in hand with urbanization—set the scene for the New Deal coalition.

As of the nineteen seventies, it is possible to pinpoint three key trends: 1) the movement of population to the Sun Belt and the northern knowledge-sector axis (New England-upper Midwest-Pacific Northwest); 2) suburbanization and the black-white polarization of the cities; and 3) the youth surge of the sixties and early seventies, followed by the rapid rise in the median age during the late seventies and eighties.

1. Regional Tides   Since the ratification of the U. S. Constitution, in 1789, the nation's population center has moved west—and a bit south—from Baltimore to Mascoutah, Illinois, near St. Louis. By 1980, the marker is likely to cross the Big Muddy into southern Missouri, and by the year 2000, it may well be in Arkansas—and on the way to Oklahoma. Power is moving the same way: south and west toward the Florida-to-California Sun Belt.

At the beginning of the New Deal era, the nation's demographic weight, like its financial weight, was centered in the industrial states of the Northeast and the Great Lakes. Chart 21 shows the shift in electoral votes away from Massachusetts, New York, Pennsylvania, and Ohio, toward the Sun Belt states of Florida, Texas, Arizona, and California.

CHART 21

The Changing Demography of U.S. Presidential Elections

Electoral Votes by Decade

	1930	1940	1950	1960	1970
Massachusetts	17	16	16	14	14
New York	47	47	45	43	41
Pennsylvania	36	35	32	29	27
Ohio	26	25	25	26	25
Florida	7	8	10	14	17
Texas	23	23	24	25	26
Arizona	3	4	4	5	6
California	22	25	32	40	45

To be sure, this is a great oversimplification of the population movement of the past few decades. The non-white shift—more on this later—has gone the other way: from the rural South to the urban North. And even white population movement, while predominantly to the South and West, has divided into several important streams. As some demographers have pointed out, residents of the center of the nation—the people of the Dakotas, Missouri, or Appalachia—have been moving toward the several rims: Not just the Florida-to-California Sun Belt but also the university districts, research parks, and ecology-scapes of the Pacific Northwest, Minnesota, the Washington-to-Boston corridor, and upper New England. The old industrial and rural heartland is losing population to the divergent strongholds of post-industrialism. And these growth poles, in turn, probably suggest the basic divisions of the future.

The top figure of Map 17 shows the states above the fortieth parallel that scored the largest 1960–70 population gains. This is the economic geography of the new class. All these areas are among the most liberal in the nation, as previous data have shown. And this local liberalism is, in many ways, a direct function of 1) shifting local economies and 2) the burgeoning population and influx of young students, white-collar workers, and professionals.*

New England is the archetype of a region *losing* population and jobs in one sector—yesteryear's manufacturing industries—while *gaining* residents and employment via the services and high-technology industries and the knowledge sector. Chart 22 shows the shift of jobs. In economic terms, the shift is a definite plus and can be expected to intensify.

Economic analyses of New England's future make no bones about the change-over. Frederick Glantz, a regional economist with the Federal Reserve Bank of Boston, believes that New England reached its industrial peak in the late 1800s and has been going downhill ever since as other regions nibble at the area's industrial base. He says that "we ought not to grieve over the loss of manufacturing jobs but realize the strength offered by development of such exportable services as education, medicine, consumer software, insurance, management consulting and tourism."[1]

Warren A. Johnson, of the Industrial National Bank of Rhode

* Colorado, which shares many of the change patterns of knowledge-sector growth areas, ought to be included with this group rather than with the South-west. Establishment-allied voting patterns, well established along the Pacific since World War II, are now spreading into some of the more fashionable areas of the Rocky Mountains. Colorado is the only clear example.

Percentage increase in state population, 1960-70

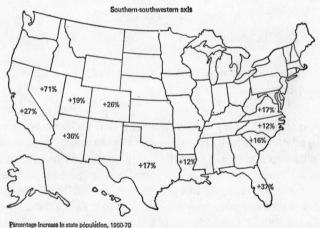

Percentage increase in state population, 1960-70

MAP 17
Areas of Principal 1960–70 Population Growth

Island, argues: "What New England is good at is management and capital. We have maintained our reputation as a center of education and research. In the long run, manufacturing simply is not cost efficient enough for New England, but the rest of the country will be looking to us for financing and managerial expertise."[2]

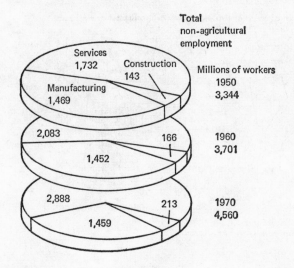

Total
non-agricultural
employment

Services 1,732
Construction 143
Manufacturing 1,469

Millions of workers
1950
3,344

2,083
166
1,452
1960
3,701

2,888
213
1,459
1970
4,560

CHART 22
The Dramatic Shift in New England's Labor Force

In a special survey published in August 1973, the editors of *Business Week* observed:

A mature economy such as New England's appears to nourish the growth of such [high-value] services. Cost and geographical liabilities to traditional manufacturing operations have little impact on medicine or insurance. And a strong sense of history boosts the Ivy League image that has helped build the great higher education complex of New England. It is estimated that these six states have 10% of U.S. colleges—including Harvard, Yale, MIT, Brown, Dartmouth and the Universities of Massachusetts and Connecticut. Such schools not only provide an export industry but generate major spin-offs in terms of technology companies, consultation businesses and educational services. . . . In short, New England may be showing how to achieve quality rather than quality growth. If it succeeds—and the six-state region faces plenty of serious problems—the results will not only enormously benefit New England, but also provide a valuable textbook for other parts of the country which, as their own younger industries mature, may be forced to look for the same kind of economic Geritol.[3]

Although manufacturing employment remains high in New England, the regional ethos has clearly shifted: No other section of the country is so clearly geared to the knowledge sector and its values. Ultimately, some economists argue, what draws people to New England is its lifestyle: a well-educated and highly skilled population, arts and culture, rather progressive state governments, and a generally pleasant environment.

If greater Boston leads the nation in asserting the knowledge-sector ethos, the upper Midwest and Pacific Northwest are not far behind (see chapter 3 for the cultural geography). And these states, too, are gaining population in sharp contrast to the stagnation of the rural farm belt and the old industrial Midwest. Oregon has gained attention for ecology, progressivism, lifestyle, and attempts to discourage settlers coming in from out of state. San Francisco is another new-morality/knowledge-sector stronghold. As for Minnesota, *Time* magazine singled the state out for an August 1973 cover story on "The Good Life in Minnesota." Culture and knowledge-industry factors topped the list:

"Over the past ten years, Minnesota has become one of the nation's leading 'brain industry' centers—more than 170 electronic and related technical businesses now employ more than 70,000 people. . . . Politics is almost unnaturally clean—no patronage, virtually no corruption. The citizens are well-educated; the high-school drop-out rate, 7.6%, is the nation's lowest. Minnesotans are remarkably civil; their crime rate is the third-lowest in the nation (after Iowa and Maine). By a combination of political and cultural tradition, geography and sheer luck, Minnesota nurtures an extraordinarily successful society."[4]

From New England to the Pacific Northwest, the basic demographic appeal is much the same: growing knowledge-sector employment, top-quality schools, progressive and civic-minded government traditions, extensive cultural facilities, and a position in the vanguard of the U.S. civil-rights, ecology, peace, and consumer movements. As indicated previously, there is also a definite overlap of this region with the historical geography of "Greater New England." People of a particular bent are already concentrated in this region—and others of similar bent appear to be drawn toward it.

If knowledge-sector areas of New England, the Megalopolis, Minnesota, and the Pacific Northwest represent one leg of the regional shift, the Sun Belt represents the other, much larger one. Map 17 shows how the largest 1960–70 increases came in the states of the southern rim. What is more, 1973 census data indicated that these areas remained the fastest-growing sections of the nation. Of the six metropolitan areas registering the biggest 1971–72 gains, all were in the Sun Belt: Fort Myers, Florida (14.9 per cent); Sarasota, Florida (12.9 per cent); Killeen-Temple, Texas (12.8 per cent); Orlando, Florida (11.7 per cent); Fort Lauderdale-Hollywood, Florida (10.4 per cent); and Tucson, Arizona (10 per cent).[5]

Like the New England-Minnesota-Pacific shift, the Sun Belt build-up is also substantially a function of post-industrial trends. First off, there are the *direct* post-industrial influences: aerospace, electronics, and related high-technology defense industries. Second, there is the impact of two industries greatly encouraged by the longer life spans and increased leisure of post-industrialism: retirement and tourism, both of great importance across the entire Sun Belt. Last, the spin-offs of rising northern labor costs: a heavy southward movement of such industries as textiles and shoes, plus a parallel shift in military bases and facilities.

Put these together, and the result is an economic transformation quite unlike that which Massachusetts or Minnesota has been experiencing. In Dixie, the great growth spur has been a tremendous increase in manufacturing. As northern costs rose, such manufacturing industries as textiles, apparel, pulp and paper, lumber, chemicals, petrochemicals, and food processing moved south in large and continuing numbers. Relatively low wages (about 80 per cent of the national average), weak labor unions, and abundant natural resources have encouraged the trend. A similar pattern carries over to the Rocky Mountains, historically linked to Dixie in low income and economic-political ideology.

Since World War II the South has been metamorphosing from an agricultural economy to a manufacturing economy. The shift was especially emphatic during the nineteen sixties, when manufacturing jobs in Dixie increased by 42.5 per cent in contrast with 15.5 per cent for the nation as a whole and a virtual standstill in post-industrializing New England. As a corollary of this growth, more than two million whites moved to the South during the sixties, twice the number of the previous ten years and a complete turnabout from the net overflow that occurred in the nineteen forties. Many of these newcomers were experienced businessmen, professionals, and technicians. Although manufacturing has been the key to southern growth, it has also triggered a regional boom in insurance, finance, research, and electronics, so that Dixie's new prosperity often seems more white-collar than blue-collar-rooted. Most economists think that, with this expanding base, recent growth has produced a self-reinforcing effect that will keep the South on track as the nation's top growth region at least through the nineteen seventies. Joseph Grant, vice-president and economist of Houston's Texas Commerce Bank, offered this explanation in 1972:

> The growth process has reached a point where we are seeing a multiplier effect. Industrialization has boosted income, which has developed markets, which in turn is inducing more industry to move South to serve the markets, which in turn stimulates further growth.[6]

Not surprisingly, Dixie's mushrooming industrialization and fast-growing regional income—shown in Chart 23—have created an increasingly commercial mentality. Corporate outlooks fast becoming unfashionable in Lexington, Massachusetts, are surging powerfully in Savannah, Georgia, and West Memphis, Arkansas. The "mechanization of Southern Baptists," described by Samuel Lubell, is a reality: Farmers now working as assistant production managers (for three and four times what their parents earned) are 100 per cent capitalists committed to "free enterprise" and dead set against welfarism and knowledge-sector social programs. Daniel Bell's "sociologizing mode" may be ascending in Oregon and New England, but the "economic mode" of industrial-society thinking prevails in the South and Southwest.

Here again, as in the knowledge-sector states, a definite regional culture is apparent. First, support for corporations, commerce, and the raw profit motive. Second, a strong nationalistic-military posture (large infusions of military bases, personnel, and spending on top of the South's existing martial tradition). Third, a considerable infusion of retired persons, definitely more conservative than the nation as a whole. Fourth, a heritage of race consciousness plus white

The South is growing faster than the United States

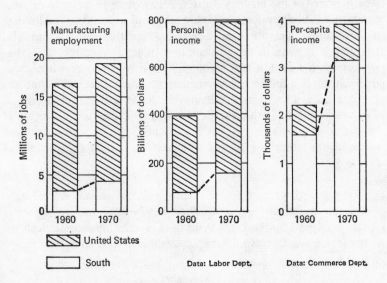

Data: Labor Dept.

Data: Commerce Dept.

Manufacturing employment has risen sharply

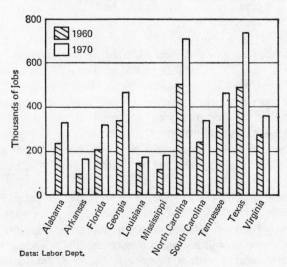

Data: Labor Dept.

CHART 23
Southern Population and Economic Trends

separation from and repression of blacks and Latins. In contrast to the northern knowledge sector, Dixie has probably been the *least* supportive of peace, ecology, consumerism, and civil-rights drives. Yet the South and the Southwest have attracted *by far and away the largest internal population migration of all.* Florida industrialist Jim Walter described the process as a "push-pull effect."[7] The push comes from the North, where crime, racial and social tension, pollution, congestion, and other factors have driven many people to migrate. The "pull" comes from the locational advantages and economic opportunities of the South.

Economists debate how long this boom will continue. The 1973–74 energy crisis hurt Florida's resort areas but generally affected the South less than other regions. Long-term energy problems might have the effect of further shifting industry to the South and Southwest. The editors of *Business Week,* in a September 1972 study, argued that "by all accounts, this southward migration of people and business will continue through this decade and well into the 1980s. It is fast earning for the 11 states of the Old Confederacy . . . the title of the New Rich South."[8]

Projections that population and economic activity would continue to shift to the South, Southwest, and Rocky Mountains were central to the assumptions of the National Goals Staff in research for their 1970 report. Chart 24, premised on the idea that government policies would encourage movement away from the old urban centers, shows the anticipated reduction in per-capita-income disparities between the various regions of the country. The major gains are expected in the South.

Census Bureau data also support the notion that U.S. population will continue to flow South and West—toward the sun. The growth of the South and Southwest is projected to outstrip the rest of the nation until the year 2000. With the sharp recent drop in the birth rate, individual estimates are unreliable, but the basic trend is clear.

Despite the possible effects of the energy crisis in retaining urban populations, the likelihood is that people will continue to move away from the old industrial areas to the new socioeconomic magnet regions. This should decrease the strength of the Old Left and Old Right and increase the relative demographic weight of the New Left and New Right, and generally further a post-industrial division in politics (especially if regional-cultural polarization continues). Within this

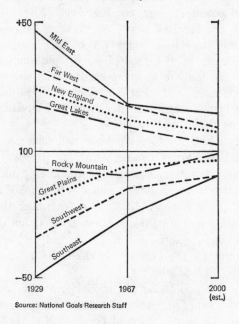

CHART 24

Relative Difference Among Regions in per-Capita Personal Income in United States

framework, the relative demographic magnitude of the movement to the South and West favors the right.

2. Suburbia and Black-White Urban Polarization   As originally established by Al Smith and Franklin D. Roosevelt, the New Deal Democratic coalition rested heavily on the white urban working class of the North—from hillbillies in Akron, Toledo, and Detroit to Italians in Pittsburgh and Irish in New York. City dwellers provided the huge urban majorities by which the Democrats overcame upstate, outstate, or downstate Republicanism in Massachusetts, New York, Michigan, or Illinois. But in the years since World War II, this base has been eroded by the move to suburbia and antagonized by the influx of southern Negroes. By the mid-nineteen seventies, high crime rates, racial tension, and polarization were the rule.

During the nineteen fifties and sixties, the phenomenon of sub-urbanization was generally assumed to help the Republicans, and this was probably more true than false. Even so, the benefit was clearly limited. By the nineteen seventies, many lower-middle-income suburbs had emerged as political extensions of urban Democratic voting patterns. However, the real diffusion of suburbia's national political impact can be linked to the shifting economics of elitism. Along the Megalopolis, from Washington to Boston, the most notable Democratic trend is frequently occurring in *affluent* suburbs (especially knowledge-sector strongholds) rather than in the middle-income tract-house neighborhoods. Southern suburbanization tends to be overwhelmingly conservative, but, in the North, the pattern is mixed, varying from suburb to suburb by dint of ethnic, vocational, and other factors. All of which is to say that in the North, suburbanization is no longer a trend that can be assigned concrete partisan implications.

Through the nineteen seventies and the nineteen eighties, more importance may once again attach to what happens in the *cities*. The combined impact of fuel shortages and rising prices plus increased house and mortgage costs has slowed the trend to the suburbs. For many young families and ethnic groups still located in the cities, the price of suburban housing is climbing out of reach. Blacks and white ethnics are both affected. Neither group can contemplate the same escape valve of suburbanization that prevailed through the sixties, and some observers have suggested the end of the American Dream.

It is a dangerous demography. In many northern cities, black populations are moving toward majority status. In each city where blacks have become a majority or near majority, and bid for control of city hall, the result has been racial polarization at the ballot box: Newark, Cleveland, Gary, Detroit, and East St. Louis. When blacks finally captured the Detroit mayoralty in 1973, the successful candidate won 94 per cent of the black vote, while the defeated contender captured 92 per cent of the white vote. Newark, Gary, and Cleveland have witnessed similar patterns. To be sure, examples of non-polarization can be found: small or middle-sized, largely white, cities electing black mayors. But once a city's black population reaches 40 per cent, and blacks begin to covet group solidarity and municipal control, politics has invariably acquired a racial cleavage.

Unless urban dynamics shift, such major cities as Philadelphia, Baltimore, Chicago, and St. Louis are likely to move into the confrontation orbit during the late nineteen seventies or nineteen eighties. Chart 10 shows the black-white ratios of city populations in 1970. By 1985–90, black majorities are expected across much of the urban North.

To some extent, these estimates reflect the impact of the black birth rate—far higher than the plummeting white birth rate. Moreover, some observers do expect the trend to be mitigated. As suburban housing becomes prohibitive in cost, the white urban exodus may slow to a comparative trickle. Secondly, as a consequence of changing lifestyles and economics, young people and even young married couples are showing new interest in the urban-renewal neighborhoods of the central cities. Not that either of these circumstances would be likely to defuse urban tension. Lower-middle-class whites stuck in urban peripheral neighborhoods tend to be especially angry political opponents of blacks, and the young professionals in the center city are likely to be liberals often allied with the blacks. This cleavage is already apparent in such cities as New York and Cleveland.

Such urban demographics lend themselves to post-industrial categorization. Fashionable downtown neighborhoods house the elite liberals of the knowledge sector: the "technologically proficient," of David Apter's classification. Black districts represent a considerable group of the technologically hopeless. And the peripheral white lower-middle-class elements parallel the "technologically obsolescent" category: motormen, tailors, and sheet-metal workers. In most big cities, as in national politics, the logical alliance is between new-class liberals and blacks, with peripheral conservative whites in opposition. Blacks may use municipal political control much as the Irish did—as an economic bootstrap. The slumping economy of the mid-seventies adds to the probability of increased racial tension.

If black-white urban cleavage continues to emerge in the above fashion, it will reinforce broader national racial divisions and dismantle the urban electoral base of New Deal liberalism. Back in 1932 and 1936, blacks and affluent urban voters supported GOP conservatism, and working-class whites—60–80 per cent of the electorate in northern cities—were the mainstay of the Democratic Party. Now blacks and affluent urbanites are the basis of liberal strength, and the countermovement among working-class and lower-middle-class whites apparent in 1968 and 1972 has eroded or eliminated the traditional liberal majorities. Changing demography makes it unlikely that racially sundered urban centers can continue to be the regular electoral base of a national presidential majority.

3. The Graying of America   Generations, like westward population movements, have played an important role in U.S. politics. Periods of massive population surge have invariably been times of political change. Two twentieth-century examples come easily enough to mind.

First, the tremendous population boom of the early-twentieth century, much of it centered in the cities and involving America's new immigrant groups, laid an important foundation for the New Deal. Samuel Lubell has described the political/demographic impact of the children born to the huge 1900–14 group of immigrants:

> Viewed in today's perspective, it is clear that those figures forecast a major political upheaval some time between 1930 and 1940. By then all of these children, plus baby brothers and sisters not enrolled in school, would have grown to voting age. Massed as they were in the states commanding the largest electoral vote, their sheer numbers would topple any prevailing political balance.
>
> No matter what else had happened, the growing up of these children of the 13,000,000 immigrants who poured into the country between 1900 and 1914 was bound to exert a leveling pull on American society. As it was, the Great Depression—striking when most of them had barely entered the adult world—sharpened all their memories of childhood handicaps. . . .
>
> Through the entire Roosevelt era the Republicans labored on the wrong side of the birth rate. Nor was there anything they could do about it, since the birth rates frustrating them were those of 1910 to 1920.[9]

During the late twenties and thirties, the median age of the U.S. population was relatively young. But, as the depression grew, the birth rate dropped sharply. By the nineteen forties, the median age was climbing. Although it began to drop again by the late forties, the political impact of the "birth dearth" of the thirties was only beginning. Just as the high birth rates of the early-twentieth century didn't begin affecting politics until the nineteen twenties and thirties, the low birth rates of the thirties did not begin to show up until the nineteen fifties. And although the conservatism of the fifties has frequently been interpreted in terms of suburbanization or Cold War psychologies, the aging of the population was also a major factor. A majority of those aged thirty to forty-five were Democrats, having come of age in the lean years, but they were less liberal in 1955, aged forty, than they had been in 1936, aged twenty-one. By the late nineteen fifties, the median *voter* was distinctly middle-aged. The 21–30-year-old electorate was small because of low 1929–40 birth rates.

	Census Bureau Series F Projections[1]					
	1972	1976	1980	1984	1990	2000
Population 20-29 Years Old (millions)	33.3	38.1	40.6	41.8	38.3	34.7
Total Population Over 20 Years Old	132	140	151	160	169	181
Percentage of Total Adult Population Constituted by 20-29-year-old Group	25%	27%	27%	25%	23%	19%

1. Series F is a low-increase projection. Other series project a larger over-all population.

CHART 25
The Graying of America

Needless to say, this pattern was soon to change. The election of 1964 saw the first, small-scale impact of the post-1940 birth surge, and by 1968, young voters were entering the electorate in droves. The big crest, of course, came in 1972. Back between 1948 and 1953, the number of babies born in the United States rose by almost 50 per cent. And by 1972, this entire mushrooming segment of the electorate was ready to vote as a result of the constitutional amendment dropping the age of eligibility to eighteen. In retrospect, the influence of the youth revolution and youth vote was profound

—not at the polls, where it had little effect in the general election of 1972, but in reshaping U.S. cultural and political behavior.

Directly and indirectly, youth played a huge role in a) the knowledge revolution—because of the schools, teachers, money, and technology needed to handle the 1950–70 surge in school enrollment; b) the civil-rights revolution—because of quite essential youthful optimism, anti-racialism, organizational willingness, and activism; c) the youth-culture syndrome—because circa-1964 young people were able or allowed to go off to college in huge numbers and nurture age-group consciousness instead of mostly joining the labor force like circa-1927 or -1939 youth; and d) the metamorphosis of liberal politics: because of time, affluence, and organization-consciousness, youth were a vital factor in sexual and racial-minority causes, anti-business psychologies, and the McGovern-New Politics shift of the Democratic Party.

In July 1971, sociologist Peter Drucker noted that the general outline of the youth revolution, if not its exact form, had been predictable. As he noted, the 1948–53 baby boom was "by far the biggest increase in births ever recorded here, or up until then, in any country."

In 1960 the center of population gravity in this country was in the 35-to-40 age group—older than it had ever been before. Suddenly, within five years, the center shifted all the way down to age 17—younger than it had been in our history since the early nineteenth century. The psychological impact of this shift proved unusually strong because so many of these 17-year-olds—almost half of the young men—did not join the work force but instead stayed on in school, outside of adult society and without adult responsibilities.

The youth revolution was therefore predictable ten or twelve years ago. It was in fact predicted by whoever took the trouble to look at population figures. No one could have predicted then what form it would take; but even without Vietnam or racial confrontation, something pretty big was surely bound to result from such a violent shift in age structure and population dynamics.

We are now about to undergo another population shift, since the 17-year-olds will no longer be the largest single group in the population. Perhaps more importantly, this is the last year in which this group will be larger than the 17-year-old group of the year before. From now on, the center of population gravity will shift steadily upward, and by 1975 the dominant age year will be 21 or 22. From 1977 to 1985, the total number of 17-year-olds in the population will drop sharply.[10]

Looking forward in time, the 1976 presidential election will stand as the high-water mark of youth influence at least through the 1996 contest, and probably longer. Estimates put 18–24-year-olds at 19 per cent of the eligible 1976 electorate. Twenty-five to twenty-nine-year-olds add another 12 per cent. By 1980, as the slumping birth rates of the sixties come into play, 18–24-year-old eligibles will represent only 18 per cent of the electorate. That will drop to just 17 per cent in 1984. By the mid-eighties, the electorate will once again be increasing its middle-aged spread. The babies of 1948–53 will be thirty-one to thirty-six years old in 1984, worried about debts, mortgages, crime, and economic pressures, and the 1924–29 mini baby boomers will be a tired, discouraged fifty-five to sixty. As of 1984, the eighteen-year-olds coming of age will be few, and by 1988, they will be fewer still, reflecting the birth dearth of the late sixties. Projecting these statistics into the elections of 1992 and 1996, which will reflect the unprecedentedly low birth rates of the seventies, one confronts an unprecedentedly *old* population and electorate. The youth influence will be negligible, and the center of political gravity in 1996 will be the 40–50-year-old group! Besides which, there is also the considerable possibility of medical advances that will increase life spans and weight the electorate further toward those over sixty-five.

Remember that the shape of the electorate through 1992–96 is already largely established. Thus, by the nineteen nineties there is the likelihood of a near gerontocracy, overwhelmingly white, reasonably affluent, and probably quite conservative. Ideological predictions are admittedly risky—the ideologies of the nineteen nineties may bear little relation to our nomenclature—but the youthful "liberals" of all previous generations have become generally conservative in middle age, and 1973 data suggest that this process has already set in among the collegians of the mid-sixties.

Although these statistics suggest an increasingly conservative political structure by the nineteen eighties, this decade's shape is less clear. But such analysts as Peter Drucker doubt that the youth surge of the sixties will be much of a liberal influence even during the seventies. He believes that "this group is even more likely than comparable age groups in the past to concern itself with the prosaic details of grubby materialism," because the youth of the sixties, after having never known anything but discretionary income through college, will face a cruel time adjusting to the overcrowded white-collar labor market of the seventies.[11] However, even though Drucker's vocational analysis is correct—two or three teachers will be fighting for every job opening—such economic pressure may well have left-liberal effects, notably pushing teachers and other young professionals into organizational militance. In coming years, economic pressures may tilt knowledge-sector workers left, while increasing the "conservatism" of traditional vocations. One thing is sure: the youth revolution is clearly spent, and the demographic balance will be shifting toward older age groups. We will see the Graying of America, not the Greening.

In sum, although the demographics of the remaining part of the twentieth century are by no means set, certain probabilities appear fairly solid. The center of population gravity is continuing to move toward the South and West; black domination (and racial polarization) may be in store for our cities; and the center of gravity of the U.S. population is about to undergo an unprecedented shift toward middle age. All these suggest a political move to what has been called the right.

D. CENTERS OF POST-INDUSTRIAL POWER

That the executive branch of the federal government is the logical repository of massive governmental power seems implicit in the nature and technology of post-industralism. And well before the upheavals of 1972–74, such analysts as Walter Dean Burnham and Samuel Lubell had arrived at a theory of emerging confrontation within the American system: a President-Manager based in the politics of the increasingly assertive white middle classes versus a Congress representing the institutionalized programs of the sixties and therefore more responsive to liberal and minority-group interests.

Notwithstanding the ignominy heaped on Richard Nixon's runaway presidency, the Burnham-Lubell thesis has a continuing validity —even to the point of being compatible with the traditional idea of

Congress as a "conservative" drag on political evolution. After all, during the nineteen thirties, the House and the Senate tended to represent the conservative interests that had been dominant in the country during the nineteen twenties but had lost access to the White House in the New Deal. More recently, in the years after 1968, Congress has continued to "conserve" the liberal interests rooted in the expansion of the sixties. As was true forty years ago, a shift in popular thinking can capture the presidency before it can dominate a House and Senate with 535 bases of election. During the nineteen seventies, Congress is likely to be the branch of government most responsive to interest-group liberalism.

This sort of conflict would be impossible in most governments around the world, because of the parliamentary system. Around the world, less and less decision making has originated in the legislative branch, and almost all of it has come to rest in the hands of prime ministers, party leaderships, and permanent bureaucracies. Divided government and hostile, separately institutionalized branches are unique to the United States. And the suspicion of executive-branch authority is probably greatest.

Even so, the triumph of the executive seems as inevitable in the United States as in the other Western democracies. What does seem likely, though, is that executive power will be put on a broader, less clique-based pattern. The key may lie in party parallelism—in the evolution of greater parallelism between the parties' executive and Congressional constituencies.

Ideally, effective party reconstitution would concentrate power in the executive branch but under *more restrained* circumstances—notably the increased influence of party (including Congress)—than prevailed during the sixties and early seventies. Inadequate parties and party lines were a major ingredient of U.S. political malfunctioning in the Johnson-Nixon era. Without them, the Madisonian system of checks and balances has proved ineffective much as foreseen by nineteenth-century theorist Frederick Grimke: In a republic, he suggested, "parties take the place of balances and checks. The latter balance the government only, the former balance society itself."[1] Arguably, it will take parties that effectively marshal and arbitrate society's forces to restore the system and keep the trend toward executive-branch hegemony under control.

But whether U.S. parties can fill this vital function in the post-industrial era is doubtful. A considerable number of historians and sociologists anticipate that the United States, and indeed much of the Western world, may be under pressure to move in an authoritarian direction. The ingredients are many: Arnold Toynbee's analysis that Western nations, denied vital natural resources by producer countries, are about to lose headway and become regimented siege economies; Richard Herrnstein's idea of a developing IQ caste system; Lewis Mumford's fear of a new dark age; the Andrew Hacker-Edward Banfield view of cities as racially divided armed camps; and the generally held, albeit milder, view that the technological complexity of post-industrial society is at very least bound to bring about an increase in government regulation and responsibility.

Some or all of these circumstances may combine to erode the traditional party system and checks-and-balances division of U.S. government. If so, any new post-industrial-era political structure will probably owe much of its shape to communications management. As of the mid-seventies, awareness of the political importance and centrality of the media is mushrooming. If politics increasingly become a struggle for influence through, and control of, the media, then not only will traditional parties play a diminishing role, but executive-branch power seems sure to increase.

The danger is obvious: that executive-branch power in the communications age will increasingly lack the institutional restraints of the industrial era: strong political parties, churches, competing elements of government, independent private-sector elites. As Office of Telecommunications Policy Director Clay Whitehead noted in 1971, "I do not know if anyone has pointed out yet that the fiftieth anniversary of the Communications Act of 1934 is 1984."[2]

An ideologically based politics resting on communications technology could easily lead in this direction; indeed, some sociologists see elements of inevitability. Thus, it is possible that the knowledge revolution may ultimately come to signify a mass-based authoritarian drift, just as the Industrial Revolution is usually linked to the evolution of middle-class democracy in lieu of aristocratic rule. It seems clear that the impact of communications and the ideologization of politics have already imposed a great strain on the traditional "genius of American politics" to disarm problems and conflicts through multiple institutions and broad-based, non-ideological parties.

The international context is also discouraging. The basic tradition that U.S. and British politics share—flowing out of the Glorious Revolution of 1688 and the constitutional caldron of the seventeenth and eighteenth centuries—has rested in no small part on the historic optimism of Anglo-America, on the safety valve of emigration to Canada, California, Australia, Rhodesia, or even Levittown, and on the continuing expansion (or at least maintenance) of a world role. From 1776 through the early nineteen sixties, Pax Britannica and then Pax Americana prevailed over much of the globe. Our institutions were formed amid, and carried along by, an upcurrent of history. But the last decade has been one of sharp, watershed contraction. Future chroniclers may remember the adventurism of the early nineteen sixties—from Britain's "pop" classless society to the U.S. "Great Society"—as a last frontier quest. Since then, with the world reach of Anglo-America shrinking, domestic social stratification has strengthened and reasserted itself in the face of contracting opportunity—regarding the United States, historian Andrew Hacker has called it the end of the American Era. Partly for these reasons, both countries have been caught up in unprecedented doubt and malaise concerning the viability of their traditional institutions.

Britain's relative decline has been taking place for many years. In the United States, the shift has been especially sudden, searing, and disheartening. But the erosion of traditional institutions and relationships seems to be occurring on both sides of the Atlantic. Conceivably, the peculiarly Anglo-American democracy that worked so well over centuries of agricultural- and then industrial-era optimism and expansion is much less suited—its institutions fish out of water— to the combined 1) ebb of Anglo-American world economic, diplomatic, and political power that has been so apparent since the sixties, 2) consequent domestic social stratification and shrinking share of world-wide economic resources, and 3) communications technology, ideologized politics, and strong-government implications of the knowledge revolution. The systems of Edmund Burke and James Madison, of Abraham Lincoln and Benjamin Disraeli, of Franklin Roosevelt and Winston Churchill, may be losing relevance. At the very least, the easygoing political traditions of the past are in for a massive strain; at most, America may be on the verge of an epochal shift in the nature of her political and governmental institutions.

NOTES

CHAPTER 1 SPINNING THE ELECTORAL COMPASS

1. David Apter (ed.), *Ideology and Discontent* (Glencoe, Ill.: The Free Press, 1964), pp. 15–43.
2. Arthur Miller, Warren Miller, Alden Raine, and Thad Brown, *A Majority Party in Disarray* (Ann Arbor, Mich.: University of Michigan Center for Political Studies, 1973).
3. Ibid.
4. Walter Dean Burnham, "The End of American Party Politics," *Trans-Action,* December 1969, p. 14.

CHAPTER 2 POST-INDUSTRIAL SOCIETY

1. "Mrs. Green Raps Her Ruler," *Christian Science Monitor,* December 16, 1970.
2. Charles Beard, *An Economic Interpretation of the Constitution* (New York: Macmillan, 1913).
3. "Herman Kahn Views the New U.S. Class Gap," Los Angeles *Times,* October 20, 1972.
4. "America's Unofficial Rulers," *National Observer,* December 29, 1973, p. 1.

   A. THE KNOWLEDGE INDUSTRY
   1. Daniel Bell, *The Coming of Post-Industrial Society* (New York: Basic Books, 1973).
   2. David Riesman, *Mass Leisure* (Glencoe, Ill.: The Free Press).

3. Ralf Dahrendorf, *Class and Class Conflict in an Industrial Society* (Stanford, Calif.: Stanford University Press, 1959).

4. Alvin Toffler, *Future Shock* (New York: Random House, 1970).

5. Fritz Machlup, *The Production and Distribution of Knowledge in the United States* (Princeton, N.J.: Princeton University Press, 1962).

6. Science Indicators 1972 (Washington, D.C.: National Science Board, 1973).

7. Paul Dickson, *Think Tanks* (New York: Ballantine Books, 1971), p. 18.

8. Ibid., pp. 13–14.

9. Congressional Record, December 3, 1969, p. H11701.

10. Richard Rosenbloom, "Thinking Ahead," *Harvard Business Review,* September–October 1973, p. 156.

11. Michael Harrington, "The Social-Industrial Complex," *Harper's Magazine,* November 1967.

12. Ibid.

13. Data from Council on Foundations.

14. Daniel Bell, op. cit., pp. 269–98.

B. A MEDIACRACY

1. Joseph Epstein, "The Media As Villian," *More,* September 1974, p. 24.

2. Lewis Lapham, "The Temptation of a Sacred Cow," *Harper's Magazine,* August 1973, p. 46.

3. Patrick Buchanan, *The New Majority* (Philadelphia: 1973), p. 15.

4. Ben Bagdikian, *The Information Machines* (New York: Harper & Row, 1971), p. 3.

5. C. Wright Mills, *The Power Elite* (New York: Oxford University Press, 1956).

6. Patrick Buchanan, op. cit., p. 18.

7. Marshall McLuhan, New York *Times,* July 29, 1973.

8. Ibid.

C. THE NEW ELITE

1. "Kahnversation," Washington *Star,* September 10, 1972, p. B-3.

2. Ibid., pp. B-3–4.

3. Paul Wieck, *The New Republic,* June 5, 1972.

4. *Christian Science Monitor,* September 13, 1972.

D. THE DYNAMICS OF LIBERAL FAILURE

1. "Walter Lippmann at 83," Washington *Post,* March 25, 1973.
2. Amitai Etzioni, "Human Beings Are Not Very Easy to Change After All," *Saturday Review,* June 3, 1972, p. 45.
3. Quoted in James Carey and John Quirk, "The Mythos of the Electronic Revolution," *The American Scholar,* Spring 1970, p. 225.
4. Quoted in David Thomson, *England in the 19th Century* (London: Penguin Books, 1950), p. 102.
5. Ibid., pp. 102–3.
6. Theodore Caplow, "Towards Social Hope," *Columbia Forum,* Spring 1973, p. 30.
7. "Mrs. Green Raps Her Ruler," op. cit.
8. Irving Kristol, "The Crisis Behind the Welfare Crisis," *Fortune,* June 1969, p. 227.
9. Gurney Breckenfeld, "Housing Subsidies Are a Grand Delusion," *Fortune,* February 1972, p. 137.
10. Ibid., p. 138.
11. Peter Henle, *Monthy Labor Review,* quoted in "Harvard Abstraction Becomes Reality," Washington *Post,* April 9, 1973.
12. Daniel P. Moynihan, *Coping: On the Practice of Government* (New York: Random House, 1973).
13. Robert L. Heilbroner, "Benign Neglect in the United States," *Trans-Action,* October 1970, p. 19.
14. Michael Harrington, op. cit.
15. Irving Kristol, "Welfare," *The Atlantic,* August 1971, p. 47.
16. Robert Webb, *Modern England* (New York: Dodd, Mead, 1969).
17. *Tocqueville and Beaumont on Social Reform,* ed. Seymour Drescher (New York: Harper & Row).
18. Christopher Jencks, *Inequality: A Re-assessment of the Effect of Family and Schooling in America* (New York: Harper & Row, 1973).
19. *U.S. News & World Report,* September 3, 1973, p. 28.
20. Martin Anderson, *The Federal Bulldozer* (New York: McGraw-Hill, 1966).
21. Data from Department of Housing and Urban Development, May 1974.

22. Gurney Breckenfeld, op. cit., p. 163.

23. Ibid., p. 166.

24. Ibid.

E. THE TRADITIONALIST COUNTERREFORMATION

1. Richard Scammon and Ben Wattenberg, *The Real Majority* (New York: Coward-McCann, 1971).

2. "Kahnversation," Washington *Star,* September 10, 1972, p. 3.

3. Ibid.

4. Dean Kelley, *Why Conservative Churches Are Growing.*

5. Christopher Booker, *The Neophiliacs* (New York: Gambit, 1970).

6. Herman Kahn, *Single* magazine (February 1974), p. 34.

7. Rhea Smith, *Spain* (Ann Arbor: Univ. of Michigan Press, 1965).

8. "Herman Kahn Views the New U.S. Class Gap," Los Angeles *Times,* October 20, 1972.

9. Andrew Greeley, *Why Can't They Be Like Us?* (New York: Dutton, 1971). Michael Novak, *The Rise of the Unmeltable Ethnics* (New York: Macmillan, 1972). Peter Binzen, *Whitetown, U.S.A.* (New York: Random House, 1971).

10. Paul Hemphill, *The Nashville Sound* (New York: Simon and Schuster, 1970), p. 180.

11. Paul Dickson, "Singing to Silent America," *The Nation,* February 23, 1970.

12. Samuel Lubell, *The Future While It Happened* (New York: Norton, 1973), p. 12.

13. "Walter Lippman at 83," op. cit.

F. A REDEFINITION OF IDEOLOGY

1. R. J. Cruikshank, *The Liberal Party* (London: Collins, 1948), p. 12.

2. Ibid.

3. William Safire, *The New Language of Politics* (New York: Collier Books, 1972), p. 126.

4. Ibid.

5. E. L. Woodward, *The Age of Reform, 1850–1870* (London: Oxford University Press, 1938), p. 92.

6. Ibid., p. 182.

7. Safire, op. cit., p. 126.

8. Paul Seabury, "The Idea of Merit," *Commentary,* December 1972, p. 44.

9. Peter and Brigitte Berger, "The Assault on Class," *Worldview,* June 1972, pp. 20–25.

G. POST-INDUSTRIAL SOCIETY CONFLICT

1. Daniel Bell, op. cit.

2. Victor Fuchs, *The Service Economy* (New York: Columbia Univ. Press, 1968).

3. *Business Week,* May 23, 1970, p. 58.

4. "Life in America," *U.S. News & World Report,* March 12, 1973, p. 46.

5. Paul Goodman, *Growing Up Absurd* (New York: Vintage Books, 1960).

6. Peter and Brigitte Berger, "The Blueing of America," New York *Times,* February 15, 1971, p. 23.

7. Seymour Lipset and Earl Raab, "The Wallace Whitelash," *Trans-Action,* December 1969, p. 26.

8. Lee Nash, "Gatsby in the Vanguard," *Human Behavior,* September 1973.

9. Washington *Post,* September 14, 1973.

10. "Herman Kahn," *Single* magazine, February 1974, p. 34.

11. "The Two Americas," *National Observer,* March 10, 1973, p. 1.

12. Herman Kahn, op. cit., p. 87.

13. St. Petersburg *Times,* April 19, 1974.

14. Samuel Lubell, *The Future While It Happened* (New York: Norton, 1973), pp. 61–66.

15. R. B. Wernham, ed., *The Counter-Reformation and Price Revolution* (The New Cambridge Modern History, 1968).

16. Richard S. Rosenbloom, "Thinking Ahead," *Harvard Business Review,* September–October 1973, p. 158.

CHAPTER 3 NEW PATTERNS IN AMERICAN POLITICS

C. EVOLUTION, NOT REVOLUTION

1. Samuel Lubell, *The Hidden Crisis in American Politics* (New York: Norton, 1970), p. 46.

D. POPULISM, CULTURE AND ECONOMICS

1. "McGovern Taps New England," *Christian Science Monitor,* September 13, 1972.

2. United Press International, October 21, 1972.

3. Richard Jensen, "The Historical Roots of Party Identification," paper presented to the American Political Science Association, September 1969.

4. Ibid., pp. 5–8.

5. Ibid.

6. Michael Rappeport, *Washington Monthly,* November 1971.

7. Russell Beeches, "The Imponderable Young," *Harper's Magazine,* March 1972, p. 62.

E. THE RISE OF TICKET SPLITTING

1. "Democrats' Bandless Wagon," *National Observer,* September 30, 1972.

2. Walter De Vries and V. Lance Tarrance, *The Ticket-Splitter* (Grand Rapids, Mich.: Eerdmans, 1972).

3. *The American Political Report,* February 14, 1972.

4. Ibid.

5. Richard Scammon and Ben Wattenberg, *The Real Majority* (New York: Coward, McCann, 1970), p. 157.

6. Jack Newfield and Jeff Greenfield, *A Populist Manifesto* (New York: Praeger, 1972).

7. Frederick Dutton, *Changing Source of Power* (New York: McGraw-Hill, 1971).

8. Walter Dean Burnham, *Critical Elections and the Mainsprings of American Politics* (New York: Norton, 1970).

9. Lubell, *The Hidden Crisis in American Politics,* pp. 32–38.

G. A NEW POLITICAL CYCLE?

1. David Broder, *The Party's Over* (New York: Harper & Row, 1972).

CHAPTER 4 THE DISRAELI ANALOGY

A. PARTIES IN FLUX

1. Moisei Ostrogorski, *Democracy and the Organization of Political Parties* (Garden City, N.Y.: Doubleday, 1964), Vol. I, p. 14.

2. André Maurois, *Disraeli* (New York: Modern Library), p. 84.

3. David Thomson, *England in the 19th Century* (London: Penguin Books, 1950), p. 58.

4. E. L. Woodward, *The Age of Reform (1815–1870)* (London: Oxford University Press, 1938), p. 154.

5. Ostrogorski, op. cit., p. 35.

6. Frederic Dutton, *Changing Sources of Power* (New York: McGraw-Hill, 1971), p. 254.

7. Herbert Spencer, *Social Statics* (London: 1850, 2nd ed., 1868), pp. 79–81.

8. Ostrogorski, op. cit., p. 53.

9. Thomson, op. cit., p. 120.

10. Ibid., pp. 120–21.

11. Woodward, op. cit., p. 175.

12. Walter Dean Burnham, *Critical Elections and the Mainsprings of American Politics* (New York: Norton, 1970), p. 169.

13. Ostrogorski, op. cit., p. 124.

14. Bell, op. cit., p. 43.

15. Ibid., pp. 364–65.

16. Ostrogorski, op. cit., p. 53.

17. "Disraeli and Nixon," *National Observer,* December 2, 1972, p. 5.

18. *Wall Street Journal,* August 21, 1972.

19. "An Interview with Edith Efron," *The Alternative,* November 1972.

20. Seymour Lipset and Everett C. Ladd, Jr., *Academics, Politics and the 1972 Elections* (Washington, D.C.: American Enterprise Institute, 1973).

21. Quoted in Allan Brownfeld, "The Irrelevance of American Politics," *The Yale Review,* October 1970, p. 5.

22. Ibid., p. 6.

23. Quoted in "What Started the Landslide," *National Observer,* November 18, 1972.

B. THE ROLE OF PARTY

1. Edgar Robinson, *The Evolution of American Political Parties* (New York: Harcourt, Brace, 1924), p. 90.

2. Ostrogorski, op. cit., p. 13.

3. Ibid., p. 74.

4. Ibid., pp. xxiv–xxv.

5. Burnham, op. cit., p. 72.

C. EXECUTIVE AND LEGISLATIVE INSTITUTIONALIZATION

1. Allen E. Goodman, "Nixon vs. Congress," *Christian Science Monitor,* April 10, 1973.

2. Nelson Polsby, "The Institutionalization of the House of Representatives," *American Political Science Review,* June 1968, p. 144.

3. Allen Drury, *Courage and Hesitation* (Garden City, N.Y.: Doubleday, 1971), p. 98.

CHAPTER 5 THE FUTURE OF AMERICAN POLITICS

A. THE PARTY SYSTEM

1. Quoted in Philadelphia *Inquirer* editorial, January 7, 1974.
2. Miller, Miller, Raine, and Brown, op. cit.

B. POST-INDUSTRIAL IDEOLOGY

1. The Ripon Society and Clifford W. Brown, Jr., *Jaws of Victory* (Boston, Mass.: Little, Brown, 1974), pp. 289–96.
2. Ibid., p. 295.
3. Ibid., p. 293.
4. Jeffrey Hart, paper submitted to American Political Science convention, Chicago, September 1974.

C. THE DEMOGRAPHY OF POWER

1. "New England: Fighting to Make a Comeback," *U.S. News & World Report,* January 1, 1973, p. 64.
2. Ibid.
3. "New England: What Replaces Old Industry," *Business Week,* Aug. 4, 1973, p. 36.
4. "The Good Life in Minnesota," *Time,* August 4, 1973.
5. U. S. Census Bureau interim reports.
6. "The New Rich South: Frontier for Growth," *Business Week,* September 2, 1972, p. 30.
7. Ibid., p. 35.
8. Ibid., p. 30.
9. Samuel Lubell, *The Future of American Politics* (Garden City, N.Y.: Doubleday, 1956), pp. 29, 32.
10. Peter Drucker, "The Surprising Seventies," *Harper's Magazine,* July 1971, p. 36.
11. Ibid.

D. CENTERS OF POST-INDUSTRIAL POWER

1. Frederick Grimke, *The Nature and Tendency of Free Institutions* (1848), quoted in Richard Hofstadter, *The Idea of a Party System* (Berkeley, Calif.: Univ. of California Press, 1970), p. 266.
2. Clay Whitehead, speech to International Radio and Television Society, New York City, October 6, 1971.

INDEX

Abolitionists (third-party group), 11, 85*ff.*, 139, 140
Activist churches, waning of, 54
Adams, John, *references to,* 9, 122
Adams, John Quincy, *references to,* 113, 147
  See also Federalists; National Republican Party
Age of Reform, The (Woodward), 155–56
Age of Revolution, 1789–1848, The (Hobsbawm), 62*n*
Agnew, Spiro, *references to,* 35, 180
Altgeld, John P., 49*n*
ABC. *See* TV networks
AFL–CIO, *references to,* 103, 108, 200
America, graying of, 221–25
American Independent Party
  campaign of 1970, 8, 143
  references to, 1, 11
  See also Wallace, George C.
American Political Science Association, 207–8
American Political Science Review, The, 184, 185*n*
American politics, future of, 191–228
  and party systems, 192–202
American Voter, The, 136
Anderson, Martin, 50
Andrews, T. Coleman, 142
Anglicans and conservative politics, 33
Anglo-American ideology, 62*ff.*
Apter, David, 3, 76, 220
Arthur, Chester A., 179
"Assault on Class, The" (Peter and Brigitte Berger), 65
AP, *references to,* 28
Auchincloss, Louis, 31

Bagdikian, Ben H., *quoted,* 28
Baltimore *Sun,* 25

Banfield, Edward, 49, 49*n*, 227
Bankhead, William P., 101
Bank of the United States, 32
  See also Biddle, Nicholas
Banks, James G., 50
Baptist Church and politics, 70, 126
  primitive, 127*ff.*
  Southern, 75
Barkley, Alben, 101
Barton, Bruce, 42
Beard, Charles, 17, 49*n*
Beer, Samuel, 18
Bell, Daniel
  on the "economic mode," 74, 75
  references to, x, 24, 35, 38, 68, 164–65, 215
Berger, Brigitte
  on liberalism, 65, 66, 70–71
Berger, Peter
  on liberalism, 65, 66, 70–71
Biddle, Nicholas, 32, 167
Bill of Rights, protection of, 30*ff.*
Binzen, Peter, 56
Birch Society. *See* John Birch Society
Birney, James G., 40
Blacks
  and political patterns, 95–101 *passim*
  and population percentages, 99
  See also Civil rights
Boas, Franz, 49*n*
Booker, Christopher, 54
Borah, William, 109
Boston *Globe,* 25
Britain
  economic unheavals in, 13*ff.*, 33*ff.*, 47*ff.*, 51–62
  Education Act of 1870, 160
  Industrial Revolution in, 154
  and liberalism, 160*ff.*

and media analyzed, 10, 26
and party upheavals analyzed, 155–57, 174
and Reform Act (1832), 153, 169; (1867), 160
Broder, David, 147
Brooks Brothers (clothiers), 95
Bryan, William Jennings
and Bryan Movement, emergence of, 11
Catholic support of, 95
nominated for President, 118, 140
references to, 36, 83–84, 115, 119, 124, 146, 148, 174
Buchanan, James, 83
Buchanan, Patrick, *quoted*, 29, 207
Buckley, William F., 205
Bundy, McGeorge, 41
Bureaucracy, unpopularity of, 77
Burnham, Walter Dean, *ix, x,* 103, 137, 164, 194, 202, 225
Business services (chart), 16
Business Week, 212, 217
Byrd, Harry, 145

Canning, George, 63
Cannon, Joe, 186
Capitalism, American, dominance of, 9
Capitalism, rise of, 13, 125–26
Caplow, Theodore, *quoted*, 42–43
Cash, W. J., 117
Catholicism and politics
Catholic-Protestant rivalry, 193
and Counter Reformation, 54
in Kennedy's administration, 118–19
references to, 33, 70, 83, 95, 102, 103, 104, 117, 126, 127, 144
Cavalier and Yankee (Taylor), 117
Center for Urban Studies (Rutgers University), 50
Changing Sources of Power: American Politics in the Nineteen Seventies (Dutton), 136
Chicago *Tribune*, 26
Christian Democratic Union, 193
Christian Science Monitor, 119
Churchill, Winston, 228
Civil rights
revolution, escalation of, 22*ff.*, 43, 50, 51–62 *passim*, 70, 89*ff.*
and school integration, 72
social engineering and race consciousness, 74
Civil War
and Clay's post-Civil War American System, 32
continues Jacksonian division, 117
GOP coalition during, 133
institutionalism during, 186
political patterns during, 85–94 *passim*, 140, 147–48, 151*ff.*
racial overtones of, 113

Republican coalition during, 106
references to, 12, 14, 101, 103, 134, *171*, 172, 173, 178–79, 200
Class and Conflict in an Industrial Society (Dahrendorf), 20
Clay, Henry, 32
Cleveland, Grover, 179, 180
Cold War, *references to*, 41, 222
Collective bargaining, *references to*, 14, 68
Colson, Charles, 4
CBS. *See* TV networks
Columbus, Christopher, 55
Committee to Re-Elect the President (CRP), 182–83, 198
Communications Act of 1934, 227
Communications industry, postwar rise of, 26–27 (chart)
Communications Revolution, *references to, v, ix, x,* 30, 146*ff.*, 177, 202
Communications technology, 201–2
Communist Party, 143
Concise Economic History of Britain from 1750 to Recent Times, A (Court), 154
Congregationalists, *references to*, 54, 117, 126*ff.*
Congress of the United States
de-institutionalization of, 189
institutionalization of, 177*ff.*
Conservatism
Danish, 193
obsolescence of, 62*ff.*
references to, 59, 71, 145, 192*ff.*, 195
See also Liberals; Republican Party
Conservative-Liberal division, beginning of, 64*ff.*, 173
Constitution of the United States
deified by Supreme Court, 17
and Fourteenth Amendment, 31
guarantees First Amendment, 30*ff.*
references to, 49*n.*, 209
Coolidge, Calvin
quoted, 42
references to, 53, 71, 109, 179
Cooper, Peter, 140
Coping: On the Practice of Government (Moynihan), 45
Corn Laws, 63
Coughlin, Father, 148
Counter Reformation (1520–1620), 76
Country and Western music, political importance of, 58
Court, W. H. B., 154
Cowles publications, 25
Critical Elections and the Mainsprings of American Politics (Burnham), 137
"Critical Theory of Elections, A" (Key), 9
Croker, John Wilson, *quoted*, 63

Cromwell, Oliver, 117
Crystal Palace exhibition (1851), 42
Culture and political patterns, 112–37
    passim
Cutting, Bronson, 109

Dahrendorf, Richard, 20
Darwinism
    conservative, 49*n*
    social, 42, 45
Davis, Jefferson, 4
Davis, John W., 148
Dean, Dwight, 71
Debs, Eugene, 141
Defense, Department of, 181
*Democracy and the Organization of
    Political Parties* (Ostrogorski),
    156–57
Democratic Congress of 1964, 60
Democratic National Committee, 182
Democratic Party
    advocates New Politics, 3
    agreements and disagreements within,
        2
    campaigns, early, 83*ff.*
    and Deep South roots, 5–6
    division of left and right wings of, 3
    embraces Populism, 6
    emergence to power of (1933), 18
    ethnic disenchantment with, 99*ff.*
    ethnic support of, 95*ff.*
    evolution of, 109–9
    and Humphrey's 1968 campaign, 119–
        20
    ideological cleavage within (1872), 3
    and Jacksonians, 139, 198
    and Kennedyites, 107
    and Kennedy's administration, 118–19
    and liberals, 185
    and McCarthyites, 107, 108
    and New Deal vote percentages (1932–
        44), 5
    new political shifts within, 223
    and 1970 campaign, 61–62
    nominates Bryan, 118
    nominates McGovern, 137
    and Peace Democrats, rise of, 173–74
    and political cycles, new, 145–49
    and post-industrial axis, moves onto,
        107
    *references to, v*ff., 60*ff.,* 73
    reform movements within, 21
    and shifting presidential geography,
        106*ff.*
    supports Nixon, 3, 137
    and ticket splitting, 130–38
    and top fifteen states, 89, 104–6
    and Wallaceites, 107–8
    and Wilson's elections (1912, 1916), 6
    See also Jackson, Andrew; Johnson,
        Lyndon B.; Kennedy, John F.;
        Roosevelt, Franklin D.; Truman,
        Harry; Wilson, Woodrow
Democratic-Republicans versus
    Federalists, divisions, 14
Depression of 1929
    causes of, 10
    and collective bargaining, ushers in,
        6–7
    and industrial Republicanism, 121–22
    references to, 12, 64, 103, 180, 221
    See also Fair Deal; New Deal
De Vries, Walter, 135
Dewey, Thomas E.
    political strategy of, 7
    presidential campaigns of, 110
Disciples of Christ in politics, 127*ff.*
Disraeli, Benjamin
    analogy, 151–89 *passim*
    conservatism discussed, 165
    references to, 13, 63, 228
Dixiecrats, *references to,* 11, 138, 142–43
Dixie presidential shift, 112
Douglas, Stephen, 115
Dow Chemical Corporation, 24
Drucker, Peter, 224–25
Drury, Allen, 188
Dutton, Frederic G., 136, 157

Economics and political patterns, 112–
    37 *passim*
Economy, New American Knowledge
    (chart), 16
Educational services (chart), 16
"Education-Poverty Industrial
    Complex," 17, 22
Efron, Edith, on media, 166
Ehrlichman, John, 167, 178
Eighty-ninth Congress, programs enacted
    by, 22*ff.*
Eisenhower, Dwight D.
    and fifties era, 39
    nomination of, 110
    and outer South victories, 103
    references to, 94, 137, 142, 159
Election cycles analyzed, 9–10
Election Men, The (Rosenbloom), 201
Elitism, 65*ff.,* 114–16
    See also Liberal elitism, rise of
*Emerging Republican Majority, The, v,
    vi,* 136
Emerson, Ralph Waldo
    quoted, 41–42
    references to, 117
Episcopalians in politics, 54, 127
Epstein, Joseph, *quoted,* 25
"Essay on Pauperism, An" (Tocqueville),
    47–48
Ethnic Factor, The (Kramer and Levy),
    82, 96
Ethnic political patterns
    and "social tension" belt, 97

references to, 95–101 *passim*
voting in presidential races, 98, 144
Etzioni, Amitai, *quoted,* 40
European economics analyzed, 51–62
passim, 63*ff.*
Evolution in political patterns, 101–12
passim

Fair Deal, *references to,* 40, 64, 118
See also New Deal; Roosevelt,
Franklin D.
Fairness Rule, focus on, 30
Family Assistance Plan, 60
Farmer-Laborites (third party), 141
Faubus, Orval, 142–43
Faulkner, William, 5
Federal Bulldozer, The (Anderson), 50
FHA, 50
Federalists, *references to,* 9, 14, 31,
113*ff.,* 168–69
See also Jefferson, Thomas
versus Democratic-Republicans,
divisions, 14
Federal spending
charitable foundations, 19, 20
education, 19, 20
research, 19, 20
Fillmore, Millard, 178
Fitzgerald, F. Scott, 71
Ford, Gerald, *references to,* 4, 81–82, 85,
180
Ford Motors, 29
Fortune magazine, 44, 50
Free-Soil (third party), 11, 139, 140
Frémont, John C., 83
French Constitution of 1795, 63
French Revolution, 62, 76, 208
Frieden, Bernard J., on federal subsidy,
44
Frost, Robert, 118
Fuchs, Daniel, 68
Fundamentalist churches, growth of, 54

Gallup, George, 96, 135
Garner, John N. ("Cactus Jack"), 101
Garrison, William Lloyd, 86
General Motors, 29, 70
George IV, King, on liberalism, 63
Gladstone, William, 64
Glantz, Frederick, 210
Glazer, Nathan, 46, 49*n*
Glorious Revolution, 14
GNP, 33
Goldwater, Barry
and anti-Goldwater landslide, 39, 98
and campaign flaws, 110–11
1964 candidacy of, 83, 106
nomination of, 93, 132, 143
Goodman, Paul, 70
GOP. *See* Republican Party
Grangers (third party), 11

Grant, Ulysses S., 179, 180
Great Depression. *See* Depression of 1929
Greater South, political division of, 5–6
Great Gatsby, The (Fitzgerald),
analyzed, 71
Great Society
programs, collapse of, 52–62 *passim*
programs, studies of, 43–44, 49
references to, 39, 40*ff.,* 80, 82, 107, 227
and Vietnam War link, 107
See also Johnson, Lyndon B.
Greeley, Father Andrew, 56
Greenbacks (third party), 139, 140
Green, Edith
on growth industries, 44
references to, 17, 22
Greenfield, Jeff, 136
Greening of America (Reich), 69–70
Grimke, Frederick, 226
Gross national product (GNP)
references to, 33

Hacker, Andrew, 227, 228
Haggard, Merle, 57–58
Haldeman, H. R., 167, 178, 188
Hale, John B., 140
Hamilton, Alexander
reference to, 9
systemization of debt, 32
Harper's Magazine, 28
Harrington, Michael, 22, 46
See also Socialism
Harris, Louis, 37, 203
Harrison, Pat, 101
Harrison, William Henry, 167
Hart, Jeffrey, on capacity of the media,
207–8
Harvard Law School, 123
and support of McGovern, 8
Harvard-M.I.T. Joint Center for Urban
Studies, 44
Harvard straw polls, 8–9
Health, Education and Welfare,
Department of (HEW)
founded (1935), 23, 181
references to, 43, 49, 60, 168
and spending, total, 23
Heilbroner, Robert L., on social welfare,
45
Henle, Peter, on individual earnings, 44–
45
Herberg, Will, 54
Herrnstein, Richard, on unemploy-
ability, 49, 227
Hobbes versus Locke, 14
Hobsbawm, E. J., 62*n*
Holmes, Oliver Wendell, 86
Hoover, Herbert, *references to,* 103, 109,
116, 120, 179, 180
House of Representatives

institutionalization of, 184*ff.*
references to, 187
Housing and Urban Development
(HUD), *references to,* 24, 60
"Housing Subsidies Are a Grand
Delusion" (Kristol), 44
Hughes, Charles Evans, 6
Humphrey, Hubert
Manhattan's support of, 8
presidential candidacies, 92, 107*ff.*,
119–20, 182
references to, 119, 180
support in 1968, lack of, 90, 129, 133

Ideological trends in politics, 138–45
passim, 196*ff.*
Ideology, redefinition of, 62–67 *passim*
Industrial Conference Board, 77
Industrial era (1896–1932)
ideological combat, 15
partisanship, 5
references to, 7, 13
See also Fair Deal; New Deal
Industrial-Labor (New Deal Democratic
Era, 1968), 10
Industrial Republican Era (1896), 10,
39, 121–22
Industrial Revolution
chronology of English, 154
creates a new elite, 24, 29*ff.*
early stages of, 53
ideological transformations because of,
151–89 *passim*
implementation of, 1
party confusion during, 2
references to, v, x, 10, 13*ff.,* 17, 32, 39,
41*ff.,* 62*ff.,* 72, 172, 227
See also Post-industrialism
Industrial Revolution-Transition
(Jacksonian Era, 1860), 10
Industrial Supremacy (Industrial
Republican Era, 1932), 10
*Inequality: A Re-assessment of the Effect
of Family and Schooling in
America* (Jencks), 48
Inflation, *references to,* 76*ff.*
Information Machine, The (Bagdikian),
28
"Institutionalization of the House of
Representatives, The" (Polsby),
185*n*
IBM, 15, 23

Jackson, Andrew
anti-, lines, 170
Catholic support of, 95
1824 defeat, 83
and Free-Soil coalition, 133, 209
inauguration of, 170
and opening of trans-Appalachian
"New West," 11

pro-, lines, 170
references to, 9, 36, 101, 113*ff.,* 119,
139, 146, 147, 179, 180, 198
triumph of 1828, 10
Jackson, Henry, 203
Jaffa, Harry, 145
Jaws of Victory, The, 206
Jefferson, Thomas
and Democratic coalition, 63, 91,
113*ff.,* 169
See also Federalists
overthrows Federalist hegemony, 9, 14
references to, 36, 168–69
Jehovah's Witnesses, growth of, 54
Jencks, Christopher, on social
engineering, 48
Jennings, M. Kent, 71
Jensen, Arthur, 49, 49*n*
Jensen, Richard, 126, 127, 172
John Birch Society, 138, 203
Johnson, Andrew, 179
Johnson, Hiram, 109
Johnson, Lyndon B.
and decision not to run for re-election,
101
and landslide victory of 1964, 22, 60,
106*ff.*
New Deal optimism of, 45
New Deal roots shown by, 39
1964 support by white voters, 90
references to, ix, 103, 118, 131, 182,
226
and War Against Poverty, 22
See also Great Society
Johnson, Warren A., 210–11
Judaism and politics, 54, 126

Kahn, Herman
on affluent young, 72–73
quoted, 34–35, 52–53, 56, 69–70
references to, x, 18, 58, 74, 167
on return to religions, 54–55
and Zone I, 78, 193
Kelly, Dean, on churches, 54
Keniston, Kenneth, 71
Kennedy, Jacqueline, 118–19
Kennedy, John F.
appoints segregationist judges, 93
and civil-rights escalation, 106*ff.*
and communications programs, 118–19
nomination of, 103, 104
references to, 39, 107, 108, 136, 161,
163, 183
Key, V. O., *quoted,* 9, 135–36
Kramer, Michael, 82, 96
Kristofferson, Kris, 58
Kristol, Irving
and "Multi-Problem Dilemma," 46–47
references to, 29
on social services, 44, 46, 49*n*
Krueger, Robert, 22

Labor
  and New England's shifting force, 212
  political shift to, 7
Labor, United States Department of
  Official Job Picture Report, 69
  Old Guard, 41
  predicts employment increases, 68
  references to, 22
Ladd, Everett C., Jr., 166, 167
La Follette, Robert
  1924 third party of, 11, 109, 138, 141–43
  See also Progressivism
Landon, Alf, 148
Legal services (chart), 16
Lemke, William, 142, 148
Levy, Mark, 82, 96
Liberal-Conservative division, 64*ff.,* 192*ff.*
Liberal elitism, rise of, 1–2, 17–18, 28
Liberalism
  British, 160*ff.,* 193
  dynamics, failure of, 38–51 *passim*
  and left-liberal tilt, 28
  and New Deal-Great Society impetus, 11
  obsolescence of, 62*ff.*
  public trend away from, 202*ff.*
  references to, 32, 59, 97
  term coined, 62–63
  youthful, 73
Life magazine, 25
Lincoln, Abraham
  1864 victory margin, 5
  election in 1860, 10
  and Republican Party emergence, 11, 146
  references to, 115, 228
  runs on Union ticket, 148
  victory margin (1864), 5, 179, 180
Lippmann, Walter, *quoted,* 38, 51, 61
Lipset, Seymour, 70, 71, 166, 167
Locke versus Hobbes, 14
Lodge, Henry Cabot, 5
Long, Huey, 148
Los Angeles *Times,* 26
Lovejoy, Elijah, 29
Lubell, Samuel
  on "mechanization of the Southern Baptists," 75
  references to, x, 59, 79, 107, 159, 168, 215, 225
Luther, Martin, 55
Lutheranism and politics
  references to, 54, 70, 126, 127
  Scandinavian, 126*ff.*

McCarthy, Eugene, 107, 108, 119
McGovern, George
  debacle of 1972, 81, 82, 130, 131
  See also Democratic Party

Harvard Law School's support of, 8
lack of voter support, 4, 36–37, 53, 90, 91, 123, 124, 137
Manhattan's support of, 8, 35
and 1970 defeat, 61–62
and populist politics, 119–20
and presidential campaign, 107*ff.,* 116, 118, 137, 161, 163, 176, 192
references to, viii, 86, 94, 96, 98, 101, 103
and social programs, 100, 223
supported by recording stars, 58
Machlup, Fritz, 20
McKinley, William
  and breakthrough of 1896, 10
  references to, 9, 115, 146, 148, 172, 174
McLuhan, Marshall
  quoted, 31
  references to, 30, 208
Madison, James, 169, 186, 228
Manifest Destiny, 40
Man Nobody Knows, The (Barton), 42
Marland, Sidney, 49–50
Marquand, John P., 31
Marriage of Figaro, The (Beaumarchais), 65
Marxism, 208
Meany, George, 203
Media and United States political conflict, 1–225 *passim*
  capacity of, 207–8
  Edith Efron on, 166
Medical health services (chart), 16
Medicare, *references to,* 40*n,* 46, 59
Methodism and politics, 54, 126
Mexican War, 157, 171
Miami *Herald,* 30
Mills, C. Wright, 29
Mind of the South, The (Cash), 117
Model Cities, *references to,* 60
Monroe, James, 91
  and "Era of Good Feeling," 10, 147, 157
Monthly Labor Review (Department of Labor's), 44
Mooney, William, 95
Mormon religion, growth of, 54
Motion pictures (chart), 16
Moynihan, Daniel Patrick
  on educational expenditures, 45
  references to, vii, 28, 47
Mumford, Lewis, 227
Murphy, Reg, 82
Murray, Paul, 167

Nation, The (magazine), 58
NBC. *See* TV networks
National Council of Churches, 54
National Observer magazine, 131
National Planning Association, 68

National Republican Party, 64
  See also Adams, John Quincy
National Review, 205
National Science Foundation, 21
Neophiliacs, The (Booker), 54
New Cambridge Modern History, 76
New Deal
  coalition, 3, 82ff., 102ff., 107
    Democratic, 209, 218
  foreshadowed by bureaucracies, 11
  and immigrant masses, importance of,
    11
  liberalism, 39, 220
  opposition to policies of, 122
  and Progressive movement, 11
  references to, 18, 33, 40, 46, 79, 97, 99,
    118, 142, 146, 209, 226
  southern breaking of loyalties to, 11–
    12
  Turnabout No. 1, 34
  Turnabout No. 2, 34
  Turnabout No. 3, 34
  years, early, 7, 87, 88, 101
New Deal-Fair Deal eras (1932–52), 7,
  34ff., 64, 89, 95, 99ff.
New elite, the, 31–38
  and "circulation of elites," 31
New England, political divisions of, 5, 6
Newfield, Jack, 136
"New Frontier," 39, 41, 64
  See also Kennedy, John F.
New Majority, The (Buchanan), 29
New Politics and knowledge-sector
  emergence, 21
New Republic, The (magazine), 28, 35
Newsweek magazine, 25, 26, 28
  See also Washington Post
New Yorker, The (magazine), 8
New York Times
  hails "big-business progressiveness,"
    23
  references to, 25, 28
Niemi, Richard G., 71
Nixon, Richard M.
  agrees to "Treaty of Fifth Avenue,"
    110
  and anti-elitist constituency, 124
  attacks radical liberalism, vii–viii
  bids for Catholic support, 95
  and cultural difference with McGovern,
    120
  Democrats' support of, 133, 137, 183
  denounced by Murphy and Spalding,
    82
  on Disraeli conservatism, 165
  and lack of interest in history, vii
  Mississippi's support of, 4
  1968 election, 182
  1970 campaign weaknesses, 61–62
  1972 victory, ix, 60, 82, 83, 90, 143, 225
    analyzed, 59, 94

references to, 29, 60, 71, 85, 98, 108,
    116, 117, 129, 138, 166ff., 176, 180,
    188, 226
  resignation of, 81
  and role in collapsing of party system,
    12
  southern voter support of, 94
  supported by Democrats, 133, 137, 183
  supported by recording stars, 58
  and war against crime, 61–62
  See also Republican Party
Nixon-Watergate era (1968–74),
    electoral analysis of, 1
Non-profit membership organizations
    (chart), 16
Norris, George, 110
North-South political divisions, 10
Novak, Robert, quoted, 28

"Okie from Muskogee" (Haggard), 57–
    58
Old Guard politicians, 8
Ostrogorski, Moisei, on British party
    divisions, 153, 156–57, 167, 171–
    72

Palmer, John, 148
Palmerston, Viscount, 160–61, 163
Pareto, Vilfredo, 31
Parker, Alton, 83–84
Party's Over, The (Broden), 147
Party systems
  upheaval of American, 2
  upheaval of British, 2
Pax Americana, 228
Pax Britannica, 228
Peel, Sir Robert
  quoted, 63
  references to, 155, 159, 170
Pentagon, references to, 70
Pentecostal churches, growth of, 54
Peoples' Party, 143
Percy, Charles, 203
Pettigrew, Thomas, 100
Phillips, Kevin P.
  and New York Times editorial, viiin
  as Nixon's voting-patterns analyst, vi
  and "Southern Strategy," vi
  as Special Assistant to the Attorney
    General, vi
Phillips, Wendell, 86
Pierce, Franklin, 178
Planning Research Corporation. See
    Krueger, Robert
Policy Research, Center for, 40
Political cycle, new, 145–49 passim
Political Studies, Center for (University
    of Michigan), 3, 200, 201
Politics, American
  future of, 191–228

patterns in, 81–149 *passim*
and systems, party, 192–202
Polk, James Knox, 157
Polsby, Nelson, 82, 184, 185*n*
Population growth, U.S., 221–25
*Populist Manifesto: The Making of a
    New Majority* (Greenfield and
    Newfield), 136
Populists
    emergence of, 11, 67, 78, 140–41, 174
    and political patterns, 112–37 *passim*,
        203, 208
    Prairie, 83
    versus Industrialists, 148
Post-industrialism
    creates liberal elite, 31
    and Democratic Party shift to, 107
    ideological transformations as result
        of, 151–89 *passim*, 202–8
    impact of, 13*ff.*
    and media political centrality, 12
    and new socioeconomy, 15
    power centers of, 225–28
    references to, v, ix, x, 12, 17, 18*ff.*,
        24*ff.*, 32–33, 77, 130, 176, 193, 199,
        214
    undercuts straight-ticket voting, 135
Post-industrial society, 13–79 *passim*
    and conflicts, 68–79
Pound, Roscoe, 49*n*
Power, demography of, 208–25
Power Elite, The (Mills), 29
Pre-Industrial Revolution (Jeffersonian
    Era, 1828), 10
Presbyterianism and politics, 126*ff.*
Presidential Cycles (19th and 20th
    Century charts), 10
Princeton University, 123
    Opinion Research Corporation of, 129
*Production and Distribution of
    Knowledge in the United States,
    The* (Machlup), 20
Professional services (chart), 16
Progressivism, *references to,* 71, 139,
    141, 142
    See also La Follete, Robert; Wallace,
        Henry
Protestant reform linked to capitalism,
    125–26

Quakerism, 73, 126*ff.*
Quarterly Review, The, 63

Radicalism, *references to,* 63
Rappeport, Michael, 129
Realignment, Scammon's battle against, 8
Real Majority, The (Scammon and
    Wattenberg), 82, 136
Reconstruction of the South, end of
    (1876), 6, 90
Recreation services (chart), 16

Reed, Clarke, 4
Reform Acts
    (1832), 63, 64, 169, 170
    (1867), 173
Reform Jews, *references to,* 73
    See also Judaism and politics
Reich, Charles, 69–70
Renaissance-Reformation, *references to,*
    67
Republican National Committee, 111,
    182
Republican Party
    broadens cultural geography, 6
    and Bull Moose split, 84
    and Capitol Hill Republicans, 182
    carries industrial North eight times
        (1896–1928), 6
    and Congress' inability to balance
        slave states, 11
    conservatism, *references to,* 38
    early campaigns, 83*ff.*
    ethnic support of, 95*ff.*
    evolution of, 110–12
    and Goldwater's campaign, 110*ff.*
    and leading Progressives, 109*ff.*
    and New Deal victory of 1936, 5
    1962 Congressional gains by, 106*ff.*
    and political cycle, new, 145–49
    references to, vff., 53, 60*ff.,* 115–16
    religious denominations and, 127*ff.*
    and ticket splitting, 130–38
    and top fifteen states, 88
    and Watergate, doubts raised by, 2
    and Yankee New England roots, 5–6
    See also Eisenhower, Dwight D.;
        Lincoln, Abraham; Nixon,
        Richard M.
R&D Resources Report, 21
Research and Development outlays, 21*ff.*
Riesman, David, 207
Ripon Society, 197, 203, 206, 207
    See also Republican Party
Rise of the Unmeltable Ethnics (Novak),
    56
Robinson, Edgar, on party guidance, 169
Robinson, Joseph, 101
Rockefeller, Nelson, 110
Romney, George, 60
Roosevelt, Franklin D.
    and coalition of 1932, 83, 84
    condemns "malefactors of great
        wealth," 31
    era economic traditions, 203
    and fireside chats, 175
    and highest ratios in South and West
        explained, 7
    pro-British policy of, 110
    references to, 18, 30, 36, 39, 95, 109,
        115, 118, 122, 146, 218, 221, 228
    and southern tilt, 101*ff.*

and victory of 1932, 9, 10, 101, 120,
    141, 142, 148
and vote percentages in New Deal
    years (1932–44), 5
    See also Democratic Party; New Deal
Roosevelt, Theodore
    and Bull Moose charge, 141
    references to, 6, 138, 168, 179
Rosenbloom, David Lee, 201
Rostow, Walt, 41
Rousseau, Jean Jacques
    and Rousseauistic philosophy, 51,
        61
    reference to, 40
Rusk, Dean, 41

Scammon, Richard
    and realignment, fight against, 8
    references to, vii, 51, 82, 136
    and "social issues," 61
Schlesinger, Arthur, Jr., 113
Schmitz, John
    candidacy of 1972, 8, 143
    top states, 144
Seabury, Paul, on liberalism, 65, 66
Sectionalism, advent of, 101, 118
Seeman, Melvin, 71
Service Economy, The (Fuchs), 68
Sindlinger, Albert, 203
"Singing to Silent America" (article
    quoted), 58
Slavery. *See* Civil War political
    patterns
Smith, Alfred E.
    rallies Catholic support, 102
    references to, 83, 95, 96, 141, 143, 148,
        218
Social-Industrial Complex (Harrington),
    22
Socialists as third party, 139, 141, 142
Socialist Workers (third party), 142, 143
Social Security, 40n, 46, 59, 118
Social Statics (Spencer), 158
Socioeconomic divisions, 3, 19, 32, 38,
    62ff., 203
Southern Baptists, growth of, 54
Southern economic trends, 216ff.
Southern presidential shifts, 112
Southern Strategy, The (Murphy and
    Spalding), 82
Spalding, Jack, 82
Spencer, Herbert, 158
Spock, Benjamin, 143
Standard Oil, 24, 172
States' Rights, *references to*, 11, 102,
    142–43
Sternlieb, George, 50
Stevenson, Adlai E., campaign defeats of,
    103
Sumner, Charles, 86
Supreme Court of the United States

overturns Miami *Herald* decision, 30
rejects "white primary," 102
Sybil, 13
    See also Disraeli, Benjamin

Taft, Robert, 110
Taft, William Howard, 6, 179, 180
Tammany Hall, 173
    founded (1789), 95
    Whisky Ring, 173
Tarrance, Lance, 135
Tawney, R. H., 125
Taylor, William R., 117
Telecommunications, Office of, 227
Television as a political propaganda
    tool, 28ff.
TVA, *references to*, 39, 102
Tennyson, Alfred, 158
Third parties
    Abolitionists, 11, 85ff., 139, 140
    American Independents, 138, 143
    Communists, 143
    Conservatives, 59, 62ff., 71, 145
    Dixiecrats, 11, 138, 142–43
    Farmer-Laborites, 141
    Federalists, 9, 14, 31, 113ff., 168–69
    Free-Soil, 11, 139, 140
    Greenbacks, 139
    Jacksonian Democrats, 139, 146
        See also Jackson, Andrew
    John Birch Society, 138, 203
    People's, 143
    Populists, 11, 67, 78, 83, 112–37,
        140–41, 174
    Progressives, 11, 71, 109, 138, 139,
        141, 142
        See also La Follette, Robert; Wallace,
            Henry
    Socialist Labor, 139, 141, 142
    Socialist Workers, 143
    States' Rights, 142–43
    Union, 142, 148
        See also Lincoln, Abraham
Thomas, Norman, 141, 142
Thomson, David, 161
Thurmond, Strom, 86, 102, 118, 138, 142
Ticket splitting
    growth of, 86, 176, 181
    new patterns in, 130–38 *passim*
    and 1968 Wallace bloc, 134
Time-Life Syndicate, 24
Time magazine, 25, 26, 213
Tocqueville, Alexis de, *quoted*, 47–48
Toffler, Alvin, 20
Tory-Whig partisanship, *references to*,
    10, 14ff., 63, 147, 149, 177
Toynbee, Arnold, 75, 227
Traditionalist Counterreformation, 51–
    62 *passim*
Transcendentalists, 41

Transportation Department, creation of, 181
Trilling, Lionel, 29
Troy, Matthew, 95
Truman, Harry
    farmer-labor support of, 102
    political strategy of, 7
    survives Dixiecrat revolt, 103
    See also Democratic Party; Fair Deal
TV networks, political importance of, 25*ff.*, 168

Union (third party), 142, 148
Unitarianism and politics, 41, 54, 73, 117, 126*ff.*
UPI, *reference to,* 28
University of Michigan
    Center for Political Studies, 3, 200, 201
    Survey Research Center, 82, 136, 199
Urban coalition, 23
Urban collapse, ingredients of, 52–62 *passim*
U.S. News & World Report, survey on mass-media by, 25, 26

Van Buren, Martin, 140
Veblen, Thorstein, 49*n*
Vietnam War
    Great Society linked to, 107
    references to, 12, 53, 59, 70, 71, 78, 201

Wallace, George C.
    and Alabama's voter support, 4, 119–20
    references to, viii, 11, 93–94, 106, 108, 117, 118, 119, 129, 138, 205
    and third-party candidacy (1968), 8, 60, 107, 111, 143
    and ticket-splitting bloc, 134, 143
    top states in support of, 144
Wallace, Henry, 103, 138, 142
Wall Street Journal, The, 165
War on Poverty, 46, 60
Wars of the Roses (1483), 14
Washington, George, 9, 62, 131
Washington *Post,* 25, 26, 28
    See also Newsweek magazine
WASP domination, 197*ff.*
Watergate
    and Massachusetts' anti-Nixon clamor, 5, 82

mentality, 62
    and post-Watergate era, 145
    See also Republican Party
    preoccupation with, *viii-ix*
    references to, 12, 85, 188–89, 203
    syndrome (1973–74), 2–3, 168, 183
Wattenberg, Benjamin
    references to, vii, 51, 82, 136
    and "social issues," 61
Weaver, James, 140
Webb, Robert, on Speenhamland, 47
Welfare, Department of, creation of, 181
Welfare states, European, 45
Whig Party
    and Democratic alignment, 10, 14*ff.,* 63, 147, 149, 178
    references to, 64, 117, 149, 170–71, 177
    and Tory-Whig partisanship, 14*ff.,* 153*ff.,* 198–99
    See also Tory-Whig partisanship
Whitehead, Clay, 227
Whitetown, U.S.A.—1970 (Binzen), 56
Why Can't They Be Like Us? (Greeley), 56
Why Conservative Churches Are Growing (Kelley), 54
William and Mary, reign of, 14
Wilson, Woodrow, and 1916 success, 102
Wolfe, Tom, 35
Woodward, E. L., on British party upheaval, 155–56
WPA, *references to,* 66, 91
    See also Roosevelt, Franklin D.
World War I
    era, 11, 37, 180
    postwar era, 71, 218–19
World War II
    decades after, 7, 28, 52, 58, 89, 122, 210*n*, 214
    federal R&D spending after, 21*ff.*
    post-industrial economic era since, 15, 17
    references to, 18, 110

Xerox Corporation, 15, 23

Yankee-led industrialism, 6
Yankelovich, Daniel, 203*n*

Zenger, John Peter, 29, 30